A Common Worship Year C Miscellany

A bumper resource for the principal seasons

Compiled by

NICK FAWCETT

kevin
mayhew

First published in 2003 by

KEVIN MAYHEW LTD
Buxhall, Stowmarket, Suffolk, IP14 3BW
E-mail: info@kevinmayhewltd.com

KINGSGATE PUBLISHING INC
1000 Pannell Street, Suite G, Columbia, MO 65201
E-mail: sales@kingsgatepublishing.com

For a list of sources from which this book was compiled
see page 493.

9 8 7 6 5 4 3 2 1 0

ISBN 1 84417 149 3
Catalogue No. 1500641

Cover design by Angela Selfe
Typeset by Fiona Connell Finch

Printed and bound in Great Britain

Contents

EASTER

ASCENSION

PENTECOST

TRINITY

ALL SAINTS

Foreword

It's been another busy week, and once again Sunday looms large on the horizon, yet you've barely had time to think about the services you're due to lead, let alone to prepare an address, family talk, prayers and so forth. Worse still, you've somehow found time, only to find your mind a blank, the wellspring of inspiration having run dry. Anyone who has been involved in the ministry or the leading of public worship will empathise with such scenarios all too well. Such moments of crisis can strike at any time, but perhaps most commonly during the great festivals and seasons of the Christian Year. Christmas, Holy Week and Easter, in particular, can be frenetic times with a host of extra events and services to organise, yet, as the years pass we can find it increasingly difficult to find new ways of approaching passages and stories from Scripture that we have already explored countless times before.

This miscellany of material has been put together as a tool for all those entrusted with the responsibility of leading worship. Drawing from such writers as Susan Sayers, Michael Forster, Katie Thompson, Mary Hathaway, Peter Dainty, Pete Townsend and Gerald O'Mahony, among many others and from my own books, it offers a resource book covering the principal seasons of the Church calendar, starting with Advent and progressing through to All Saints' Day. Beginning with an up-to-date translation of the recommended Gospel reading for Year C of Common Worship (generally taken from the Katie Thompson resource book *Hear the Good News*), it provides a variety of prayers, all-age-talk suggestions, service outlines, poems, meditations, sketches and other reflective material, together with introductory comments concerning key festivals and practical suggestions as to how these might be celebrated.

Most of the material can be used as it stands, though some – the all-age-talk material in particular – will require further thought and preparation. Nobody can provide a complete off-the-shelf package, and of course we would not want that, for we need to make worship our own, prayerfully seeking God's guidance as we weave diverse threads into a single tapestry. My hope, though, is that this book will help provide some of these threads, and so serve as a tool to all given the responsibility and privilege of leading the worship of God's people.

NICK FAWCETT

Advent

The First Sunday of Advent

Preparing ourselves for the glorious return of Christ

Luke 21:25-36

(also Jeremiah 33:14-16; Psalm 25:1-9; 1Thessalonians 3:9-13)

A reading from the Gospel of Luke (21:25-28, 34-36)

Jesus said:

> Before the Son of God returns, there will be signs in the sun, moon and stars, and people will be afraid and bewildered by all that they see. There is nothing to fear; instead, give thanks to see the power and glory of God. Hold your heads high because your salvation is near. Stay awake and always keep yourselves ready to meet the Son of God, so that you are not taken by surprise when he comes unexpectedly.

This is the Gospel of the Lord
Praise to you, Lord Jesus Christ   KATIE THOMPSON

Introductory material

'Come, thou long-expected Jesus.' 'O come, O come Emmanuel.' So we sing year after year at Advent. But do we mean it? Are we really looking forward to the coming of Christ? Do we truly believe one day he will return? And if so, what will it all mean? It is questions such as these that Advent puts to us, for above all this is a season of expectation, a season which reminds us of the promise Jesus gave to come again in glory. Soon we shall be celebrating once more the coming of Jesus in a stable in Bethlehem – a coming his people had looked forward to for so long yet which, when it finally happened, they failed to recognise. It is with that sobering truth in mind that we ask ourselves today: 'What do *we* expect? And what *should* we expect?'   NICK FAWCETT

Prayers

Praise and petition – The Christ who will come again

Gracious God,
>   we praise you that you came to our world in Christ,
>   fulfilling your promise of old,
>   vindicating the long-held expectations of your people.
>   We praise you that you came again to the Apostles in the risen Christ,
>   appearing when you were least expected
>   bringing new hope and immeasurable joy.
>   We praise you for the promise that you will come again in Christ
>   to establish your kingdom
>   and to give life to all your people.
>   **Come, Lord Jesus, come!**

>   Yet we recognise there were many
>   who were not ready for the coming of Jesus –
>   many who were not as prepared as they thought they were,
>   whose lives were not what they could have been
>   and whose response was not what it should have been.
>   Help *us* to be prepared –
>   to live such lives that at any moment we would be happy
>   to be confronted by the returning Christ.
>   Help us to examine ourselves –
>   our words and deeds, thoughts and attitudes;
>   living each day and moment
>   as though Jesus were visibly by our side –
>   and so may we commit ourselves wholeheartedly to his service.
>   **Come, Lord Jesus, come!**

Gracious God,
>   we pray not only for ourselves but our world,
>   and those many people who have no thought
>   of Christ or his coming –
>   those who live only for themselves,
>   who seek fulfilment solely in material satisfaction,
>   or who have no spiritual dimension to their lives.
>   **Come, Lord Jesus, come!**

>   We pray for those who profess to love
>   but who have drifted away from your side –
>   their faith shallow and empty,
>   their hearts full of bitterness, pride, envy,
>   or their minds troubled by doubts and disillusionment.
>   **Come, Lord Jesus, come!**

We pray for those who work against your kingdom –
   who knowingly cheat and deceive,
   who serve self at the cost of others,
   who spread hatred and incite violence in pursuit of their aims.
Come, Lord Jesus, come!

We pray for those who long for your kingdom –
   who hunger for a new beginning,
   who pray for a fresh chance,
   or who simply see no hope for themselves in this world.
Come, Lord Jesus, come!

And finally we pray for those who work towards your kingdom,
   who strive for peace and harmony,
   who campaign for freedom and justice,
   who demonstrate love and compassion in action.
Come, Lord Jesus, come!

Gracious God,
   we thank you for the assurance
      that your kingdom shall come and your will be done –
      the knowledge that we do not hope or wait in vain.
   Teach all your people to live always
      as those ready for Christ's coming,
      so that those who have no faith may hear and respond
      to your word of challenge.
   Grant to those who despair
      the knowledge that you are with them,
      and to all who work to bring your kingdom nearer
      the assurance that in your own time it will come.
   In that faith we pray:
   Come, Lord Jesus, come!
   Amen.   NICK FAWCETT

Petition – The challenge of Advent

Lord of all,
   you tell us to wait and pray for that time
      when Christ shall come again to establish his kingdom;
      that time when your purpose shall be fulfilled
      and your name made known and worshipped on all the earth!
   You challenge us to live in the light of that promise –
      help us to respond.

Teach us, we pray, never to lose sight of your purpose,
    never to stop believing that you are at work,
    never to lose confidence in your kingdom.
Teach us that, as Christ came, so he shall come again.
You challenge us to live in the light of that promise –
    help us to respond.

But teach us also not to waste the present moment,
    not to place all our hope in the future,
    or to imagine that you are unconcerned
    for us and your world now!
Teach us to recognise that Christ is with us always,
    by our side to the end of time.
You challenge us to live in the light of that promise –
    help us to respond.

Help us to live and work for you always,
    rightly and responsibly enjoying your many gifts,
    and seeking to do your will and follow your ways.
Help us to live each day
    as though Christ were coming back at that moment,
    until that day when he returns in glory
    and you are all in all.
You challenge us to live in the light of that promise –
    help us to respond.

For his name's sake.
Amen.   NICK FAWCETT

Intercession – The hope of Advent

Lord Jesus Christ,
    we remember today
        how so many looked forward to your coming,
        but we remember also
        how it became harder to go on believing
        as the years went by;
        how hope started to splutter and dreams began to die
        until, finally, you came –
        the fulfilment of prophecy,
        the culmination of God's purpose,
        the definitive expression of his love.
    Lord of all,
        the Word made flesh,
        bring hope to your world today.

We remember with gladness
    how you brought hope throughout your ministry,
    a sense of purpose to those for whom life seemed pointless –
    the poor, sick, outcasts and broken-hearted –
    light shining in their darkness,
    joy breaking into their sorrow,
    new beginnings in what had seemed like the end.
Lord of all,
    the Word made flesh,
    bring hope to your world today.

Hear now our prayer for those caught today in the grip of despair –
    those for whom the future seems bleak,
    optimism seems foolish,
    and trust seems futile.
Reach out in love,
    and may light shine into their darkness.
Lord of all,
    the Word made flesh,
    bring hope to your world today.

Hear our prayer for those whose goals in life have been thwarted,
    whose dreams have been shattered,
    who have grown weary, cynical and disillusioned.
Reach out in love,
    and rekindle their faith in the future.
Lord of all,
    the Word made flesh,
    bring hope to your world today.

Hear our prayer for those who mourn,
    or who wrestle with illness,
    or who watch loved ones suffer.
Reach out in love,
    and grant them your strength and comfort.
Lord of all,
    the Word made flesh,
    bring hope to your world today.

Hear our prayer for those whose lives are blighted by injustice,
    crushed by oppression, poverty, hunger,
    and encourage all who work against the odds
    to build a better world.
Reach out in love,
    and grant the assurance of your coming kingdom.
Lord of all,
    the Word made flesh,
    bring hope to your world today.

Lord Jesus Christ,
    we remember your promise to come again in glory,
        the culmination of God's purpose,
        the ultimate victory of love.
    May that conviction bring new faith,
        new vision,
        and new purpose wherever life seems hopeless.
    Lord of all,
        the Word made flesh,
        bring hope to your world today.

In your name we pray.
Amen.   NICK FAWCETT

All-age-talk material

Read Luke 21:25-36

It doesn't seem as if a week goes by without reports of something happening in the sky, news of tidal waves or treacherous storms at sea, or even the threat of asteroids hitting the earth! Earthquakes, tornadoes, flash floods cause many people to be frightened and panic. There is a problem. Weather forecasts and predictions try to warn us of what may happen, but if they are so accurate, why do so many people get caught out?

Guessing what the weather will do can be a tricky business. It's no joke walking in a crowd of people when you're dressed in waterproof coat, wellington boots, plastic bags wrapped around your legs and a bucket on your head, and everybody else is wearing short sleeves and sunglasses. So, you ignore the weather forecast of torrential rain, go out in short sleeves and sunglasses and promptly get soaked. Sometimes you just can't win.

But, let's be honest, most of us would prefer to know what to expect rather than be kept guessing. Some surprises are OK, such as a birthday or Christmas, provided you've given everyone enough hints.

In the Bible reading, Jesus said that there would be lots of warnings and signs about his return but no one will know for sure when it's going to happen. Some of the things that Jesus referred to happen very frequently, almost too frequently. For instance, people in San Francisco, America, know they live in a major earthquake area. Earthquakes have happened before and occasionally earth tremors hint at what may be to come. But no one knows exactly when 'the big one' will happen. They prepare for it, they rehearse possible scenarios and plan how they may react to a major earthquake. But still no one knows when.

Even if you know it's going to happen sometime, isn't it possible that you can become a bit bored with wondering when it's going to happen? Rather like having a fire drill – the alarm sounds and you evacuate the building . . . eventually. Well, it's only a rehearsal, isn't it?

In San Francisco, they know history is going to repeat itself and another major earthquake will hit the city. They can't live every day in fear and they can't live every day ignoring the evidence. They watch, wait and prepare. Pretty much just what Jesus asks of us.   PETE TOWNSEND

Hope

Reading
Luke 21:25-36

Aim
To explore the key theme of Advent – hope!

Preparation
In large letters print the following riddle:
> My first is in HIDDEN but not found in SEEN.
> My second's in COMING but not there in BEEN.
> My third's in PROMISE and also EXPECTANT.
> My last is in EASTER as well as in ADVENT.
> My whole is a word that can mean many things,
> from confident trusting to wishful thinking.

Display this in a prominent position from the start of the service.

Talk
Invite the congregation to solve the riddle – some may already have done so. The answer, of course, is HOPE. Run through the riddle again for the benefit of those who haven't solved it, showing how this answer is reached.

Hope is one of the loveliest words in the English language, and something we all need to have in life. So perhaps that is why Advent is such a special time for so many – for it is all about hope: hope that one day Christ will come again and establish his kingdom.

As in the riddle, the truth of that promise is HIDDEN to many, rather than SEEN. Yet, trusting in what has BEEN, we are confident Christ is COMING again. We have that PROMISE from Christ himself, and this season reminds us always to be EXPECTANT, for we do not know when that time will be.

Advent is a time full of HOPE – not just vague WISHFUL THINKING but CONFIDENT TRUSTING in the Christ who shall come again!

NICK FAWCETT

Be ready to welcome Jesus!

Luke 21:25-36

Jesus will come again – but only God knows when

Write the letter that is missing from the second word in the box

In **BEAR** but not **ARE**

In **MILE** but not **MILL**

In **ROSY** but not **POSY**

In **SWEET** but not **SWAT**

In **SAIL** but not **SILL**

In **DANCE** but not **PRANCE**

In **YELLOW** but not **FELLOW**

What must we remember to do? _____

KATIE THOMPSON

Jesus told us how we will know that the end of time has come

Use the code to fill in the blanks and find out what we must watch for!

A B C D E F G H I J K L M N O P Q R S T U V W X Y Z
1 2 3 4 5 6 7 8 9 10 11 12 13 14 15 16 17 18 19 20 21 22 23 24 25 26

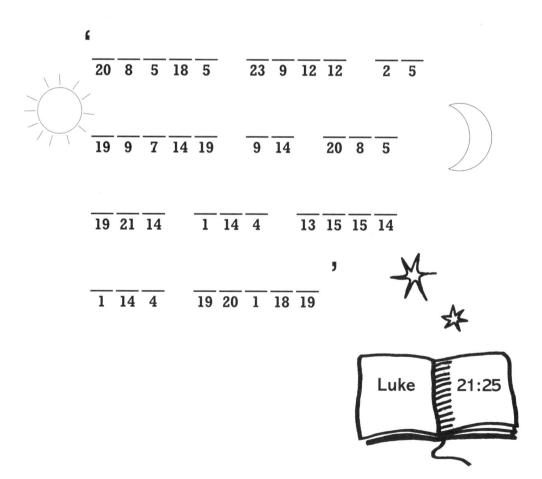

'
____ ____ ____ ____ ____   ____ ____ ____ ____   ____ ____
20 8   5   18 5   23 9 12 12   2   5

____ ____ ____ ____ ____   ____ ____   ____ ____ ____
19 9   7   14 19   9 14   20 8   5

____ ____ ____   ____ ____ ____   ____ ____ ____ ____
19 21 14   1 14 4   13 15 15 14

,

____ ____ ____   ____ ____ ____ ____ ____
1 14 4   19 20 1 18 19

Luke   21:25

KATIE THOMPSON

The word 'Advent' means 'coming'. Today is the First Sunday of Advent when we light the first candle on our wreath

Find the words missing from the poem below

**WAIT   CHRISTMAS   BIRTHDAY   CANDLES
PINE   FIRST   GREEN   UNENDING   BIRTH**

Jesus' _____ is not far away,

and we must be ready for _____ Day.

As we light the _____ candle on our Advent ring,

we begin to prepare for the _____ of our King.

Like the ring of _____ holly and _____

that we see,

God's love is _____ , and will always be.

As the light from the _____ grows brighter and

strong,

we watch and we _____ as time draws on.

KATIE THOMPSON

Reflective material
(sketches, meditations and poems)

Give us time

(This is a dialogue between the human race and God and could be read by two people.)

Human race:
Lord, give us the time and we'll do something great;
   we'll banish all evil and violence and hate;
   we'll march on to freedom, bring justice and peace;
   we'll feed all the hungry and warfare shall cease.
Give us time, give us time.

God:
I've given you time and what have you done?
You've marched into battle with bomb and with gun;
   you've built up your empires and revelled in war;
   you've trampled on freedom, forgotten the poor –
all the time, all the time.

Human race:
Just give us the time and we'll do and we'll dare;
   we'll transform this earth to a paradise fair;
   we'll tame all the deserts and farm all the seas,
   abolish all suffering and outlaw disease;
given time, given time.

God:
But I give you the time, and what do you do?
You scar what is beautiful, twist what is true;
   you build concrete deserts and chop down the trees;
   you poison the earth and the air and the seas.
Waste of time, waste of time.

Human race:
Only give us the time and we'll do all we can
   to conquer the world for the glory of man.
Technology's servants will spend every breath
   in reaching the stars and in mastering death,
with more time, with more time.

God:
I'll give you the time, but you'll need something more,
   if you're going to end poverty, famine and war;
   you'll need hands that are willing and hearts that are good,
   and eyes that are fixed on the Kingdom of God.
Now's the time, now's the time.

PETER DAINTY

Meditation of a first-century Christian

He was wrong, wasn't he?
Let's be honest about it,
    he made a promise which he hasn't been able to keep.
There have been wars and rumours of wars,
    chaos, confusion, unrest and upheaval,
    all the things he predicted,
    but a generation has come and a generation has gone
    with neither sight nor sound of his coming.
We've seen nation rise against nation,
    famine,
    earthquake,
    flood.
There's been persecution,
    sorrow,
    untold suffering;
    brother betraying brother,
    families divided among themselves,
    just as he said it would be –
    in fact, there's only one thing missing,
    one piece left to complete the jigsaw,
    and that's him,
    the one it should all be about!
So that's it, isn't it –
    the end of the story,
    the death of the dream –
    no point believing any longer?
Unless, maybe, we've missed something,
    misunderstood what he was trying to say.
Is it possible?
Is that why he spoke of heaven and earth passing away
    but his words standing for ever?
Could it be that, though the fulfilment is yet to come,
    the kingdom is here now,
    growing all around us if only we have eyes to see it?
Come to think of it, isn't that what he said:
    'The kingdom is among you'?
In every act of love and deed of kindness,
    every word of witness and testimony to his saving grace,
    bit by bit it's taking shape;
    another brick in the wall,
    another thread woven into the tapestry,
    each bringing the day of fulfilment a little closer.
It may not be quite the time-scale we imagined,
    nor the one *he* had in mind, either,

but, if that causes us to doubt,
    maybe we're looking for the wrong thing
    in the wrong place at the wrong time.
The signs are there, plain enough,
    just as he promised they would be.
Do not despair.
Do not lose hope.
Springtime is upon us.
The summer is near.

NICK FAWCETT

Thought for the day

Keep alert, because much is demanded of those to whom much is entrusted.

Aim

To explore the practicalities for keeping alert for when Jesus comes.

What's in store

Characters

Manager, Assistant, Customer, Boss.

Provide a jacket and tie for the manager, various items of the store's produce and some authentic cardboard cartons. The manager and shop assistant are moving cartons from one place in the shop to another.

Manager	Easy does it, Fred.
Assistant	Yes, sir.
Manager	Always bend your knees, rather than your back.
Assistant	Yes, sir.
Manager	I take my responsibilities seriously, you know; and as a shop assistant your back is one of my heavy responsibilities.
Assistant	Yes, sir. These chocolate and nut cookies weigh a ton, don't they, sir?
Manager	Ah yes, more heavy responsibilities the boss left me with, eh . . . ha, ha!
Customer	Hallo, Harold! The boss gone away and left you in charge, has he? How about a packet of chocolate and nut cookies for friendship's sake? I'll buy you a pint this evening at the Crown.

Manager	You owe me a pint as it is, you old skinflint! And anyway, what do you think the boss would think if he came back and found me dishing out his stock. He's left me in charge because he reckons I'll look after things properly for him.
Customer	I don't think you'll see the boss in a hurry. He's languishing in the sun somewhere I expect. Anyway, I'll have some chewing gum. *(He buys chewing gum, thanks the manager and leaves)*
Manager	What's that grinding noise, Fred?
Assistant	That's my stomach, sir. It seems a long time since breakfast. *(He strokes one of the packets of cookies)*
Manager	Yes, I'm rather peckish, myself. Oh, come on, let's split a packet of these between us! Bill's probably right – the boss won't be back yet. *(They do so and start eating)*
Boss	*(Comes in and stares amazed at what is going on. Then he coughs to get their attention)* So this is the man who was so sure I could trust him, is it?
Manager	*(Trying to hide biscuits)* Mr Taylor! I . . . I wasn't expecting you!
Boss	Evidently. Mr Woodman . . .
Manager	Yes, sir?
Boss	You're fired.

Discuss and list suggestions for practical ways to stay alert and avoid falling into temptation.

Discussion starters

1. Obedience is something most of us find very hard. How is it linked to selfishness and what factors make it easier / more difficult for us to do?

2. When is obedience a matter of life and death? How can we practise obedience in little ways so we're ready for the Big Event?   Susan Sayers

The Second Sunday of Advent

John the Baptist, the voice in the wilderness foretold by Isaiah

Luke 3:1-6

(also Malachi 3:1-4; Luke 1:68-79 (canticle); Philippians 1:3-11)

A reading from the Gospel of Luke (3:1-6)

When Pontius Pilate was governor of Judea, a man appeared in the wilderness and began to preach the Word of God; his name was John. He called the people to turn away from sin and to ask for God's forgiveness, and he baptised them as a sign of turning back to God. All this happened just as the prophet Isaiah had foretold:

> A voice cries out in the wilderness,
> prepare a path for the Lord.
> Make it straight and smooth
> and all people will see God's salvation.

This is the Gospel of the Lord
Praise to you, Lord Jesus Christ   Katie Thompson

Introductory material

We are here today at one of the best-loved times of the Christian Year – the season of Advent. But what does Advent mean to us apart from Advent candles, traditional hymns, and a sense that Christmas is getting closer? All too often that's about it; yet it shouldn't be, for Advent is above all a time for preparation, a time for looking back to the Christ who came, and looking forward to the Christ who shall come again. It is an invitation to reflect not simply on Christmas, but on the whole of the Gospel, and to ask ourselves the all-important question: 'What does it mean for me?'   Nick Fawcett

Prayers

Praise – Receiving the word

Gracious God,
    we praise you today for the power of your word,
        the way you have spoken to so many people
        throughout history.

    You called the universe into being –
        heaven and earth,
        night and day,
        the sea and the dry land,
        life in its multitude of manifestations.
    You spoke,
        and it was done,
        our world and our very existence owing to you.
    For your word of life,
        we praise you.

    You called Abraham, Isaac and Jacob,
        Moses and Joshua,
        judges, kings and prophets,
        Apostles, disciples, preachers and teachers –
        a great company of saints,
        each testifying to your sovereign purpose,
        your awesome power
        and your merciful love;
        each hearing your voice and responding in faith.
    For your word of life,
        we praise you.

    You came in Jesus Christ, the Word made flesh,
        identifying yourself with our humanity,
        sharing our joy and sorrow,
        experiencing our life and death.
    You came in fulfilment of your promises of old,
        revealing the extent of your love
        through everything he said and did,
        demonstrating your gracious purpose for all.
    For your word of life,
        we praise you.

    You speak still through the pages of Scripture;
        through their record of your involvement in history
        and their testimony to your will for the world.

You speak through dialogue between Christians,
   through the witness of your Church and personal testimony,
   through study and reflection,
   and through the sharing of fellowship.
You speak through the grandeur of the universe
   and the wonder of life,
   your still small voice breaking into our experience
   to challenge and inspire.
For your word of life,
   we praise you.

Gracious God,
   we rejoice at the ways you have spoken to us in the past
   and the way you continue to speak today.
We receive your word with joyful thanksgiving,
   and we pray for strength to make it so much a part of us
   that your voice may be heard through all we are and do,
   to the glory of your name.
For your word of life,
   we praise you.

Through Jesus Christ our Lord.
Amen.   NICK FAWCETT

Petition – Advent witness

Loving God,
   we remember today how prophets foretold the coming of Christ –
   how they declared their faith in your purpose,
   their confidence in your love,
   their assurance of your final victory.
They did not keep their faith to themselves;
   they shared it with others:
   teach us to do the same.

We remember how shepherds responded
   to the message of the angels –
   how they hurried to Bethlehem
   and found the baby lying in a manger,
   and how they went on their way praising and glorifying you
   for everything they had seen and heard.
They did not keep their faith to themselves;
   they shared it with others:
   teach us to do the same.

We remember how John the Baptist
    prepared the way of Christ in the wilderness –
    how he proclaimed a baptism of repentance,
    a new beginning,
    the coming of one far greater than he could ever be.
He did not keep his faith to himself;
    he shared it with others:
    teach us to do the same.

We remember how you came to us in Christ –
    how he brought light into our darkness,
    hope into our despair,
    joy into our sorrow.
He did not keep his faith *to* himself.
He did not live his life *for* himself;
    he shared it with others:
    teach us to do the same.

In his name we pray.
Amen.
                                      NICK FAWCETT

Intercession

The Word of God has been gradually unfolded all through the Old Testament, throughout the New Testament and ever since.

Father, we think of the difficulties facing the church;
and pray for all who minister your love.
Silence for prayer
We believe and proclaim:
Jesus is Lord in every situation

Father, we think of the way our world
is torn apart by war and lack of love.
Silence for prayer
We believe and proclaim:
Jesus is Lord in every situation

Father, we think of those
whose lives are hard and twisted.
Silence for prayer
We believe and proclaim:
Jesus is Lord in every situation

Father, we think of the great pressures
on this generation to abandon your ways,
and of all those who feel lost
and without real value.

Silence for prayer

We believe and proclaim:
Jesus is Lord in every situation

Father, we think of those we find it hard to relate to,
and of those who sometimes find us
difficult to get on with.

Silence for prayer

We believe and proclaim:
Jesus is Lord in every situation

Father, we think of all
who fill our days with love and friendship.

Silence for prayer

Merciful Father,
accept these prayers
for the sake of your Son,
our Saviour Jesus Christ, Amen.   SUSAN SAYERS

A short prayer

Loving God,
　you called your servant John
　to go out into the wilderness
　to prepare the way of the Lord;
　not to be the light you promised,
　but to point to the one who was coming,
　who would bring light to all.
You call us in turn to share in this responsibility,
　to prepare the way of Christ
　in the wilderness of the world today.
Give us the courage, the faith and the humility
　we need to respond,
　and may our lives bear witness in word and deed
　to the life-giving power of Christ,
　in whose name we pray.
Amen.   NICK FAWCETT

All-age-talk material

Read Luke 3:1-6

Verses 4-6 of this reading are taken from Isaiah 40:3-5. These words were spoken to the people of Israel while they were exiled in Babylon. Exile meant that they were far from home and that many of the young Israelites were born in exile and didn't know anything other than the land of their exile.

Exile also meant living as captives: never knowing freedom. The ability of the Israelites to promote their culture and traditions was severely limited. They couldn't live as they wanted to or behave in any way that might annoy their captors. They would often be made to work in situations that were at best unpleasant and at worst so bad they'd reduce their life expectancy to zero! The exiles' lives were not their own; they belonged, body and soul, to their captors.

The words in verses 4-6 announce the end of captivity and the start of a new life of freedom.

At the time of John the Baptist, Galilee and Judea were under Roman rule. Although the people weren't physically in exile they were captives in their own land. The Romans brought with them traditions, customs, beliefs, politics and a lifestyle that were distinctly 'foreign'. No wonder that John the Baptist's words were greeted with such enthusiasm. Most of the people wanted an end to the Roman occupation and were fed up with being 'exiles' in their own land.

However, John was referring to the people's emotional and spiritual exile. It was an exile that had seen the people become so busy with customs and traditions that they had gradually lost sight of who God was. The people had become captives of a society that presented many alternatives to God and as many ways to God as there were roads to Rome.

John announced the coming of 'one' who would 'straighten the crooked paths and smooth out the rough roads' (verse 5). John was preparing the way for the people to return to God and know what it was to be where they belonged, no longer captives to fear, suffering and death, allowing their lives to be cared for and guided by the Heavenly Father.   PETE TOWNSEND

Books of the Bible

Reading

2 Timothy 3:14-4:5

Aim

To get across the message that God speaks through the Bible – and that we need to read it!

(This talk is suitable for any Sunday of the year, but is especially suited for Bible Sunday.)

Preparation

On large pieces of paper or card reproduce the following 'Catchphrase' clues.

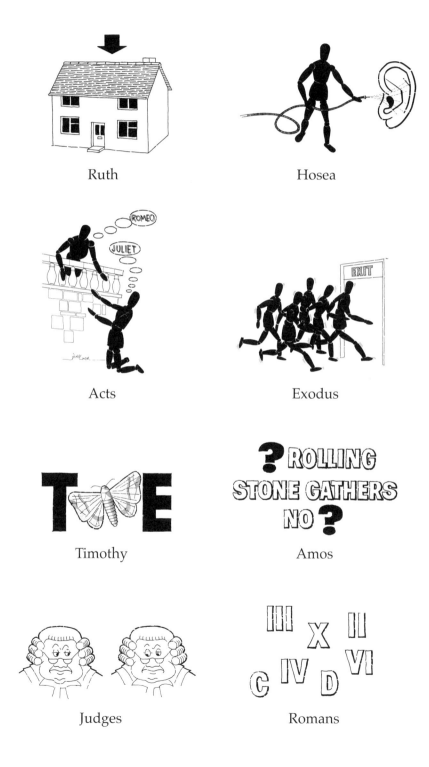

Ruth

Hosea

Acts

Exodus

Timothy

Amos

Judges

Romans

Numbers

Isaiah

Proverbs

Lamentations

Nehemiah

Esther

Ephesians

1 Peter

Talk

Begin by asking the congregation how many books there are in the Bible (66), how many in the Old Testament (39), and how many in the New Testament (27). Explain that you have chosen sixteen books for them to identify from your 'Catchphrase' drawings.

When all the answers have been revealed, explain that there is a serious message in all this and ask if anyone has spotted it – 'Read your Bible through'.

These are just some of the books of the Bible, but, as we were reminded earlier, there are 66 books in all. How many of these could they name? And, more important, how many have they read?

Reading the Bible isn't always easy, especially some of the lesser known books in it, and there will be times, as with the clues above, when we spend time wondering just what a particular passage means. We need help, advice and support if we are to get the most out of our Bibles. But as Christians we believe the Bible is a record not only of the way God has spoken to his people in times past, but his word to us now; a book which has a message for everybody and every part of our lives; a book which opens the way to knowing God and living life as he wants us to live it.

It's true that the Bible can be hard to understand, but if we make time to study it we will find the effort more than worth it, for we will discover God speaking his word to us!   NICK FAWCETT

Be prepared

God sent John
the Baptist to prepare the
way for Jesus

Use the code to find out what Isaiah said John would do

CODE	A	F	O	T
△	A	F	O	T
○	D	H	P	W
□	E	L	R	Y
	1	2	3	4

Luke 3:4

' __ __ __ __ __ __ __
3○ 3□ 1□ 3○ 1△ 3□ 1□

__   __ __ __   __ __ __
1△   4○ 1△ 4□   2△ 3△ 3□

                        ,
__ __ __   __ __ __ __
4△ 2○ 1□   2□ 3△ 3□ 1○

KATIE THOMPSON

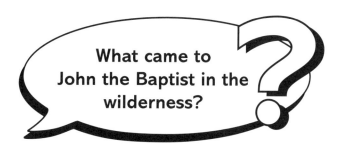

What came to John the Baptist in the wilderness?

Use the clues to find the missing letters and decode the answer

A place where trees grow

△ ⊡ ◇ ○ ⋁ ↑

What a kangaroo does

𝖫 ⊡ ✷ ⋁

Cricket bats are made from this

∼ ⊡ ⊡ ⩘

A very thick mist

△ ⊡ ꞊ₒ꞊

Opposite of enemy

△ ◇ ✽ ○ ∩ ⩘

Season following autumn

∼ ✽ ∩ ↑ ○ ◇

↑ 𝖫 ○   ∼ ⊡ ◇ ⩘

⊡ △   ꞊ₒ꞊ ⊡ ⩘

Luke 3:2

KATIE THOMPSON

Today is the
Second Sunday of Advent
and we light two candles
on our wreath

**Write the first letter of each picture to
find the missing words in the poem!**

On this _ _ _ _ _ _ Sunday,

_ _ _ candles we light,

The _ _ _ _ _ from our wreath,

Is now twice as _ _ _ _ _ _ ,

_ _ _ sent John the Baptist,

To help change our _ _ _ _ _ _

And show us the _ _ _ to make a fresh start

In the words of _ _ _ _ _ _ , 'prepare a way',

So that we will be ready for

_ _ _ _ _ _ _ _ _ _ day!

KATIE THOMPSON

Reflective material
(sketches, meditations and poems)

Meditation of Zechariah, father of John the Baptist

How did we feel about him?
Well, you don't really need to ask, do you?
We were more proud than words can say.
To think that our lad, John,
    should be the one spoken of by the prophet,
    chosen to proclaim the coming of the Messiah,
    to announce the dawn of his kingdom.
What an honour!
What a privilege!
The very thought of it still takes our breath away!
To tell the truth, we've had to be careful sometimes
    not to get carried away,
    not to put our son on a pedestal
    as though *he* was the one God had promised;
    heaven knows he's special enough to us.
Yet if ever we fell into that trap, he soon put us right,
    reminding us, in no uncertain terms,
    just what his role is in the great scheme of things.
It's funny how he knows,
    for we've never spelt it out to him,
    never had any need to –
    he seems to have understood from the very beginning
    what God expects from him.
You only had to see him as a boy to recognise that;
    the way he acted towards Jesus, especially –
    it was as though he had a special responsibility towards him,
    and I swear sometimes there was a hint of admiration in his eyes,
    even awe as they played together!
If anything, it's become more apparent as the years have passed;
    a special bond developing between them,
    but there's always been an element of distance too,
    a sense, on John's part anyway,
    of getting this close and no further,
    as though there's a gulf in status between them
    which he would never presume to cross.
Not everyone could do that, could they? –
    accept a supporting role rather than a position centre-stage –
    but there's never been a hint of resentment,
    still less any desire to thrust himself forward.
A voice in the wilderness, that's how he describes himself,

sent to prepare the way of the Lord,
   to make straight his path in readiness for his kingdom –
   and he's shown since exactly what that means.
Not that he's the only one who longs for that day –
   we've all prayed for it for as long as I can remember.
The difference is that John doesn't simply talk about it,
   he's helping to make it happen,
   his actions as well as his words,
   his whole life, in fact,
   a daily witness to the change God requires of us –
   a foretaste, if you like, of that transformation he holds in store.
You think you're ready for his coming,
   ready to welcome the Messiah?
Well, maybe you are,
   but before you get too complacent
   just ask yourself this:
   what are you doing to bring his kingdom closer?
For until you can answer that, take it from me,
   you're nowhere near ready at all.   NICK FAWCETT

The Wrinklies at the Park

Characters	Two wrinkled grumps who like nothing better than to have a whinge about anything and everything.
Scene	The two Wrinklies sitting on a park bench watching all the people passing by on their way to hear John the Baptist.
Props	two old raincoats hats walking stick umbrella park bench pair of tatty sandals for Old 1

Old 1	Gracious me, would you just look at that!
Old 2	What's that, then?
Old 1	Over there, look. (*Points into distance*)
Old 2	(*Rubs eyes and stares into distance*) What?
Old 1	Are you blind or summat?
Old 2	Nah, just takes me eyes a few moments to get adjusted, that's all. Now, what are you on about?

Old 1	Her over there *(points)* see?
Old 2	*(Nods head)* Oh her. Haven't seen her about for a while. Last I heard she'd taken to her bed after a drop too much of the falling-over juice.
Old 1	*(Cackles)* Must be summat good to get her out of bed.
Old 2	Usually a jumble sale. Haven't heard of one, have you?
Old 1	Nah, *(waves sandals under nose of Old 2)* got these last time. They've seen a few sights.
Old 2	*(Holds nose)* Smells like they've stepped in a few as well.
Old 1	It's them donkeys. Don't care where they do their business. You'd think the authorities would do summat about it. Pays me taxes, regular.
Old 2	Don't give me authorities. Right bunch of parasites. It's all take, take, take.
Old 1	Too right. As long as they're all right, nothing and nobody else matters.
Old 2	It's about time somebody stood up to them. Told 'em a few things, put 'em straight. *(Waves walking stick in the air)* If I were a few years younger, I'd make them see sense, good smack around the head, that's what they need.
Old 1	Steady on, who's rattled your cage?
Old 2	Well, it ain't right.
Old 1	What ain't?
Old 2	Anything you care to think of.
Old 1	Got out of bed the wrong side, eh?
Old 2	Wasn't worth going to bed. Couldn't sleep.
Old 1	Your old trouble playing up again?
Old 2	*(Looks at knees)* Nah, they're all right. It's all those folk walking past my house.
Old 1	What they up to, then?
Old 2	They're traipsing off to see that weird bloke, you know, the one who keeps shouting his mouth off about getting ready for summat or other.
Old 1	Who, Zec and Liz's lad?

Old 2	That's the one. Been living in the desert, so I hear.
Old 1	That's not all I've heard.
Old 2	*(Nudges Old 1)* Go on, what have you heard? I enjoy a bit of gossip. Did ya hear about old Ben and that mix up with the goat's cheese?
Old 1	What was that, then?
Old 2	Turns out he'd been milking old Joe's goats at night, making the cheese and selling it.
Old 1	Didn't Joe think summat was wrong when he didn't get any milk from his goats?
Old 2	Nah, he just thought the goats had run dry. He spent a fortune in vets' bills.
Old 1	What did old Ben say when he got caught?
Old 2	He reckoned the goats were wild and anyone could have milked 'em.
Old 1	Were they running wild?
Old 2	Nah, they were in Joe's backyard.
Old 1	What's old Ben like, eh?
Old 2	Well, at least he dresses properly, not like that fella in the desert. All dressed up in camel hair.
Old 1	Bit itchy.
Old 2	Doesn't seem to bother him. Reckons the only thing that bothers him is all the bad things people have done and that they should turn back to God.
Old 1	Who does he think he is?
Old 2	Well, he's said to be the creator and . . .
Old 1	Not God, you dozy lump, this desert fella.
Old 2	Oh, John they call him, John the Baptist.
Old 1	The Baptist?
Old 2	Yeah, tells people they're dirty inside and throws 'em in the river.
Old 1	Don't think I'd want to swallow much of that River Jordan; too many people wash their feet in there, including you.

Old 2   I'll ignore that. Anyway, this John fella caused a bit of a stir when those Pharisees and Sadducees went up to see him.

Old 1   What did he do?

Old 2   Called 'em a load of snakes.

Old 1   Bet that rattled 'em!

Old 2   He wants to be careful what he says, could get himself into trouble saying the wrong things. *(Stands up)* Right, I'm off then.

Old 1   Me too. Gonna go and see this John fella. I reckon my feet could do with a wash.

PETE TOWNSEND

The Third Sunday of Advent

A call to repentance and promise of forgiveness

Luke 3:7-18

(also Zephaniah 3:14-20; Isaiah 12:2-6 (canticle); Philippians 4:4-7)

A reading from the Gospel of Luke (3:10-18)

The people listened to John the Baptist's words and asked him, 'What must we do?'

John told them, 'Be generous and kind, and always ready to share whatever you have with others.' To the tax collectors he said, 'Take no more than you are owed,' and to the soldiers he said, 'Force no one to give you what is not yours. Be content with what you already have.'

The people grew excited and many began to think that John might be the Messiah, promised by God.

But John told them, 'I baptise you with water, but someone is coming who will baptise you with the Holy Spirit. He is filled with the power of God, and I am not good enough to undo his sandals. Just as the wheat and the chaff are separated at harvest time, he will separate the good from the bad.'

This is the Gospel of the Lord
Praise to you, Lord Jesus Christ   KATIE THOMPSON

Introductory material

We come today to hear again familiar words of scripture, words which pointed centuries beforehand to the coming of Jesus Christ, the Word made flesh. We come rejoicing that God still speaks today, through the same scriptures and the same Lord, able to challenge and guide, to encourage and inspire, to comfort and bless, to teach and nurture. We come, seeking to understand more of everything God has spoken across the centuries, and so asking that we may hear his voice today; his word speaking to our lives, here and now.

NICK FAWCETT

Prayers

Petition – The way of Christ

Lord Jesus Christ,
  you came to our world, sharing our humanity,
    identifying yourself with us,
    expressing through actions and self-sacrifice your love for all.
  Teach us to follow in your footsteps.

  Yours was the way of service, compassion and reconciliation.
  Despite the rejection of so many,
    you saw the best in people,
    the good,
    the worth that others overlooked.
  Teach us to follow in your footsteps.

  You loved all,
    without prejudice,
    without passing judgement,
    without any strings attached.
  Teach us to follow in your footsteps.

Lord Jesus Christ,
  you come to our world still each day,
    but to do that fully you need our co-operation,
    our willingness to be used for your purpose.
  Teach us to follow in your footsteps.

  You need us to speak for you,
    to act for you,
    to show your love and share your life
  Teach us to follow in your footsteps.

  You need us to take that way of service,
    to break down barriers,
    to bring people together.
  Teach us to follow in your footsteps.

  You need us to take the Way of the Cross –
    valuing people for what they are,
    offering them trust and encouragement,
    helping them to believe in themselves.
  Teach us to follow in your footsteps.

Lord Jesus Christ,
   you came to our world to establish a new kingdom,
     a new era,
     a new dimension to life.
   Help us through who we are
     and all we do to bring that kingdom nearer.
   Teach us to follow in your footsteps,
     for in your name we ask it.
   Amen.   NICK FAWCETT

Thanksgiving and Intercession –
Sharing the Good News

Living God,
   we thank you for the great message of the Gospel,
     the glad tidings of your love,
     the good news of your coming to our world
     through your Son Jesus Christ.
   May that message inspire us again this Christmas-time
     and in the days to come.
   Speak your word of love,
     and move in the hearts of all who hear it.

We thank you that the Good News of Christ
   has challenged people across the ages,
     and that though it has been proclaimed countless times,
     though we have heard it ourselves so many times before,
     it continues to be news for us and news for all –
     able still to speak to individuals across the world
     and change their lives.
   Speak your word of love,
     and move in the hearts of all who hear it.

So now we pray for those you have specially called
   to proclaim the Good News –
   ministers,
   preachers,
   evangelists,
   teachers –
   all those with the special gift and responsibility
   of communicating your word.

Grant them wisdom,
   dedication,
   inspiration,
   and courage,
   that they may faithfully witness to you
   in the power of the Holy Spirit.
Speak your word of love,
   and move in the hearts of all who hear it.   NICK FAWCETT

Petition and Intercession

Lord Jesus Christ,
   at this time supposedly of goodwill among all,
     we pray for peace in our world –
     an end to division and discord,
     hatred and hostility,
     death and destruction.
   Prince of Peace,
     hear our prayer.

Lord Jesus,
   we speak of peace
     but in our hearts we do not believe it possible.
   When we look at our world
     we see little hope of an end to its troubles.
   We are sceptical,
     uncertain,
     filled with doubts,
     cautious about expressing any optimism.
   Even where there are signs of hope,
     moves towards reconciliation,
     we know it will take many years
     before we dare believe it is really possible.
   But, we pray in this Advent season,
     renew our ability to look forward,
     rekindle our belief in the future,
     and restore our capacity to hope for better things.
   Prince of Peace,
     hear our prayer.

   Help us –
     as we remember your coming,
     as we serve you now,
     and as we look forward to your coming again –

to anticipate your kingdom
  through the service we offer and the lives we live.
Prince of Peace,
  hear our prayer.

Teach us to work for that day
  when your throne shall be established,
  your justice prevail,
  and the earth be filled with the knowledge of you
  as the waters cover the sea.
Prince of Peace,
  hear our prayer,
  for your name's sake.
Amen.   NICK FAWCETT

Short prayer

Loving God,
  you promised Abraham that through his offspring
  all the earth would be blessed – and it was.
You promised through your prophets
  that the Messiah would come – and he came.
You promised Mary
  that she would give birth to a son – and she did.
You promised the disciples
  that death would not be the end – and it wasn't.
You promised your followers
  that they would receive the Holy Spirit –
  and it happened.
Loving God,
  you promise that when two or three are gathered
  in the name of Christ,
  he will be there among them.
Help us, remembering the faithfulness you have
  always shown,
  to trust in that promise too –
  to know you are here and to meet with you now.   NICK FAWCETT

All-age-talk material

Read Luke 3:7-18

You have to imagine the scene: out of the desert comes this large, hairy man, dressed in clothes made of camel's hair, a leather strap around his waist and living on a diet of grasshoppers and wild honey (see Matthew 3:4). Not only does he look a tiny bit different, but he's shouting his head off about all manner of things!

After quoting the prophet Isaiah, John then goes on to call a load of people 'snakes who come running from judgement'.

John had spent a long time in the desert, some might say too long! The desert was covered in brushwood, twigs and dry stalks of dead plants. At times a spark could set the desert alight, burning anything that could be burnt. When this happened, it was common for vipers to slither out of the nooks and crannies where they lay hidden, and attempt to escape the flames. It was this picture that John must have had in his head when the people rushed to hear what he had to say. Some thought he was the Messiah, a claim he quickly denied by saying that he was not good enough to untie the sandals of the one to come. (The act of undoing someone's sandals was the act of a servant.)

The people who came to John wanted to know what they had to do to escape the 'coming judgement' (see verse 7). John didn't tell them to get down and pray, go to church as often as they could or read the scripture continuously; he directed his comments at their lifestyle. John told the tax collectors not to overcharge to line their own pockets, he told the soldiers not to charge protection money and he told those who were well-off to share what they had with the poor. These were all issues that Jesus later tackled.

John was trying to make it clear that just appearing to act 'godly', by going to church, reading the Bible and praying, was not what God required. God wanted a change of heart which would be reflected by the way people lived.

What do the group think about the way that John spoke to the people who came to see him? Wasn't he making enemies rather than encouraging people to turn back to God and be baptised (verse 3)? Eventually, John did use a few too many words when he criticised Herod Antipas, ruler of the area, for marrying Herodias (who was, at one time, Herod's sister-in-law and his niece). Herod Antipas met Herodias, who was married to another bloke called . . . Herod. He seduced her and later married her. Now, Herod Antipas was related to Herod who was married to Herodias (!) In one way and another, Herod, Herod Antipas and Herodias were all related through Herod the Great. It gets confusing (not to mention a severe lack of imagination when it comes to names), but by the standards of Jewish law and opinion the marriage of Herod Antipas and Herodias was well out of order. Using a few choice words, John the Baptist pointed out that Herod Antipas' actions were wrong, which resulted in John being shoved in prison for his failure to compromise his message.

Are there any areas of our lives where John's lack of compromise would embarrass us?

PETE TOWNSEND

Turn back to God

God sent John the Baptist to tell the people about Jesus his Son

John baptised people in the River _ _ _ _ _ _ ?

Find the letters hidden in the picture!

KATIE THOMPSON

The people asked
John what God wanted them to
do. Last week did you find out
what he told them?

Add or subtract letters to find out whether you were right!

A B C D E F G H I J K L M N O P Q R S T U V W X Y Z

1. _____   _____

M+6D+4G−6P?2Q−12   Z−3G+1F−5 X−4D+1S+3G?2 V−4

_____   _____

Z−1D+11P+5   G+1L−11T+2D?1

2. _____   _____

C−1A+4   N−6L+3P?2 J−5 Q+2Y−5

3. _____   _____

F−4 F−1   A+2K+4A+13V−2F?1M+1X−4

KATIE THOMPSON

Some people thought that John was the Saviour promised by God

Use the code to find out what he told them

○	P	U	S	M	K
◇	I	T	O	L	R
☽	E	N	H	W	Z
□	Y	B	A	C	G
	☀	♡	☺	△	☆

'SOMEONE IS COMING

WHO WILL BAPTIZE

YOU WITH THE

HOLY SPIRIT'

Luke 3:16

KATIE THOMPSON

Luke 3:1-20

Aim

To help people see the relevance of John the Baptist's teaching in their own lives.

Begin by asking them to line themselves up in order of height, then in order of shoe size, then by number of beans they can hold in one hand (dried, or baked if you are feeling adventurous or gross). They will find that the way they line up varies according to the standard or yardstick.

Now read the Luke passage together, asking them to look out for the standard John the Baptist wanted them to use in getting their lives lined up. Keep note of the suggestions made after the reading.

Have a look at yourselves and your church against this standard – God's standard of love and respect for one another.

Discussion starters

1. The people of Israel knew that Elijah would return to herald the coming of the Messiah. In what ways is John the Baptist similar to Elijah?

2. What makes us repentant? Why doesn't repentance lead to despair?

SUSAN SAYERS

Reflective material
(sketches, meditations and poems)

Meditation of John the Baptist

Shall I tell you something strange?
Almost funny you might call it, were it not so sad.
It's about me,
   the voice in the wilderness,
   the baptiser in the Jordan,
   the one sent to prepare the way of the Lord.
Well, I managed that, didn't I?
Or at least so they'll tell you –
   I made straight a path in the wilderness,
   I paved the way for his coming,
   and, yes, I have to say I made a good job of it,
   too good in a sense,
   for, much to my embarrassment, many were so impressed
   they followed me instead of him.
But it wasn't just them who got it wrong,

it was me,
   for when Jesus finally came I was as unprepared as any.
Oh, I didn't realise it at the time,
   far from it –
   in fact, I thought I was an example to them all,
   the one who, more than any other,
   understood who he was and what he came to do.
'Behold the lamb of God!' I told them,
   'the one who comes to take away the sin of the world.'
A good speech, wouldn't you say?
But it was just words,
   sounding impressive,
   but belying the truth beneath.
And it wasn't long after –
   when his ministry had begun and mine ended,
   when he was travelling the byways of Judah
   and I was rotting in prison –
   that I found myself questioning everything.
'Could he be the Messiah?' I asked,
   'the one we'd so long waited for?'
If he was, then why was so little happening –
   why so little evidence of his kingdom getting closer?
I should have known different, of course I should,
   and, yes, you may well say a hint of jealousy
   coloured my judgement.
But, honestly, how would you have felt in my position,
   knowing that, having given your all,
   more would be asked,
   even life itself?
It won't be long now before they come for me,
   I'm under no illusions.
There's no escape,
   no possibility of a last-minute reprieve;
   that wife of Herod's won't rest
   until she sees me dead and buried,
   the voice in the wilderness silenced for ever.
I wasn't prepared for that when I started,
   and I still wouldn't have been, just a day ago.
But thank God he's given me time to think,
   to hear what Jesus is doing,
   to understand what it's all leading up to,
   and I'm ready now,
   at last I'm ready,
   prepared for anything
   prepared for everything!

NICK FAWCETT

Meditation of Zechariah, father of John the Baptist

I wanted to believe it, honestly!
After all those years trying,
   all those false hopes and crushing disappointments,
   there was nothing I wanted to believe more.
A child!
A son!
At our time of life!
Wonderful!
But that was the trouble –
   we were too old,
   not just *over* the hill but well down the other side,
   and we'd both accepted we just weren't meant to be parents.
It hurt, of course it did,
   but little by little we'd come to terms with it,
   the pain easing as we threw ourselves into what was left us.
So why suddenly this strange vision,
   this sense of God speaking to me
   in a way so real and powerful
   it was as though an angel was there in person,
   spelling out the message word for word?
To be frank I felt we could do without it, both of us,
   and, whatever else, there was no way I intended
   to go running back to Elizabeth,
   opening up old wounds.
So I just laughed it off,
   shrugged my shoulders and carried on
   as though nothing had happened.
Let's face it, I reasoned,
   a few more years and we'd be pushing up the daisies,
   an end to life's mysteries once and for all.
Well, I couldn't have been more wrong, could I?
For it happened,
   every last word of it,
   down to the final detail!
How did I feel?
Well, you can imagine.
Ecstatic!
Just about beside myself with joy!
It was the proudest and most wonderful moment of my life,
   and for a time after the birth I could think of nothing else,
   every moment too precious to waste.
Yet I've been thinking recently
   about those words spoken by the angel,
   for when he spoke of John's coming,

he talked also of the role he was destined to fulfil:
   'He will turn many of the people of Israel to the Lord their God.
   With the spirit and power of Elijah he will go before him,
   to make ready a people prepared for the Lord.'
I forgot that afterwards in all the excitement,
   too much else going on to give it a second thought.
But do you think it could possibly mean what I think it does?
God's promised Messiah, coming at last?
A child, born to *me, that* was wonderful!
But for us *all,*
   a child to change the world –
   could that really be?   NICK FAWCETT

The Fourth Sunday of Advent

Nothing is impossible with God

Luke 1:39-45 (46-55); Luke 1:26-49
(also Micah 5:2-5a; Psalm 80:1-8 (or Magnificat); Hebrews 10:5-10)

A reading from the Gospel of Luke (1:39-44)

After the angel Gabriel had appeared to Mary, she set off at once to visit her cousin Elizabeth. When Elizabeth saw Mary coming, she ran to welcome her, and the baby inside her leapt for joy at the sound of Mary's greeting.

Elizabeth was filled with the Holy Spirit and said to Mary, 'Of all women you are the most blessed, and blessed is the child you will have, because you believe in the power of God and he has chosen you to be the mother of our Saviour.'

This is the Gospel of the Lord
Praise to you, Lord Jesus Christ   KATIE THOMPSON

Alternative reading: Luke 1:26-49

This is St Luke's adaptation of the Song of Zephaniah to announce the birth of Christ – the guarantee that God is with us.

God sent his angel to the town of Nazareth in Galilee,
to a young woman called Mary
who was engaged to a man called Joseph,
a distant descendant of King David.

The angel said to her,
'Shout for joy, Mary, beloved of God!
The Lord is in your midst.'
Mary was startled,
and wondered what these words could mean.
The angel said,
'Do not be afraid, Mary.
God has chosen you to be mother of his Son.
You must give the baby the name "Jesus",
which means "God has come as our Saviour".
He will inherit the throne of his ancestor David,
and rule over God's people for ever.'

Mary said,
'How can this come about? I am not yet married.'
The angel replied,
'The power of God will enfold you.
Nothing is impossible for God.'
Mary said,
'I am here to serve the Lord.
Let it be as you have said.
The Almighty has worked this marvel for me.'   H. J. RICHARDS

Prayers

Approach – God's need of us

Living God,
    you promised to come to your people of old
        through the Advent of the Messiah.
    You promise to come to each of us
        in the triumphant and glorious return of your Son.
    Open our hearts to his coming.

Loving God,
    you came into our world through Mary,
        entering our world of space and time.
    You want to come afresh through each of us,
        Christ made real in our day to day lives.
    Open our hearts to his presence.

Gracious God,
    you needed Mary's assent
        before you could work through her.
    You need our willingness
        to let you work through us.
    Open our hearts to your Spirit.

Sovereign God,
    you called Mary to believe that with you
        nothing is impossible.
    You need us to show that same faith
        if your kingdom is to come.
    Open our minds to all that you can do.

Mighty God,
  you brought a new beginning to Mary,
    to Joseph,
    to your people Israel,
    to all the world.
  You offer a new beginning to each of us,
    this and every day.
  Open our lives to your renewing, transforming love,
    through Christ our Lord.
  Amen.   NICK FAWCETT

Carol service approach – Coming to see

Father God,
  we thank you for this day of praise and celebration –
    this day on which we set aside time
    to relive that first Christmas long ago,
    on which we remind ourselves
    of the wonder of the birth of Christ,
    on which we remember once more the glad tidings
    proclaimed to the shepherds,
    witnessed by the wise men,
    made possible through Mary.

Loving Father,
  we come to give thanks for this season –
    to rejoice at your great love in sending your Son,
    to see for ourselves the truth discovered by the shepherds,
    to worship Christ and offer our gifts
    as wise men came before us.

  We come asking you to use us,
    just as you used your servant Mary to enter our world.
  Take our faith, small though it is,
    take our gifts, few though they are,
    take our love, poor though this seems,
    take our lives, weak though we may be.

Loving Father,
  speak to us through this service.
  May all we hear draw us closer to you,
    may all we share remind us of your love,
    and so may the message of Christmas
    come alive in our hearts,
    to the glory of your name.
  Amen.   NICK FAWCETT

Christmas intercession

God of love,
we pray for all those many people
who will be celebrating Christmas this year,
enjoying presents, parties, food and fun,
yet not having heard or accepted or understood
what Christmas is all about.
Speak to them now,
and help them to respond.

We pray for those who have never heard the Gospel,
or received a distorted picture of its message,
or failed to recognise it is good news for them.
Speak to them now,
and help them to respond.

We pray for those who have closed their hearts and minds to Christ,
refusing to listen or consider further,
rejecting your Son as so many rejected him at his coming.
Speak to them now,
and help them to respond.

We pray for those who have come to faith
but barely realised what that means,
seeing perhaps just a small part of all you have done,
or seeking to know more but troubled by doubts and questions.
Speak to them now,
and help them to respond.

God of love,
come again to our world this Christmas,
breaking through our cosy traditions,
our narrow horizons,
our neatly packaged celebrations.
Speak to *us* now,
and help *us* to respond.

Help us and all people
to glimpse the wonder of your awesome love –
a love revealed in the Christ who came and lived among us,
who suffered and died on the Cross,
who rose and reigns with you,
and who shall come again to draw all things to himself.
Speak to *us* now,
and help *us* to respond,
for in his name we pray.
Amen.   NICK FAWCETT

Closing prayer – A time for others

Gracious God,
    we have heard the good news of this season,
        the glad tidings of the birth of your Son,
        our Saviour, Jesus Christ,
        and we have rejoiced in everything which that means.
    Yet we know that this message is not just for us but for everyone –
        your love for all the world,
        your concern for all people,
        your purpose without limits.
    Help us then to go now with joy in our hearts
        and wonder in our eyes,
        to share the love that you have shown,
        and to make known the great thing that you have done in Christ.
    May Jesus be born again in our hearts
        and made known through our lives.

Through the words we say and the deeds we do,
        the love we share and the compassion we show,
        the faith we proclaim and the people we are,
        may his light shine afresh in the world,
        bringing hope, healing, joy and renewal.
    Grant that all may come to know you for themselves,
        and so celebrate the news of great joy,
        your coming among us in Christ
        to bring us life in all its fullness.
    May Jesus be born again in our hearts
        and made known through our lives.

In his name we go,
        to live and work for him,
        with joyful thanks and grateful praise.
    Amen.   NICK FAWCETT

All-age-talk material

Read Luke 1:39-45

Most people are really pleased when someone tells them about an eagerly awaited pregnancy. There's weeks of planning and preparation, every conversation seems to be centred around the coming event and it's hard to think about anything else (especially if you're the parents!).

It's much the same for an unplanned pregnancy, except that the conversation isn't always too encouraging! In fact, the conversation, or gossip, isn't always very complimentary.

You can imagine how Mary felt. Here she was, a teenager, engaged to a respectable bloke and along pops an angel to tell her she's pregnant. It didn't help matters that she came from an area that had a bit of a rough reputation to start with. Mary came from Nazareth, which was considered to be a no-go area for any respectable Jew. Nazareth was full of non-Jews (and some Jews) who didn't observe all the requirements of the Jewish law. Nazareth also attracted 'foreigners' who brought with them customs and traditions that were thought to be a bit dodgy for Jews.

So, after discovering that she is pregnant, Mary goes off to another town to visit her cousin Elizabeth. Elizabeth's husband is a priest and is respected in his community. Elizabeth opens the door and immediately Mary greets her with the news that she's engaged to Joseph (how nice for you, dear!), she's a virgin (Joseph will be pleased) and she's pregnant (Joseph will definitely not be pleased).

You would imagine Elizabeth would be shocked but she isn't! Instead her baby (to be born John the Baptist) moves in her womb and Elizabeth celebrates the news!

Elizabeth isn't a stranger to the unusual. She and her husband, Zechariah, were both harvesting wrinkles (getting old) and didn't have any children, and this in a society that considered children a blessing and to be without children a punishment from God.

Put simply, Zechariah moaned to God about not having children, God sent an angel to tell Zechariah that Elizabeth would have a son, Elizabeth became pregnant, Zechariah moaned to God (who said 'typical man'?), and God caused Zechariah to be dumb (lucky Elizabeth) until the birth of John.

Because of her own situation, Elizabeth was able to understand what Mary was going through and called her 'fortunate' because Mary chose to believe God. Both Elizabeth and Mary chose to believe and trust in God in situations that were far from normal.

Ask the group to imagine how Zechariah might have reacted to Mary's news. He is a respected member of the community and his wife's cousin arrives with some disturbing news. Could he have thought: 'Well, what do you expect, coming from Nazareth?' or 'What are the other priests going to say about this?'

How do we react to news that's a little hard to believe or is something we don't really want to hear? Do we dismiss it straightaway or think for a few seconds and then dismiss it?   PETE TOWNSEND

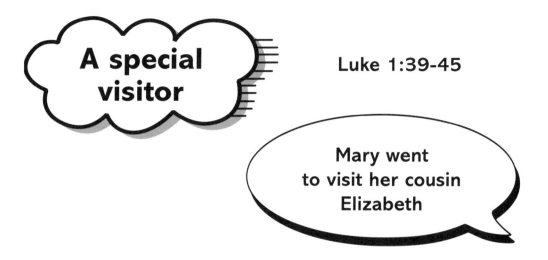

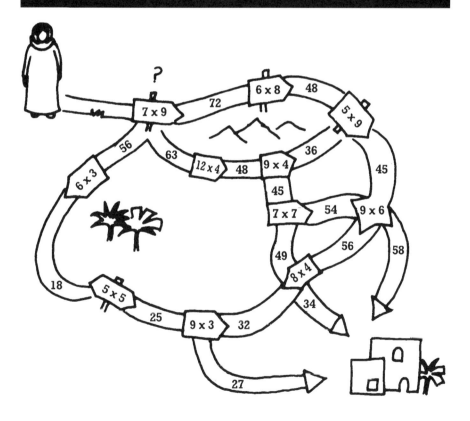

KATIE THOMPSON

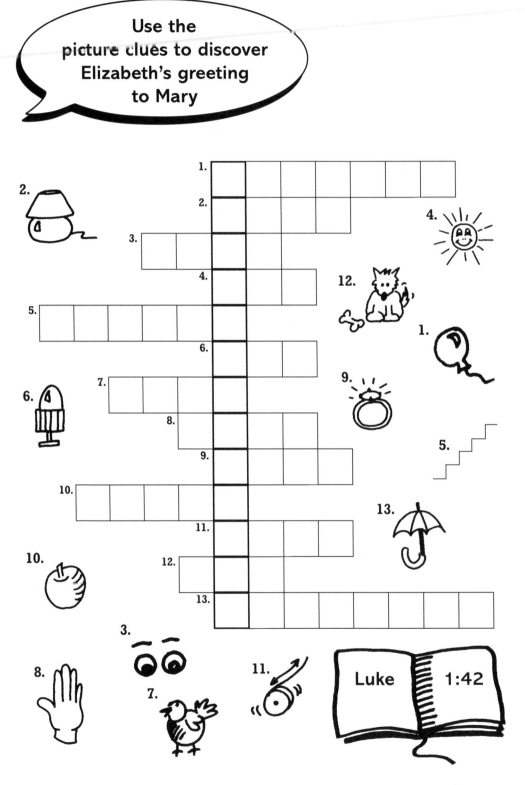

Use the picture clues to discover Elizabeth's greeting to Mary

Luke 1:42

KATIE THOMPSON

Today is
the Fourth Sunday of
Advent. Four candles are
lit today!

Complete the dot-to-dot and add four flames to the picture

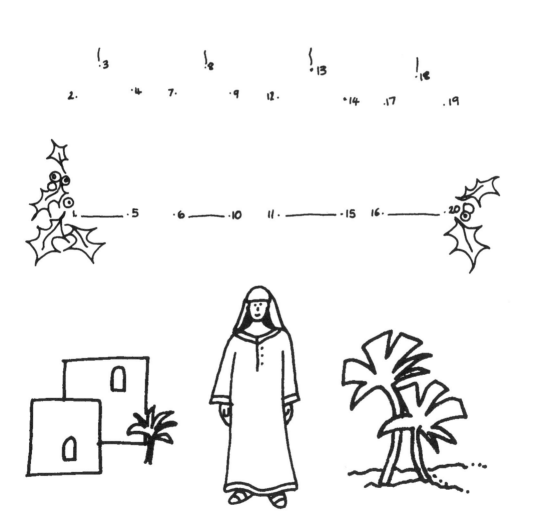

Reflective material
(sketches, meditations and poems)

Meditation of Joseph

I didn't know what to think,
 not when she first told me –
 my sweet innocent Mary, pregnant!
I suppose I should have been angry,
 and I was later,
 extremely!
But that wasn't my first reaction;
 it was shock, more like,
 disbelief,
 an inability to take it in.
You see, I just couldn't see her playing around,
 deceiving me behind my back –
 not Mary.
Other girls perhaps,
 but she wasn't like them;
 I'd have trusted her with my life if necessary.
So when she started chattering on about this angel,
 about being with child by the Holy Spirit,
 do you know what?
I listened!
No, honestly, I really did!
Maybe that does sound daft,
 but I just couldn't believe she was making it all up,
 inventing an excuse to get her off the hook,
 the wagging tongues.
Maybe, of course, I wanted to marry her anyway,
 or just didn't want to hurt her.
Maybe I simply liked the thought of being a dad,
 and wanted to believe that story of hers,
 incredible though it seemed.
To be truthful
 there were probably all kinds of reasons behind my decision;
 yet perhaps it's through such things as those,
 our everyday thoughts and feelings,
 just as much as through dreams and visions,
 that God chooses to speak to us.
Perhaps through those most of all.

NICK FAWCETT

Meditation of Elizabeth, mother of John the Baptist

Read Luke 1:39-43

In those days Mary set out and went with haste to a Judean town in the hill country, where she entered the house of Zechariah and greeted Elizabeth. When Elizabeth heard Mary's greeting, the child leapt in her womb. And Elizabeth was filled with the Holy Spirit, and exclaimed with a loud cry, 'Blessed are you among women, and blessed is the fruit of your womb. And why has this happened to me, that the mother of my Lord comes to me?'

Meditation

My baby jumped for joy, I swear it!
Oh I know you often feel them kicking,
 and you may well say it was only shuffling about in the womb,
 but this was different, I'm positive.
It was the first time I'd ever felt it move for a start,
 a wild lurch as Mary approached,
 almost as if it knew even then
 she was carrying the child who would shape its life.
Yes, I know that sounds ridiculous,
 and I wouldn't have given it another thought myself –
 I'm not usually given to romanticising.
But you see, when I saw Mary coming,
 I knew something special had happened,
 something quite out of the ordinary.
I realised she was pregnant for one thing,
 but then we women do spot those things, don't we?
Not that it was showing yet, mind you,
 but it was there in her eyes,
 in her expression,
 in the spring in her step,
 just as it had been in mine a few months earlier.
I knew,
 and I ran to embrace her,
 sharing her joy.
Yet there was more to it than that,
 I could feel it in my bones even before she began to speak.
I could sense that her child would be different,
 not just from mine but from every child,
 born to set us free,
 the fulfilment of our hopes,
 the answer to our prayers.
You think that's over the top?
Well, I may have over-reacted, I accept that,
 let my imagination run away with me.

I'd been a bit on edge, it's true,
  ever since that queer business with Zechariah –
  that day before I conceived when he came back from the temple,
  eyes staring,
  shaking his head in disbelief,
  unable to say a word until after John was born.
It got me down, I don't mind admitting it,
  and yes, perhaps I was a little overwrought,
  perhaps just plain excited.
But I still say it,
  despite what anyone may think –
  my child leaped in my womb,
  positively jumped for joy!   NICK FAWCETT

Christmas

Christmas Day

The Saviour is born in Bethlehem

Luke 2:1-14 (15-20); Luke 2:1-7

(also Isaiah 9:2-7; Psalm 96; Titus 2:11-14)

A reading from the Gospel of Luke (2:15-20)

After the angels had left them, the shepherds hurried to Bethlehem and soon found the stable. There in the manger lay a tiny baby. They told Mary and Joseph what they had seen and heard that night, and they shared their amazement. Mary listened carefully and cherished all these things in her heart. The shepherds went back to their sheep on the hillside, singing God's praises because everything had been as the angel had said.

This is the Gospel of the Lord
Praise to you, Lord Jesus Christ   KATIE THOMPSON

Alternative reading: Luke 2:1-7

Our cosy Christmas cribs do not always catch the spirit of St Luke's story. Jesus' first appearance in our world is as a representative of the world's poor, homeless and refugees.

It was the year that the Roman Emperor had ordered
a census of the whole Empire.
Everyone had to be registered
in the town his family came from.
So Joseph set out from Nazareth in Galilee
to go to Bethlehem, in Judea,
the hometown of descendants of David,
so that he could register there
with his fiancée Mary, who was pregnant.

While they were in Bethlehem
the time came for Mary to have her baby.
It was a boy, her first.
She wrapped him in a blanket
and laid him in a manger,
the animals' feeding trough,
because there was no room for them in the house.   H. J. RICHARDS

Prayers

Praise and Thanksgiving

Loving God,
we thank you for this day and all it speaks of –
your promise of old to send a Messiah to your people,
the fulfilment of that promise through the sending of your Son,
the realisation of those long years of expectation,
the glad tidings proclaimed by the angels,
the wonder and mystery of that first Christmas.
For all this time means and will always mean,
we praise you.

We thank you for this season's power to move, inspire and challenge,
to gladden the hardest of hearts and most broken of spirits,
to stir our minds and capture our imagination.
For all this time means and will always mean,
we praise you.

We thank you for the special things we associate with Christmas –
the spreading of goodwill,
the sharing of friendship,
the longing for peace,
and the expressing of love.
For all this time means and will always mean,
we praise you.

But above all we thank you for the truth behind this day –
the message that you have come to us,
that you love us,
that you have shared our humanity,
and that you want us to share in your everlasting life,
For all this time means and will always mean,
we praise you.

Loving God,
accept our praise,
receive our thanksgiving,
bless our celebrations,
and may the wonder of the Gospel
come alive in our hearts this day,
through Jesus Christ our Lord.
Amen.

NICK FAWCETT

Petition

Almighty and loving God,
  in the name of your Son Jesus,
    we join together to worship you.

  Through his coming you have blessed us
    with the light of your love,
    you have filled our world of darkness with your light,
    you have illuminated our hearts with Good News,
    you have made your glory shine upon us,
    so that nothing shall ever overcome it.

  So now we come,
    with glad thanksgiving,
    with eager expectation,
    with heartfelt praise.

  Help us, as we sing your praise and hear your word,
    to kneel before the manger in our hearts,
    to offer our gifts,
    to bring our worship,
    to recognise you are with us now.

  And so help us to go on our way this and every day,
    glorifying and praising you
    for all that we have seen and heard.
    In the name of Christ.
  Amen.
                                                    NICK FAWCETT

Intercession

Lord Jesus Christ,
  born an outcast and refugee,
    in weakness and frailty,
    as we rejoice today hear our prayers
    for all those who have no cause for celebration.
  Lord, in your mercy,
    hear our prayer.

  We pray for the hungry and the homeless,
    the poor and the unemployed,
    the oppressed and the exploited,
    the lonely and the downhearted.
  Lord, in your mercy,
    hear our prayer.

We pray for the sick and the dying,
   the sorrowful and the bereaved,
   victims of violence and war,
   all whose lives have been shattered
   by tragedy and disaster.
Lord, in your mercy,
   hear our prayer.

Lord Jesus Christ,
   born to set your people free,
     come again to our world,
     bringing reconciliation where there is division,
     and comfort where there is sorrow,
     hope where there is despair,
     and confidence where there is confusion.
Lord, in your mercy,
   hear our prayer.

Come and bring light where there is darkness,
   and love where there is hatred,
   faith where there is doubt,
   and life where there is death.
Lord, in your mercy,
   hear our prayer.

Lord Jesus Christ,
   come again to our world,
     and bring that day nearer when your kingdom will come,
     and your will be done.
Lord, in your mercy,
   hear our prayer,
   for we ask it in your name.
   Amen.

NICK FAWCETT

Short prayers

Approach

Loving God,
   you have come to us in Christ.
So now we come to you,
   to offer our worship,
   to hear your word,
   to reflect on your love.
Help us through all we share today
   to hear the great story of Christmas
   speaking to us as though for the first time.

May words that we know of old
    take on new meaning
    so that the joy given to Mary,
    the glad tidings told to the shepherds,
    the Christ-child visited by the wise men,
    becomes Good News for us!   NICK FAWCETT

Thanksgiving and petition

Sovereign God,
    we thank you for all those
    who have borne witness to your coming in Christ,
    all who have shared their faith
    so that others might come to know him
    and experience his love for themselves.
We thank you for those
    from whom we first heard the gospel,
    and all those who have nurtured
    and encouraged us in the years following.
Help us, now, to play our part
    in that continuing ministry,
    sharing what Christ means with those around us,
    and making known the way he has worked
    in our lives.
Send us out in his name,
    to his glory.
Amen.   NICK FAWCETT

Blessing

God of Mary and Joseph,
    God of the shepherds and the magi,
    God of the baby lying in a manger,
    God with *us*,
    touch our hearts
    with the living presence of Christ,
    fill us with the love and joy
    which he alone can bring,
    and send us out to proclaim his kingdom,
    glad tidings for all.
In his name we pray.
Amen.   NICK FAWCETT

All-age-talk material

A different kind of lamb!

Luke 2:15-21: The shepherds hear about Jesus.

Equipment:

large cards or A4 sheets
music and lyrics or drama sketch

Take ten cards and write the following headlines:

'Budgie eats tube of Smarties!'
'Sales of coloured tissues drop'
'Two injured in ice-cream fight!'
'Forty witnesses to chocolate bar theft'
'Lorry carrying paint overturns. Multicoloured motorway'
'Police fear local car thief may strike again'
'Government declare national holiday every Monday'
'Island disappears after volcanic eruption'
'United Nations calls for world-wide nuclear testing ban'
'Local man swallows Guinness book of records!'

Show each headline to the group. For each headline ask the group whether it should be reported in the local newspaper or national newspaper; on local radio or national radio; local TV or national TV?   PETE TOWNSEND

The heart of Christmas

Reading

Luke 2:1-7

Aim

To show that unless Jesus is at the heart of our Christmas celebrations, we will fail to understand what this time is all about.

Preparation

Print the following combinations of letters on to small pieces of card: SA, AUS, R, F, DE, ONS, MI, ES, TU, Y, T, EL, WR, PER, C, OLS, ST, NG, CR, RS, PR, TS. Attach magnetic tape to the back of each, and place on a magnetic whiteboard as follows:

```
SA          AUS
RU     F
DE          ONS
MI        ES
TU     Y
T     EL
WR              PER
C    OLS
ST        NG
CR        RS
PR     TS
```

Then print these combinations: NTA CL, DOL, CORATI, NCE PI, RKE, INS, APPING PA, AR, OCKI, ACKE, ESEN.

Again, stick magnetic tape to the back of each piece of card, but keep these separate, ready to stick on the board during the talk.

Finally, print the following: CHRIST, CHRIST, CHRIST, WHITE, MAS, FATHER, MAS, HAPPY, MAS.

Again attach magnetic tape and keep separate for later use.

Talk

Show the congregation the combinations of letters you have arranged on the board, and ask if they can make sense of them? Offer the clue that they are all to do with Christmas. Invite suggestions, and fill in the missing letters as each correct answer is given, as follows:

```
SANTA CLAUS
RUDOLF
DECORATIONS
MINCE PIES
TURKEY
TINSEL
WRAPPING PAPER
CAROLS
STOCKING
CRACKERS
PRESENTS
```

All of these words are familiar terms associated with Christmas, but when we take the centre out of them suddenly they no longer make sense. And the same is true with the following, only this time it's much easier to spot what's missing?

```
WHITE        MAS
FATHER       MAS
HAPPY        MAS
```

The missing word, of course, is CHRIST. And just as 'Christ' here makes sense of these letters, so Christ also makes sense of this time of year. Unless we have Christ at the centre of our Christmas it really doesn't make sense, for there will always be the most vital part missing.

We may enjoy all these other things we have talked about, for they are all a part of our Christmas celebrations; but we will not discover the happiness and the joy God wants us to discover if Christ is missing.

It is only when we put Christ at the heart of Christmas that we will understand what this time really means.   NICK FAWCETT

Do you know why they had to go to Bethlehem?

Moving clockwise around the circle, write down every other letter. Do this twice to find the answer

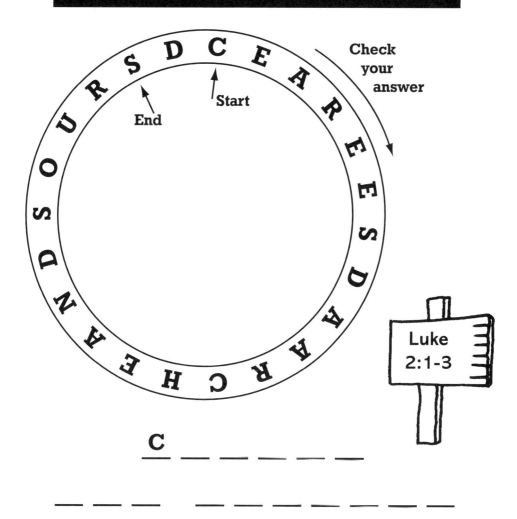

Check your answer

Start

End

Luke 2:1-3

C _ _ _ _ _   _ _ _   _ _ _ _ _ _   _ _   _ _ _ _ _ _   _ _   _ _ _ _ _ _ _ _

KATIE THOMPSON

While in Bethlehem the time came for Mary to have her baby. They named him Jesus, just as the angel had told them

The name Jesus means 'God is with us'

Find the letter missing from each group to spell out another name given to Jesus

CDFGHI   _____

JKLNOP   _____

LNOPQR   _____

XYZBCD   _____

IJKLMO   _____

RSTVWX   _____

BCDFGH   _____

HIJKMN   _____

Matthew 1:23

KATIE THOMPSON

Reflective material
(sketches, meditations and poems)

Meditation of Mary, mother of Jesus

He looked so tiny lying there,
    so vulnerable –
    like a little china doll,
    like thistledown swaying in the breeze –
    and I wanted simply to hold him in my arms
    and protect him from the world outside.
Could this be God's Son, I asked,
    the one destined to be great,
    the Prince of Peace,
    a ruler over Israel?
Surely not!
It had been hard enough to believe at the start,
    when the angel first broke the news –
    to think that I, Mary, had been chosen above all others,
    singled out to bear in my womb the Messiah –
    but now, as I gazed down into the manger,
    and saw those little arms waving,
    that sweet innocent face wrinkled up in sleep,
    and those eyes so tightly shut,
    it seemed doubly impossible,
    out of the question,
    a foolish fancy of my fevered imagination.
Be sensible, I told myself,
    there's no way God could take such a gamble,
    no possibility, if the fate of the world truly hung in the balance,
    that he would stake it all on a helpless child,
    least of all one born where we found ourselves –
    a stable of all places!
And, as if to prove the point, that very moment Jesus awoke,
    tears filling his eyes,
    a scream of protest on his lips,
    and I realised he was hungry,
    well past his usual feed.
It dawned on me then, the staggering implications –
    he needed me, this child,
    not just for food, or warmth, or protection,
    but for everything,
    his very future in my hands.
Would God allow that?

Could he ever need *us* as much as *we* need him?
No, there had to be some mistake –
   it just couldn't be, could it?
Could it?   NICK FAWCETT

Please do not adjust

Luke 2:8-14; John 1:10-11

While people watched their sets one night,
   all seated round the screen,
   the angel of the Lord appeared
   where evening news had been.
'Fear not,' said he (for flashing light
   had altered the transmission;
   this strange, celestial visitor
   had interfered with vision).
'I bring good news of peace on earth
   for all mankind,' he said;
   but crackling sparks zigzagged the screen
   and every set went dead.
So angry viewers growled and cursed
   and electricians fumed,
   until as soon as possible
   normal service was resumed.   PETER DAINTY

He humbled himself

Luke 2:7

The newborn king arrived
   at twelve o'clock midnight precisely
   (Middle Eastern Time),
   a rather feeble 4lbs 5oz
   (but what could you expect
   from an undernourished peasant girl?)
No district nurse was present;
   there was no delivery bed,
   no injections,
   no gas and air,
   no shiny, sterile instruments,
   no hints on correct breathing,
   no attendant doctors;
   only soiled straw, and cobwebs,
   and staring animals

and a farmyard smell;
and awkward Joseph's shaking hand,
holding a shivering lamp
for the innkeeper's wife,
who was busy
with her rough, well-meaning fingers.
So the new red king entered his kingdom
to the pricking of hay, and the tight warmth
of the long swathing bandage.
There was no dignity about it,
except the dignity that attends
every human birth;
no mystery, except the normal mystery
of a new life; no wonder
except the wonder of excited shepherds
with half-mad stories of angelic visions.

For God stooped low, and will stoop lower,
even to the oozy bottom of the human ocean,
to raise the sunken treasure
of lost souls.

PETER DAINTY

The secret

I carry a secret,
a wonderful secret,
it lives and moves and stirs in me.
We created a person,
a new human being,
it grows in my body so silently.

Christ grew in secret,
the world's greatest secret,
part of his mother, hidden inside.
Then born as a baby,
a perfect little baby,
helpless, dependant, he fed and cried.

But while still in the womb
this tiny baby's fingers
reached out in love and touched every land.
He was creation,
not just one of its creatures,
and he held the world in his unborn hand.

MARY HATHAWAY

No room

Based on Luke 2:1-7

Narrator	Simon and Susannah ran the local Bed and Breakfast, in Bethlehem. They were very caring people, and Simon certainly never meant to be unkind. But sometimes he did unkind things without meaning to – and this was one of them. So, not for the first time, he was getting a good telling off from Susannah.
Susannah	D'you mean to tell me that you turned that poor young couple away on a night like this – and her expecting a baby at any minute?
Simon	But we haven't any room, what else was I to do?
Susannah	Where there's a will, there's a room. I'm going to get that couple back here, and by the time I do, you'd better have thought of something.
Narrator	With that, Susannah went out into the night to look for the couple. Can you help her to look?

- She *looked to the left*
- She *looked to the right*
- She *turned her head from side to side*

And eventually she saw the couple. Their names were Mary and Joseph. They had been getting very worried, because it seemed as though Mary was about to have her baby any minute!

Susannah	Don't worry! I'm afraid that husband of mine is a bit silly sometimes, but he means well.
Mary	We don't want to be any trouble, but we really do need to find somewhere very soon.
Susannah	No trouble at all. You come with me. And if Simon hasn't thought of something by now, he'll be sorry!
Narrator	When they arrived, Simon was looking very pleased with himself.
Simon	I still haven't got a room, but there's a shed out the back – not much in it, just a cow and a couple of goats, so it smells a bit. But there's plenty of straw, and anyway, it's all there is.
Mary	It will have to do. We're far too tired to go on looking.
Narrator	So Mary got comfortable on a pile of straw, but she didn't get a lot of sleep. Just as she and Joseph had expected, their baby son, Jesus, was born that night. They realised there was nowhere to put him, where he could sleep. Then Susannah had an idea.

Susannah	I know! We could put some clean straw in that feeding trough the animals are using.
Narrator	The animals weren't happy. They kept trying to get closer to the manger. No one was sure whether they were trying to see the baby or eat the straw!
Susannah	I think we'd better tie them up somewhere out of the way.
Narrator	So that's what they did. The stable didn't seem quite so bad as it had at first, but I think I'd rather have my own nice warm home, wouldn't you? MICHAEL FORSTER

Christmas means . . .

Aim

To show that Christmas is not just toys and Father Christmas, but that it is when Christians celebrate the time that God came to the world he created.

Song

A band of angels

Puppet sketch

Micky	Guess what!
John	What?
Micky	It's nearly Christmas and you know what Christmas means, don't you? Presents! *(Micky bounces around full of excitement)*
John	Yes, Micky, but you know Christmas means more than just presents, don't you?
Micky	Of course! Christmas means Father Christmas and you know what he brings – presents!
John	Well, yes, but Christmas means more than Father Christmas and presents.
Micky	I know. Christmas means parties and guess what you get at parties – PRESENTS !
John	Oh, Micky! Christmas means more than parties, Father Christmas and presents.
Micky	I know. Christmas means trees – and what do you find at the bottom of most Christmas trees? PRESENTS!

John   Oh, Micky!

Micky   I know what else Christmas means!

John   You do?

Micky   Aunties and uncles – and guess what they bring.
              P – R – E – S – E – N – T – S !

John   Micky, read this *(he hands him a Bible open at Luke 2)*. It will tell you
              about a very special baby. He's what Christmas is all about!

Micky   Excellent! *(Micky excitedly dashes into the bag with the Bible)*

John   I wonder how well you know the Christmas story. I'm going to tell
              you the story, but I'm going to put in a few mistakes. See if you can
              spot them and at the end we'll put them right.

Bible story

Luke 2:4-14

Once upon a time there was a grand knight. His name was Sir Joseph. He was a brave, handsome man who rode a white stallion, a fine horse!
He was madly in love with a beautiful young lady. Her name was Princess Mary. They decided to marry and not long after she gave birth to a boy. They named him Jesus.

They went to the palace and placed him in a golden cot. Many kings, queens and important lords and ladies came to celebrate his birth. The town crier went into the streets to announce the birth of the new king. They all lived happily ever after. The end.

Did you spot any mistakes? There were quite a few of them.

First of all, it's not a fairy story, it's a true story.

Joseph wasn't a brave knight on a white horse. What was he and what did he have to ride? He was a carpenter and he rode a donkey.

Was Mary a princess? No, she was just a normal young girl.

Jesus was a special baby, but was he born in a palace and did he have a golden cot? No, when he was born, he was put in a manger because there was no room for them in the inn.

There were no lords and ladies, but there were visitors. Who were they? Shepherds and wise men.

There wasn't a town crier, but who did announce the birth of Jesus to the shepherds? . . . A band of angels!

Sing: A band of angels

Round-up

If Jesus had been born in a palace the shepherds wouldn't have been allowed in, but Jesus was born in a place where all could go and see. Christmas is for everyone – everyone is welcome to celebrate the birth of Jesus.

Prayer

Father God, thank you for this special time of year. Help us to remember what Christmas really means! Amen.   JOHN HARDWICK

Additional Christmas Material
(First and second weeks after Christmas or Candlemas)

Luke 2:41-52
(also John 1:1-9, 10-18; 1 Samuel 2:18-20, 26; Psalm 147:12-20)

A reading from the Gospel of Luke (2:41-52)

Every year Joseph and Mary went to Jerusalem to celebrate the Jewish Passover. When Jesus was 12 years old, he made the journey with them.

After the feast, Mary and Joseph set off for home, but that evening, when they realised that Jesus was missing, they returned to Jerusalem to look for him. After searching for three days, they finally found Jesus in the Temple. He was sitting with the Jewish teachers, listening to them and asking them questions, and they were filled with admiration for him.

Mary and Joseph were astonished when they saw him and said, 'Son, we have been so worried for three days! Why have you done this to us?'

Jesus answered, 'Why were you looking for me? Did you not realise that I would be in my Father's house?' But they did not understand what his answer meant.

The family returned to Nazareth, and Mary kept all these things in her heart. Jesus grew in height and wisdom, and was loved by God and all who knew him.

This is the Gospel of the Lord
Praise to you, Lord Jesus Christ   KATIE THOMPSON

Prayers

Praise – Receiving the word

Gracious God,
   we praise you today for the power of your word,
     the way you have spoken to so many people
     throughout history.

You called the universe into being –
     heaven and earth,
     night and day,
     the sea and the dry land,
     life in its multitude of manifestations.
You spoke,
     and it was done,
     our world and our very existence owing to you.

For your word of life,
  we praise you.
You called Abraham, Isaac and Jacob,
  Moses and Joshua,
  judges, kings and prophets,
  Apostles, disciples, preachers and teachers –
  a great company of saints,
  each testifying to your sovereign purpose,
  your awesome power
  and your merciful love;
  each hearing your voice and responding in faith.
For your word of life,
  we praise you.

You came in Jesus Christ, the Word made flesh,
  identifying yourself with our humanity,
  sharing our joy and sorrow,
  experiencing our life and death.
You came in fulfilment of your promises of old,
  revealing the extent of your love
  through everything he said and did,
  demonstrating your gracious purpose for all.
For your word of life,
  we praise you.

You speak still through the pages of Scripture;
  through their record of your involvement in history
  and their testimony to your will for the world.
You speak through dialogue between Christians,
  through the witness of your Church and personal testimony,
  through study and reflection,
  and through the sharing of fellowship.
You speak through the grandeur of the universe
  and the wonder of life,
  your still small voice breaking into our experience
  to challenge and inspire.
For your word of life,
  we praise you.

Gracious God,
  we rejoice at the ways you have spoken to us in the past
    and the way you continue to speak today.
  We receive your word with joyful thanksgiving,
    and we pray for strength to make it so much a part of us
    that your voice may be heard through all we are and do,
    to the glory of your name.

For your word of life,
   we praise you.
Through Jesus Christ our Lord.
  Amen.
NICK FAWCETT

Closing prayer – In the footsteps of faith

Almighty God,
  we have heard once more the wonderful message
    of your coming to us in Christ –
    tidings of great joy,
    Good News for all people.
  As you have come to us,
    so may we go for you.

We thank you for that message,
    the well-loved words we have heard and sung again today –
    so familiar,
    so often repeated,
    yet still so special and meaningful.
As you have come to us,
    so may we go for you.

We thank you for the faith and trust of Mary –
    her willingness to accept your will;
    for the pilgrimage and gifts of the wise men –
    their determination to seek and respond;
    for the simple actions of the shepherds –
    who, hearing the message and seeing its truth for themselves,
    shared with others what they had experienced!
As you have come to us,
    so may we go for you.

Teach us, we pray, as we celebrate this Christmas-time,
    to learn from their example,
    to follow in their footsteps,
    to share their faith.
As you have come to us,
    so may we go for you.

Teach us to know the reality of Christ born for *us*,
    and in our turn to pass on
    what we have discovered through him to those around us!
As you have come to us,
    so may we go for you,
    in the name of Christ.
  Amen.
NICK FAWCETT

Intercession – first Sunday after Christmas

Laying his glory and majesty aside, God is content to enter human life as a vulnerable baby.

Father, breathe your life
into every worshipping community,
and heal all disunity in your church.

Silence for prayer

God of glory:
we thank you for loving us

Father, breathe your peace into our world
both in individuals and in nations.

Silence for prayer

God of glory:
we thank you for loving us

Father, breathe your joy into our homes
and places of work and leisure.

Silence for prayer

God of glory:
we thank you for loving us

Father, breathe your comfort into all who suffer,
whether mentally, physically,
emotionally or spiritually.

Silence for prayer

God of glory:
we thank you for loving us

Father, breathe your hope into those
who feel they have little to live for.

Silence for prayer

God of glory:
we thank you for loving us

Father, breathe your refreshment and delight
into our attitudes,
until we live in thankfulness.

Silence for prayer

Merciful Father,
accept these prayers
for the sake of your Son,
our Saviour Jesus Christ, Amen.

SUSAN SAYERS

Intercession – second Sunday after Christmas

God's salvation is for all peoples and nations; everyone is eligible.

Father, into your care we commit all Christians,
all in ministry and all church leaders.

Silence for prayer

O Lord, our God:
it is good to be safe in your love

Father, into your care we commit our world,
with its needs and failures,
hope and despair.

Silence for prayer

O Lord, our God:
it is good to be safe in your love

Father, into your care we commit those we love,
and those we could love more.

Silence for prayer

O Lord, our God:
it is good to be safe in your love

Father, into your care we commit those of all ages
who are in danger,
and live in fear.

Silence for prayer

O Lord, our God:
it is good to be safe in your love

Father, into your care we commit
those who have recently died
and all who mourn for them.

Silence for prayer

O Lord, our God:
it is good to be safe in your love

Father, we rejoice in the way you look after us,
and thank you for providing for all our needs.

Silence for prayer

Merciful Father,
**accept these prayers
for the sake of your Son,
our Saviour Jesus Christ, Amen.**

SUSAN SAYERS

All-age-talk material

God's house

Reading

Luke 2:41-52

Aim

To show that while the place in which we worship is only a building, it can also rightly be called 'the house of God'.

Preparation

No preparation is needed for this talk, unless you want to add to the list of questions suggested.

Talk

Tell the congregation that you have prepared a quiz about houses. All they have to do is tell you who lives in each of the places you are going to mention. Invite responses.

- Who would you hope to meet in 10 Downing Street? *(The Prime Minister)*

- Who would you hope to meet in Buckingham Palace? *(The Queen)*

- Who would you hope to meet in Lambeth Palace? *(The Archbishop of Canterbury)*

- Who would you hope to meet in the Vatican? *(The Pope)*

- Who would you hope to meet in the White House? *(The President of the United States)*

- Who would you hope to meet in 11 Downing Street? *(The Chancellor of the Exchequer)*

- Who would you hope to meet in Highgrove House? *(Prince Charles)*

Although many of these places are not these people's real or only homes, they can nonetheless be found in these places at some time during the year.

Now ask whom we hope to meet in church? (God.) Ask whose house Jesus told his parents he had been in when they returned to Jerusalem to find him sitting in the Temple. (His Father's house.)

While God isn't limited to any one place or time, and although the Church is more about people than bricks and mortar, a church building is a special place where we come to focus our thoughts on God; a place set apart where we recognise his presence, where we speak to him and where we worship him. That is why we call our church building 'the house of God' – a place where we can come and meet *our* Father, and enjoy his presence.   NICK FAWCETT

Jesus went missing in Jerusalem! Where did Mary and Joseph eventually find him?

Use the code to find out

⚒	M	N	H
✋	E	P	I
✂	L	T	E
	❀	✹	O

Luke   2:46

‾‾‾ ‾‾‾ ‾‾‾   ‾‾‾ ‾‾‾ ‾‾‾

‾‾‾ ‾‾‾ ‾‾‾ ‾‾‾ ‾‾‾ ‾‾‾

How long did they search for him?

$(4 \times 3) - 10 = $ _____ $\times 8 = $ _____ $\div 4 = $ _____ $- 1 = $ _____ **days**

KATIE THOMPSON

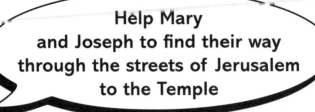

KATIE THOMPSON

Jesus sat listening and asking questions in the Temple

Circle eight things which are different in the bottom picture

KATIE THOMPSON

Underline the word in each group which doesn't belong. Write these words on the lines

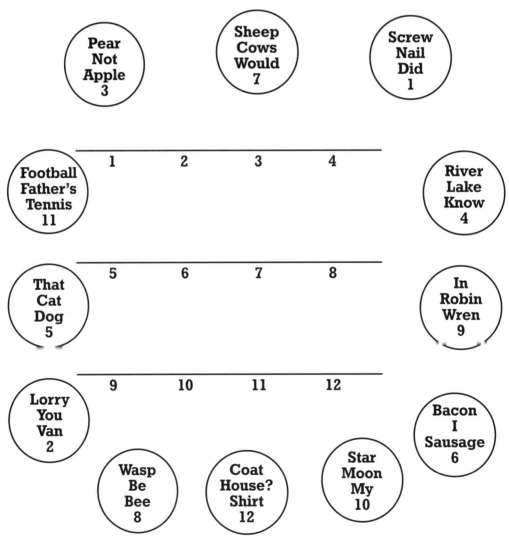

Pear
Not
Apple
3

Sheep
Cows
Would
7

Screw
Nail
Did
1

1 ___ 2 ___ 3 ___ 4 ___

Football
Father's
Tennis
11

River
Lake
Know
4

5 ___ 6 ___ 7 ___ 8 ___

That
Cat
Dog
5

In
Robin
Wren
9

9 ___ 10 ___ 11 ___ 12 ___

Lorry
You
Van
2

Bacon
I
Sausage
6

Wasp
Be
Bee
8

Coat
House?
Shirt
12

Star
Moon
My
10

KATIE THOMPSON

Read Luke 2:41-52

Before we start to think about this account, by Luke, of Jesus getting himself into grief with his parents, it's worth trying to understand a little of the background.

At the age of 12, a Jewish boy officially becomes a man and takes on the associated duties and obligations. Jesus and his parents had travelled to Jerusalem to attend his first Passover (a meal to commemorate the exodus of the Israelites from captivity in Egypt). When it was time to go home, the women would have travelled together and set out earlier than the men. The men would follow later and both parties would meet up at the evening camp. You can imagine that both Mary and Joseph thought Jesus was travelling with the other parent: 'I thought he was with you!' 'No, I thought he was with you!'

Eventually, Jesus was found in the temple where the Sanhedrin (the supreme Jewish court) was meeting in public to discuss religious and theological questions. After three days' search, Mary and Joseph found Jesus listening to the discussions and asking questions. It was significant that at the same time as he reached adulthood, Jesus also acknowledged who he was and who his father was (see verse 49).

Jesus became aware of his status as an adult and the value that God placed upon him. It was this knowledge that gave him the motivation to return home with his parents, continue to learn the trade of a carpenter and allow his future to remain secure in God's hands.   PETE TOWNSEND

Read John 1:10-18

If you ever get around to reading the book of Proverbs, in the Old Testament, you will find loads of comments about friendship. One in particular has a neat way of putting across the value of friends:

'The sweet smell of incense can make you feel good, but true friendship is better still' (Proverbs 27:9).

In other words, a temporary pleasant smell can surround us and be pleasing and possibly disguise some bad odours (!) but it doesn't last. A real friend is someone who hangs around even when things don't look or smell too clever. You can easily find out who your real friends are – by the time you've finished spelling the word 'trouble' see how many of your supposed friends are left standing next to you.

The song 'What a friend I've found' has one line which says: 'What a friend I've found, closer than a brother'. That's some statement to make.

In John's Gospel we can find a similar awesome statement. In verse 14 of the reading, John writes that:

'The Word became a human being and lived here with us.'

John the Baptist was saying that Jesus was God's spoken Word, the Word which gives light and life, and that God chose, through Jesus, to come and live with us.

The original word used in John's Gospel for 'live' is 'tabernacle' which literally means 'putting a tent up'. A tent isn't usually a permanent place to live. John the Baptist understood that Jesus was only going to be 'living' with them for a short time (33 years from birth to crucifixion). But the message that Jesus brought was that he now wanted to come and live with us permanently, to become a part of us, to share our every experience and be with us every step of every day.

Jesus doesn't just want to move into the neighbourhood, or even move in next door, he wants to become an essential part of our life, a central part of our existence.

Equipment:

postcards (sufficient for most members of the group to take part in the game)
paper and pens

Each of the postcards should have a word on with two or three different definitions. This is a kind of biblical *Call My Bluff*. For example:

SPIKENARD

Definition 1. During Old Testament times, people would travel around by riding on a donkey. When the travellers reached their destination they would tie the donkey to a special post which was usually found at the rear of a house. The word *Spikenard* was the name given to this type of post.

Definition 2. In biblical times people didn't wash their hair as often as we do today. Rather than allow their hair to look or smell unclean, people would use a perfume, *Spikenard*, to comb through their hair.
(Correct definition.)

MIZPAH

Definition 1. When guests visited unexpectedly, the host would offer a small cake with some wine. The cake, or *Mizpah*, was similar to a mini doughnut and flavoured with honey

Definition 2. In Old Testament times it was important always to be on the lookout for thieves or potential enemies who might attempt to sneak up and attack a village or encampment. A tower would be built to provide a look-out point. Such a tower is called a *Mizpah*.
(Correct definition.)

You can write other zany definitions using a Bible dictionary with a large dose of imagination. Divide the group into teams and give each team a selection of words. Each player reads out a definition and the other team have to decide which is the correct definition.

PETE TOWNSEND

Lord, my eyes have seen your salvation. (Luke 2:30)

Crack the code to find some good advice for Christians.

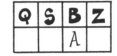

Simeon is not alone. Colour the dotted shapes to reveal who is with him.

WORDSEARCH
Find the following words in the grid:
WATCH AND PRAY, SIMEON, HOPE,
ANNA, PROPHET, PROMISE, VIGIL,
MARY, JOSEPH, JESUS, TEMPLE,
SALVATION, SAVIOUR,
NAZARETH.

```
P S A L V A T I O N O E
P R O P H A T E M P L E
J V O E M I S A L J P B
E I S M E T E H P O R P
S G I L I I V G H S O R
U I M E O S V I G E E O
S B V I O I E O R P H M
S A L V G M A R Y H E I
S N V I O E R O P H M S
X N L R U O I V A S Y V
Y A R P D N A H C T A W
N A Z A R E T H A T C H
```

MICHAEL FORSTER

Reflective material
(sketches, meditations and poems)

Just Christmas

Just a girl
  with an outlandish message,
  just a relationship
  strained to breaking point,
  just two people
  facing the betrayal of love
  – just Christmas.

Just busy roads
  and hotels overbooked,
  just the pain
  and the mess of childbirth,
  just the cry of the newly born
  – just Christmas.

Just low-paid workers
  doing long hours at night,
  just stillness
  and the stars shining in the cold,
  just the uneducated
  seeing visions
  – just Christmas.

Just travellers
  coming from the east,
  just a quest
  riddled with doubts,
  just seeking
  in loneliness of heart
  – just Christmas.

Just soldiers
  patrolling the streets,
  just political unrest
  and corruption in high places,
  just the innocent
  suffering under those in power
  – just Christmas.

Just truth
  in small fragments,
  just heaven
  in the ordinary,
  just God,
  ignored and unnoticed
  – just Christmas.

MARY HATHAWAY

The boy in the temple

Beware, old men,
  of the boy who asks questions
  in the Temple.
Beware of his probing mind,
  like the prodding finger of God
  unplayfully poking holes
  in your ancient dignity.
Hide those antique laws
  before he sees the spirit
  beneath the letter.
Protect those sacred truths with iron fear,
  or he will fan them into life
  with the breath of his living faith;
  and the fire of their knowledge
  will destroy both you
  and your solemn system.
Beware of this boy who asks questions,
  the inquisitive Son
  of a disturbing Father.
Others there are
  whom you need not fear –
  they ask no questions,
  but tread traditional ways
  like sleep-walkers, blindly following
  the easy path of custom,
  each predictable today
  a reprint of a ritual yesterday.

But this boy,
  who so amazed with his insight,
  is stirring the dust of ages
  with the eternal broom of truth,
  for he is God's boy,
  already about his Father's business.

PETER DAINTY

The innocents

John 1:10

(For up to five readers.)

What do we do with the babe in the cradle;
   the babe in the cradle, the hope of the world?
House it in shanty town, hovel and stable;
   a refugee camp for the hope of the world.

How do we care for the infant so helpless;
   the infant so helpless, the young one so frail?
Give it no doctors, no fit sanitation;
   and raise it in squalor, the young one so frail.

How do we nourish the seed of the future;
   the seed of the future, the heir of mankind?
Feed it with charity soya bean mixture;
   a cupful of rice for the heir of mankind.

How do we nurture the child full of promise;
   the child full of promise, the light of the world?
School it in prejudice, half truths and falsehood;
   and quench with dark hatred the light of the world.

Where are the wise men with gifts for the baby;
   with gifts for a baby, but fit for a king?
Bring him the best of the world's wealth, and maybe
   our great expectations will blossom in him.
Treat him with reverence, the tender young sapling;
   then great expectations will blossom in him.   PETER DAINTY

Meditation of the innkeeper

There was something about that couple,
   something that caught my attention the moment I saw them.
Happiness, I suppose it was,
   the joy of sharing a newborn baby.
Only it was more than that,
   for I've seen a multitude of parents over the years,
   each coming bubbling with excitement,
   skipping with delight,
   and yet none had that look of wide-eyed wonder which these had.
It was as though they thought their child different from any other,
   a unique gift from God to be handled with infinite care,
   treasured beyond all price.

Oh, I know every parent feels their baby's special –
   in their eyes the most beautiful thing ever born –
   yet with these two it was more than that.
It was almost as if they were in awe of the child,
   elated yet terrified at the responsibility of parenthood.
You think I'm exaggerating,
   reading too much into an innocent moment?
Well, possibly.
She was very young after all,
   and this was their first child –
   everything new,
   unknown, unexplored.
Yet I still say I've never seen a look quite like they had.
Probably it will always remain a mystery,
   for though no doubt they'll come back
   for the occasional festival or ceremony,
   I'm not sure I'll recognise them when they do.
Yet perhaps I may find the answer despite that,
   for when his mother handed me the child,
   and announced his name – Jesus –
   she did so as if it should mean something to me,
   as if I would understand straightaway
   why the child was so important,
   as if he was a gift not just to *them*,
   but to *me*,
   to *you*,
   and to *everyone*.

NICK FAWCETT

Meditation of Anna the prophetess

I really felt I'd missed it,
   truthfully.
I mean, I wasn't just old,
   I was ancient!
And still there was no sign of the Messiah,
   no hint of his coming.
I began to wonder whether all those years of praying and fasting
   had been worth it,
   or simply one almighty waste of time.
I doubted everything,
   questioned everything,
   despite my outward piety.
Why hadn't God answered my prayers?
Why hadn't he rewarded my faithfulness?
Why believe when it didn't seem to make a scrap of difference?

I still kept up the facade mind you –
   spoke excitedly of the future,
   of all that God would do –
   but I didn't have much faith in it,
   not after so many disappointments.
Until that day when,
   hobbling back through the temple after yet more prayers,
   suddenly I saw him,
   God's promised Messiah.
Don't ask me how I knew,
   I just did,
   without any shadow of a doubt,
   and it was the most wonderful moment of my life,
   a privilege beyond words.
It taught me something, that experience.
It taught me never to give up,
   never to let go,
   never to lose heart.
It taught me there is always reason to hope
   no matter how futile it seems.
It taught me to go on expecting
   despite all the blows life may dish out.
It taught me God has never finished
   however much it may feel like it.
I nearly lost sight of all that.
I was right on the edge,
   teetering on the brink,
   fearing God had passed me by.
But he'd saved the best till last,
   and I know now, even though the waiting is over,
   that there's more to come,
   more to expect,
   more to celebrate.
For though my life is nearly at an end,
   it has only just begun!

NICK FAWCETT

Simeon's vigil of hope and prayer: Luke 2:21-40

(See page 109 for a dramatised version of this story.)

Never give up hope

Around the time that Jesus was born in Bethlehem, there was an old man living in Jerusalem called Simeon. Although he was sad, Simeon was also full of hope. 'I just know that God's going to do something about all this trouble we're having, before I die,' he used to say. 'God's going to send his special Saviour into the world, and I'm going to live to see it.'

Simeon's neighbours all liked him – you couldn't help liking old Simeon – but, to be honest, they thought he was a little bit dotty. And Maggie, who lived just across the street, was no exception, although she admired him very much.

'I don't know where you get this faith from,' she said to him. 'We've been conquered by the Romans, and their soldiers are everywhere – you can't breathe out of turn without someone telling the governor you're plotting against Rome. Every day, people get tortured to death just for believing something different, and we all know God's given up on us – all of us with any sense, that is.'

'God never gives up,' said Simeon, quietly. 'He always keeps his promises – and he's promised me I'll be around to see it when the Saviour comes.'

'Well, I've got to admire your faith,' said Maggie, 'even if I do think you're crackers. Anyway, I've baked you a few little cakes to cheer you up.'

Simeon smiled. 'Just because I'm old, you think I need cheering up,' he said, 'but you're the one who's saying there's no hope. But thank you, anyway – you're very kind.' Then he stopped for a moment. 'Actually, I'll eat them later,' he said. 'I get the feeling I ought to be at the temple. I think something interesting's happening.'

'Another little message from the Spirit of God, is it?' Maggie laughed, kindly. 'Off you go, then, Simeon – just don't be disappointed, that's all.'

'Oh, don't worry,' Simeon answered, 'I won't be.'

Simeon got to the temple just in time to see a young woman and her husband carrying a baby.

'Hey, look at this, Mary,' the man was saying. 'Just look at the craftsmanship in this cedar chest. I wonder how they get that effect in the carving – I must try it when we get home.'

'Typical!' Mary smiled. 'Even now, you can't get carpentry out of your mind.'

'I'm going to teach Jesus everything I know,' Joseph beamed, proudly.

'Well, let him grow up a bit, first,' Mary laughed. 'And right now, we've got to get him blessed properly.'

Simeon knew these were the people God had brought him here to meet. He just knew, that's all. 'Excuse me,' he said, 'would you mind if I had a look at your baby?'

'Of course not,' Mary answered. 'We're getting used to this – ever since he was born people have been saying how special he is. It's been the most amazing eight days of my life.'

Simeon took the baby from her – very carefully, so as not to drop him. 'Just keep your hand under his head,' Mary advised. 'His neck isn't very strong, yet.' Simeon looked at the tiny baby. 'So this is the one,' he said quietly. 'Well, Lord, I've waited a long time, but you can let me go now. I can die happy, because I've seen the beginning of your saving work for all nations. This is the one – absolutely, the One! And I've seen him and held him! He's going to bring light into the whole world – and a special kind of glory to your people right here in Israel. Thank you for keeping your promise.'

Then Simeon turned to Mary. 'There are tough times ahead,' he said. 'No quick fix – that's not how God works. This little bundle's going to grow up to change lives – he'll bring joy to a lot of people, but he'll upset some, as well. Sometimes the truth's painful, but that won't stop him telling it. And it won't be any picnic for you, either, I'm afraid.'

Just then an old woman came up. 'This is Anna, a prophet,' said Simeon. 'She's been living day and night in the temple waiting for this moment.'

Anna was almost crying with joy. 'This is the one,' she said. 'This is the Saviour. After all the trouble we've had, God really is doing something. Haven't we always said, Simeon – God keeps his promises?'

Mary and Joseph took Jesus home to their place in Nazareth, where he grew up strong, and wise, and full of faith in God's love for everyone. Even though life was hard, and many people were unhappy, he always had hope. 'God can bring hope out of any amount of trouble,' he used to say. 'Trust me.'

Respond to the story

Discussion

How do the children think Simeon and Anna had felt during all those years of watching, waiting and praying?

- Hopeful?
- Confident?
- Had they sometimes felt impatient?
- Had they perhaps sometimes felt let down when things didn't seem to be happening?
- Might they, perhaps, have been tempted to give up?

How do the children think they felt when they finally saw Jesus?

- Elated?
- Grateful to God?

Song

One or more of the following songs might be used in the all-age worship:

Be the centre of my life, Lord Jesus
I'm gonna walk by faith
Hang on, stand still, stay put, hold tight
Seek ye first the kingdom of God
There was one, there were two
Watch and pray (Taizé)
We're going to shine like the sun

Art and craft

Make a simple graphic on a flip chart or whiteboard. Draw a circle, diamond or other shape in the middle and write '(Simeon and Anna) WATCH AND PRAY', making those last three words larger and more prominent than the names. Explain to the children that people who do this are often at the centre of God's saving activity in the world, which is why you've put this in the centre of the page. In the service, the congregation will add the other crucial events of the Christmas story around it.

Draw or paint a picture of Simeon holding the baby Jesus.

This is the key picture, but you might want to do others in addition to it, such as:

- Simeon and/or Anna at prayer
- Mary and Joseph carrying Jesus into the temple

Drama – Never give up hope

Narrator	Around the time that Jesus was born in Bethlehem, there was an old man living in Jerusalem called Simeon. Although he was sad, Simeon was also full of hope.
Simeon	I just know that God's going to do something about all this trouble we're having, before I die. God's going to send his special Saviour into the world, and I'm going to live to see it.
Narrator	Simeon's neighbours all liked him – you couldn't help liking old Simeon – but, to be honest, they thought he was a bit dotty. And his neighbour, Maggie, was no exception, although she admired him very much.
Maggie	I don't know where you get this faith from. We've been conquered by the Romans, and their soldiers are everywhere. Every day, people get tortured to death just for believing something different, and we all know God's given up on us – all of us with any sense, that is.
Simeon	God never gives up. He always keeps his promises – and he's promised me I'll be around to see it when the Saviour comes.
Maggie	Well, I've got to admire your faith, even if I do think you're crackers. Anyway, I've baked you a few cakes to cheer you up.
Simeon	Just because I'm old, you think I need cheering up, but you're the one who's saying there's no hope. But thank you, anyway – you're very kind. Actually, I'll eat them later – I get the feeling I ought to be at the temple. I think something interesting's happening.

Maggie	Another little message from the Spirit of God, is it? Off you go, then, Simeon – just don't be disappointed, that's all.
Simeon	Oh, don't worry, I won't be.
Narrator	Simeon got to the temple just in time to see a young woman and her husband carrying a baby.
Joseph	Hey, look at this, Mary – just look at the craftsmanship in this cedar chest. I wonder how they get that effect in the carving – I must try it when we get home.
Mary	Typical! Even now, you can't get carpentry out of your mind.
Joseph	[*Proudly*] I'm going to teach Jesus everything I know.
Mary	Well, let him grow up a bit, first! And right now, we've got to get him blessed properly.
Narrator	Simeon knew these were the people God had brought him here to meet. He just knew, that's all.
Simeon	Excuse me, would you mind if I had a look at your baby?
Mary	Of course not. We're getting used to this – ever since he was born people have been saying how special he is. It's been the most amazing eight days of our life.
Narrator	Simeon took the baby – very carefully, so as not to drop him.
Mary	Keep your hand under his head; his neck isn't very strong, yet.
Simeon	So this is the one. Well, Lord, I've waited a long time, but you can let me go now. I can die happy, because I've seen the beginning of your saving work for all nations. This is the one – absolutely, the One! And I've seen him and held him! He's going to bring light into the whole world – and a special kind of glory to your people right here in Israel. Thank you for keeping your promise.
Narrator	Then Simeon turned to Mary.
Simeon	There are tough times ahead. No quick fix – that's not how God works. This little bundle's going to grow up to change lives – he'll bring joy to a lot of people, but he'll upset some, as well. Sometimes the truth's painful, but that won't stop him telling it. And it won't be any picnic for you, either, I'm afraid.
Narrator	Just then an old woman came up.

Simeon	This is Anna, a prophet. She's been living day and night in the temple waiting for this moment.
Anna	This is the one. This is the Saviour. After all the trouble we've had, God really is doing something. Haven't we always said, Simeon – God keeps his promises?
Narrator	Mary and Joseph took Jesus home to their place in Nazareth, where he grew up strong, wise, and full of faith in God's love for everyone. Even though life was hard, and many people were unhappy, he always had hope. 'God can bring hope out of any amount of trouble,' he used to say. 'Trust me.'

MICHAEL FORSTER

Shepherds – unexpected guests (Luke 2:8-20)

(See page 113 for a dramatised version of this story.)

God's gentle revolution

Abi and Sam were shepherds, and they both wanted a change. 'It's not the job itself,' Sam said, 'I just don't like being looked down on all the time.'

Abi tried to encourage him. 'Don't worry, Sam,' she said. 'Come the revolution *we'll* be calling the shots.'

'Oh, you and your revolution!' scoffed Sam. 'You've got to change people's *attitudes* – and no revolution is going to do that. No, shepherds have always been the bottom of the heap and we always will be. Face it, Abi – no one wants us, not nowhere, not nohow.'

'Now, what sort of a way is that to speak?' came a voice. 'Just because you're a shepherd doesn't mean you have to talk nonsense!' Abi and Sam stared in amazement; the speaker was about ten feet tall, in a long white robe with a pair of enormous wings and a ring of light around his head that lit up the entire night sky.

Abi and Sam threw themselves flat on the ground in fear. 'It's God, come to punish us,' Sam trembled. 'It's all your fault, going on about revolutions and things.'

'Well, if you didn't moan all the time . . .,' Abi retorted.

'Oh dear,' said the angel. 'I was afraid this would happen. That's the trouble with ceremonial dress, it frightens people. Look, I can't change in the middle of a mission – it's not allowed – but just don't be frightened, OK? I've got good news for you.'

Slowly, Abi and Sam raised their heads. 'Good news?'

The angel didn't look so terrifying any more – just impressive. 'Sure thing,' he said. 'Good news for you and for the whole world. It's about your Saviour – you know, the one everyone's been on about for centuries? Well, he's here – well, near here – in Bethlehem, to be exact.'

Abi was thrilled. 'That's it – it's started,' she crowed. 'Up the revolution!'

'Oh, you and your revolutions!' scoffed Sam. 'Don't you know a hallucination when you see one?'

The angel interrupted. 'Oh, it's true enough – you don't think I get all dolled up like this for just any old ceremony, do you? I mean, this is really mega – and I suppose it is a *kind* of revolution, but not the kind you're after. *You're* the ones God wants to be the first to know. He's chosen *you* to be the first visitors. I mean, the priests aren't even going to be told, and the king's being kept well in the dark – I'd say that was pretty revolutionary! Go to Bethlehem and look for a baby wrapped in strips of cloth and lying in a donkey's feeding trough. You don't get many of those to the postal district, so you'll know it's the right one.'

The angel raised his hands and snapped his fingers. 'Cue music!' Instantly, the night air was filled with the most wonderful singing – it was a kind of mixture of every different sort of music they'd ever heard – and quite a lot that they hadn't, as well. And for some reason, it all sounded great together! The angel raised his hand again. 'And . . . action!'

'Good grief!' exclaimed Abi. 'There's thousands of them!' And there were – angels stacked up as far as the eye could see, singing, dancing and generally making whoopee. 'Glory to God in heaven!' they thundered. 'Peace to his people on earth!' Peace? No chance, with all that racket! Strangely, though, the sheep didn't seem at all frightened – just went on chewing the grass as though nothing was happening.

'No one else can hear it!' Sam exclaimed – 'All this is being laid on just for us.'

Abi was as amazed as Sam. 'They wouldn't allow that kind of stuff in the synagogue,' she said, as a troupe of angels did a conga across the horizon, while another group rocked to the heavy beat of some instruments Sam and Abi had never seen before. Gradually, the music and the angels became more distant – their last sight was of the angel who'd talked to them high-kicking his way into the nearest cloud. 'Come on!' Sam gasped. 'Let's go to Bethlehem.'

Suddenly, minding the sheep didn't seem so important. They set off on the trot, expecting to find a party in full swing, but when they got there, there were just the parents and the baby. Sam and Abi were awe-struck. 'So all that was just for us!' said Sam. 'So much for not being important!'

Abi looked puzzled. 'I don't know what's going on,' she said, 'but I'm sure it's *some* kind of revolution.'

Respond to the story

Discussion

Can the children remember why Abi wanted a revolution?

- To give her a chance to be important?
- So that she could make people look up to her, instead of down?

Why did Sam think a revolution wouldn't work?

- Because you have to change people's attitudes?
- Because you can't force people to like you?

Song

One or more of the following songs might be used in the all-age worship:

Come and join the celebration
God was born on earth
Hee, haw! Hee, haw!
See him lying on a bed of straw
There's a star in the East (Rise up, shepherd, and follow)
While shepherds watched

. . . and anything else you care to think of – you hardly need me to suggest songs for Christmas Day, I'm sure!

Art and craft

Prepare outfits and props for a simple role play. The children could dress up in elaborate costumes or could use simple, representative props or badges; for example: a homeless beggar with a notice slung round the neck saying, 'Two children to support' and a begging bowl in hand; an unemployed person could just carry a placard saying, 'Work wanted – cheap rates'; someone else could carry a notice saying, 'Fresh horse manure, £1 per bag'. (Perhaps the children can think of other examples of people who would be less than welcome in many places.) The 'postie' simply needs a bag, a badge saying 'Royal Mail', and of course a letter to hand to you.

Beyond this, you can be as elaborate as you like, but don't forget to leave time to prepare the children for their role in the service.

Draw or paint a picture of the shepherds around the manger.

This is the key picture, but you might want to do others as well, such as:

- the shepherds shivering on the hillside
- the angel talking to the shepherds
- the choir of angels

Drama – God's gentle revolution

Narrator	Abi and Sam were shepherds, and they both wanted a change.
Sam	It's not the job itself. I just don't like being looked down on all the time.
Abi	Don't worry, Sam – come the revolution *we'll* be calling the shots.

Sam	Oh, you and your revolution! You've got to change people's *attitudes* – and no revolution is going to do that. No, shepherds have always been the bottom of the heap and we always will be. Face it, Abi – no one wants us, not nowhere, not nohow.
Angel	Now, what sort of a way is that to speak? Just because you're a shepherd doesn't mean you have to talk nonsense!
Narrator	Abi and Sam stared in amazement; the speaker was about ten feet tall, in a long white robe with a pair of enormous wings and a ring of light around his head that lit up the entire night sky. Abi and Sam threw themselves flat on the ground in fear.
Sam	God's sent an angel to punish us. It's all your fault, going on about revolutions and things.
Abi	Well, if you didn't moan all the time . . .
Angel	Oh dear, I was afraid this would happen. That's the trouble with ceremonial dress, it frightens people. Look, I can't change in the middle of a mission – it's not allowed – but just don't be frightened, OK? I've got good news for you.
Abi and Sam	Good news?
Narrator	The angel didn't look so terrifying any more – just impressive.
Angel	Sure thing. Good news for you and for the whole world. It's about your Saviour – you know, the one everyone's been on about for centuries? Well, he's here – well, near here – in Bethlehem, to be exact.
Abi	That's it – it's started! Up the revolution!
Sam	Oh, you and your revolutions! Don't you know a hallucination when you see one?
Angel	Oh, it's true enough – you don't think I get all dolled up like this for just any old ceremony, do you? I mean, this is really mega – and I suppose it is a *kind* of revolution, but not the kind you're after. *You're* the ones God wants to be the first to know. He's chosen *you* to be the first visitors. I mean, the priests aren't even going to be told, and the king's being kept well in the dark – I'd say that was pretty revolutionary! Go to Bethlehem and look for a baby wrapped in strips of cloth and lying in a donkey's feeding trough. You don't get many of those to the postal district, so you'll know it's the right one.
Narrator	The angel raised his hands and snapped his fingers.
Angel	Cue music!

Narrator	Instantly, the night air was filled with the most wonderful singing – it was a kind of mixture of every different sort of music they'd ever heard – and quite a lot that they hadn't, as well. And for some reason, it all sounded great together! The angel raised his hand again.
Angel	And . . . action!
Abi	Good grief! There's thousands of them!
Narrator	And there were – angels stacked up as far as the eye could see, singing, dancing and generally making whoopee.
Chorus*	Glory to God in heaven! Peace to his people on earth!
Narrator	Peace? No chance, with all that racket! Strangely, though, the sheep didn't seem at all frightened – just went on chewing the grass as though nothing was happening. Then Sam realised.
Sam	No one else can hear it! It's just for us – all this is being laid on just for us.
Abi	(*Amazed*) They wouldn't allow that kind of stuff in the synagogue.
Narrator	As she spoke, a troupe of angels was doing a conga across the horizon while another group rocked to the heavy beat of some instruments Sam and Abi had never seen before. Gradually, the music and the angels became more distant – their last sight was of the angel who'd talked to them high-kicking his way into the nearest cloud.
Sam	Come on! Let's go to Bethlehem.
Narrator	Suddenly, minding the sheep didn't seem so important. They set off on the trot, expecting to find a party in full swing, but when they got there, there were just the parents and the baby. Sam and Abi were awe-struck.
Sam	So all that was just for us! So much for not being important!
Abi	I don't know what's going on, but I'm sure it's *some* kind of revolution.

* A chance, if a brief one, for everybody to be involved!   MICHAEL FORSTER

Epiphany

The Epiphany

Jesus – the light of the world and the hope of the nations

Matthew 2:1-12

(also Isaiah 60:1-6; Psalm 72:(1-9) 10-15; Ephesians 3:1-12)

A reading from the Gospel of Matthew (2:1-12)

Jesus was born in Bethlehem, a small town in Judea when King Herod ruled the land. Some wise men from the east travelled to Jerusalem and asked King Herod where they could find the newborn King of the Jews whom they had come to worship.

Herod was greatly troubled because he didn't want anyone else to be king, so he sent for his advisers. 'Tell me where this child, the so-called King, will be born,' he said.

'It has been foretold by the prophets that he will be born in Bethlehem,' they answered.

For the prophets had written:
And you, Bethlehem in Judea,
are not the least important among Judean cities,
for from you a leader will come,
a shepherd for my people Israel!

King Herod sent for the wise men privately, and asked them to tell him exactly when the star had first appeared. Then he said to them, 'I will allow you to search for this child, but you must come back and tell me where to find him. Then I too can go and honour him.'

The wise men set off again on their journey. They followed the bright star until it appeared to stop over a house, where they found Mary with the baby Jesus. They were filled with wonder and joy, and, falling to their knees to worship him, they gave him gifts of gold, frankincense and myrrh.

An angel warned them in a dream not to return to Herod's palace, so they went back to their own country a different way.

This is the Gospel of the Lord
Praise to you, Lord Jesus Christ   KATIE THOMPSON

Introductory material

After Christmas, Epiphany; after shepherds, wise men – the end of a marathon journey and an arrival long after the events of Bethlehem. But one thing was unchanged – the light which had begun to shine then was shining still, as strongly and brightly as that first day; a light which nothing, not even death itself, would ever be able to extinguish. We come to remember that journey of the magi, and to consider the meaning both of their pilgrimage and the gifts they brought. We come to give our homage to the one at the centre of it all, Jesus Christ, the light of the nations, the Saviour of the world.   NICK FAWCETT

Prayers

Praise – Light in our darkness

Everlasting God,
    we celebrate your coming to our world in Jesus Christ,
        your light that continues to shine
        in the darkness of our world.

We praise you for the way your love shone
    in so many lives during his ministry;
    through the healing he brought to the sick,
    comfort to the distressed,
    promise to the poor,
    and forgiveness to the lost.
Receive our worship,
    and shine in our lives today.

We praise you for the light
    that has shone in so many lives since,
    the faith you have nurtured in innumerable hearts;
    new beginnings,
    new purpose,
    new life born within them.
Receive our worship,
    and shine in our lives today.

We rejoice that you are at work in our lives here and now,
    inviting us to bring our hopes, fears and concerns
    before you in the knowledge
    that you will always meet our needs,
    no situation beyond your power to transform and redeem.
Receive our worship,
    and shine in our lives today.

We praise you for the assurance that evil will be overcome;
    that hope will replace despair,
    joy come after sorrow,
    and life triumph over death –
    that even the deepest darkness shall be turned to light!
Receive our worship,
    and shine in our lives today.

Fill us now with the light of Christ.
May it illumine our worship and guide our footsteps,
    so that we may live as a lamp for others,
    to the glory of your name.
Receive our worship,
    and shine in our lives today.

In his name we ask it.
Amen.   NICK FAWCETT

Confession – Footsteps of the wise men

Lord Jesus Christ,
    this is a day which reminds us
        of the journey of the wise men –
        their determination to greet you
        which inspired them to persevere
        despite difficulties and disappointments along the way.
    Forgive us that we lack their sense of vision,
        their willingness to undertake a pilgrimage
        into the unknown
        in the confidence that you will lead.
    Forgive us if our response to you has lost its initial sparkle,
        the flame which once burned so brightly within us
        now grown cold
        and our hearts no longer stirred
        by the prospect of one day seeing you face to face.
    Lord, in your mercy,
        hear our prayer.

This is a day which reminds us
    of how you led the magi on their journey,
    your light always with them –
    a guiding star,
    a sign of your presence,
    a call to follow until they came to the place where the child lay.
Forgive us that we are so often closed to your guidance,
    unable or unwilling to see your hand,
    more concerned with our own way than yours,
    reluctant to commit ourselves to anything
    when the final goal is not clear.
Forgive us for talking of faith as a journey
    but turning it instead into a comfortable destination.
Lord, in your mercy,
    hear our prayer.

This is a day which reminds us of the magi's worship –
> their falling to their knees before you,
> their bowing in homage,
> their mood of joy and exultation, wonder and privilege.
Forgive us for losing such feelings –
> for being casual,
> complacent,
> even blasé when we come into your presence,
> taking it all for granted.
Forgive us for offering our worship out of habit or duty,
> outwardly correct but inwardly empty.
Lord, in your mercy,
> **hear our prayer.**

This is a day which reminds us of the magi's gifts,
> their presents of gold, frankincense and myrrh,
> each one an expression of love,
> a token of esteem,
> a symbol of all you meant to them.
Forgive us that, though we have received so much,
> we give so little,
> our thoughts more for ourselves than for you,
> our offering made out of routine
> rather than as a sacred act of consecration.
Forgive us that we give what we feel we can afford
> rather than what your great love and goodness deserves.
Lord, in your mercy,
> **hear our prayer.**

Lord Jesus Christ,
> we come to recommit ourselves to the journey of faith,
> to follow where you would lead,
> to bring you our worship
> and to offer ourselves in joyful service.
Receive us in all our weakness
> and go with us on our way,
> that we may live and work for your kingdom.
Lord, in your mercy,
> **hear our prayer.**

For we ask it in your name.
Amen.

NICK FAWCETT

Intercession – Seeking and finding

Lord Jesus Christ,
    you promised that those who seek will find,
      and in the pilgrimage of the magi
      we find proof of that promise.
    So now we bring you our prayers for all in our world,
      known and unknown to us,
      who, in different ways, are searching.
    May your light shine upon them:
      a beacon of hope and a lamp to their path.

We pray for those who search for meaning,
    their lives empty,
    devoid of purpose,
    hungry for something or someone to put their trust in.
In the bewildering variety of this world's voices,
    each claiming to offer the answer,
    may your love break through
    and the message of the gospel touch their hearts,
    so that they might find in you
    the one who is the Way, the Truth and the Life.
May your light shine upon them:
    a beacon of hope and a lamp to their path.

We pray for those for whom the journey of life is hard,
    beset by pain, sickness and sorrow,
    or overwhelmed by disaster, deprivation and injustice.
In the trials they face and the burdens they struggle with
    may your love break through
    and the message of the gospel bring strength and comfort,
    help, healing and inspiration.
May your light shine in the darkness:
    a beacon of hope and a lamp to their path.

We pray for those unsure of the way ahead,
    faced by difficult choices and vital decisions,
    troubled by situations in which they can see no way forward
    or doubting their ability to cope
    with the demands the future will bring.
In the uncertainties of this ever-changing world,
    may your love break through
    and the message of the gospel bring a new sense of direction,
    an inner peace,
    and the assurance which you alone can give,

so that, whatever they may face,
they will know that nothing will ever separate them
from your love.
May your light shine upon them:
a beacon of hope and a lamp to their path.

We pray for those who have gone astray –
betraying their principles,
or their loved ones,
or, above all, you.
In this world of so many subtle yet powerful temptations,
may your love break through
and the message of the gospel bring new beginnings,
so that, however low they might have fallen,
they will know themselves forgiven,
accepted and restored.
May your light shine in the darkness:
a beacon of hope and a lamp to their path.

Lord Jesus Christ,
hear our prayer
for all who seek purpose, help, guidance and mercy.
May they find in you the answer to their prayer
and the end to their searching.

In your name we ask it.
Amen.   NICK FAWCETT

Intercession

In Jesus we see God's secret plan revealed.

We pray for all who spend their lives
leading others to you,
supporting and encouraging them on their journey;
give them your ideas, their love for others,
your joy and your humility.

Silence for prayer

Father, today and every day:
lead us to yourself.

We pray for our leaders and advisers in politics,
business, education and health;
for good values, integrity and compassion,
for courage to stand up for what is right.

Silence for prayer

Father, today and every day:
lead us to yourself.

We pray for our relationships with our neighbours,
colleagues and those in our family;
for the grace to forgive readily,
listen attentively and to be available
whenever you need us.

Silence for prayer

Father, today and every day:
lead us to yourself.   SUSAN SAYERS

Short prayers

Loving God,
    inspire us, as you inspired the magi,
    to journey in faith,
    following where you would lead
    until we reach our goal.
Though we do not know the way ahead,
    and though the path may be hard,
    keep us walking in the light,
    travelling steadfastly to our journey's end.
Teach us to live as a pilgrim people,
    fixing our eyes on Jesus,
    and running the race with perseverance
    for the joy set before us,
    until that day when we kneel
    before the throne of grace,
    and offer our homage to Christ our Lord.
Amen.   NICK FAWCETT

Light of the world,
　shine in our darkness today.
Where there is pain and sorrow
　may the brilliance of your love bring joy.
Where there is sickness and suffering,
　may sunshine come after the storm.
Where there is greed and corruption,
　may your radiance scatter the shadows.
Where there is hatred and bitterness,
　may your brightness dispel the clouds.
Lord Jesus Christ, light of the world,
　rise again upon us we pray,
　and illuminate the darkness of this world
　through your life-giving grace.
In your name we ask it.
Amen.   NICK FAWCETT

All-age-talk material

Where is he?

Reading
Matthew 2:1-11

Aim
To demonstrate that Christmas isn't simply about celebrating the coming of Jesus long ago, but more importantly about our personal response to him, now.

Preparation
Fold in half eight A4 pieces of stiff paper to make A5 cards. On the front of these write the following words in bold letters:

JUDEA
BETHLEHEM
MANGER
STABLE
HOUSE
NAZARETH
JERUSALEM
EGYPT

On the inside of each card, again in bold letters, write 'NOT HERE!' Place the cards prominently around the front of the church so that the word on the front of each can be seen.

Also prepare eight pieces of A4 paper with one of the following written in large, bold letters: E, I, H, H, S, R, E, E.

You will also need a question mark sign and an exclamation mark sign.

Talk

Ask the congregation if anyone can remember what the wise men asked Herod when they came to Jerusalem? (Where is the one born King of the Jews?) Explain that you want to ask this question again today, and that to do so you need eight helpers. Invite volunteers to come to the front, and pin one of the single letters (E, I, H, H, S, R, E, E) on the front of each.

Invite each volunteer in turn to look behind one of the cards to discover where 'the King of the Jews' has been born. After each unsuccessful attempt ask the volunteer to display the words inside – NOT HERE! – and to stand at the front of the church until all eight volunteers are standing side by side in a line.

Observe that, despite the volunteers' help, your question remains unanswered. Ask the congregation to look again very carefully, and see whether they might have missed something. Allow time for people to think, then line the volunteers up so that the letters pinned to their fronts spell 'HE IS HERE'.

That's the answer to our question. Or is it? Well, not quite, for it all depends on what comes after these words. (Position yourself at the end of the line.) Is it a question mark (hold up '?'), or is it an exclamation mark (hold up '!')?

We all know Jesus was born in Bethlehem of Judea; we all know he was born in a stable and laid in a manger because there was no room in the inn; we all know his parents came from Nazareth, and that they took Jesus later to Jerusalem; and we probably know that after Jesus' birth they fled to Egypt to escape Herod.

All that is part of the wonderful Christmas story we know and love so well. But unless there's another chapter in that story, then all the rest doesn't finally mean anything. It is only when Jesus can also be found here in our hearts, in our lives, in each one of us, that Christmas truly comes alive.

Where is the one born King of the Jews? Is he simply here (point to one of the cards), or here (point to one of the volunteers), or here (point to the congregation)? Or can we point to ourselves and say, honestly and without hesitation, 'He is here!'

That's the question we need to ask this Christmas, and the answer we need to give.

Nick Fawcett

The Wise Men come to Jesus

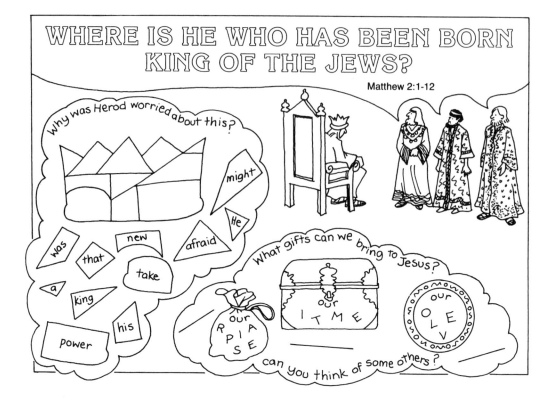

SUSAN SAYERS

Herod is surrounded by traitors.
Can you find six of them hidden in this room?

He will reign . . . for ever. (Luke 1:33)

Help the wise men get back home
without passing Herod's palace.

Home

WORDSEARCH

Find the following words in the grid:

BETHLEHEM, HEROD, FRANKINCENSE,
EGYPT, JESUS, PROPHECY, WISE,
LOVE, POWER, ANGEL,
GOLD, MYRRH,
JOSEPH, MARY.

```
B E T H L E H E T I S B
E G Y P L O N E W I S E
J O S E P H P O W E S T
Y E G G T Y C E P O R H
R N S Y G P O W D R D L
A H F U X O Y G O L D E
M R R B S I L G R I S H
F R A N K I N C E N S E
G Y N O V E L O H E F M
Y M K R E W O P E G N A
P R I O W E V H E W O D
T I N N Y C E H P O R P
```

MICHAEL FORSTER

God is awesome

Have seven large cards available. On each card write one letter from the word 'awesome'. Place the first card on the flipchart and ask the group to think about their dreams and ambitions. While they are thinking, turn the card over to reveal the word: 'Almighty'. Do this with each of the other cards.

A: Almighty

W: Wonderful

E: Everlasting

S: Saviour

O: Omnipotent

M: Majestic

E: Everywhere

After you have revealed each word and the group have recognised each one as telling us a little bit about God's character, finish with the following prayer:

God, you are
Almighty, creator of all things seen and unseen.
You are Wonderful, absolutely amazing, totally astounding.
You are Everlasting in your love for each one of us.
You are our Saviour, our rescuer from everything
    that would try and put a barrier between us.
You are Omnipotent, powerful, able to do
    the impossible, able to love me.
You are Majestic, royalty above all royalty.
You are Everywhere, all around, with us in everything we do
    and watching out for us every step of the way.
God, you are
AWESOME.

PETE TOWNSEND

Read Matthew 2:1-12

Every Christmas we see them, dressed in dressing gowns and wearing paper crowns. The three 'wise men' take their tinsel-covered shoe boxes and present them to the plastic doll lying in the cot. Everybody sighs at the little boy dressed as a donkey and laughs at the two girls fighting with the black-and-white sheet that allows them to pretend they are a cow. It's all part of the Christmas story. It's familiar, safe and we wouldn't feel the same without it.

What's that got to do with 'awesome'? Take the three 'wise men'. These 'wise men' or magi, were religious leaders and scholars from an area we now know as Iran and the surrounding countries. We always think of them as being only three, but there were more than likely up to a hundred of them travelling together (we think of three wise men because of the three gifts).

The magi travelled a huge distance, covering mountains and desert, through storms and possible encounters with bandits along the way. We are told they followed a 'star' which came to rest over Bethlehem. Chinese astronomers recorded a comet around 5 BC which travelled slowly across the sky and its 'tail' pointed towards Bethlehem. This comet became visible on the first day of the Egyptian month Mesori. Mesori literally means 'birth of a prince'. With this knowledge, the magi set off on a long and hazardous journey to see who this prince could be.

The magi walked away from everything that was safe and familiar so that they could find this special child and offer their worship. They brought with them the three gifts that would signify the role of the child: gold for royalty; frankincense for priesthood and myrrh for death.

For the magi to leave their homes and travel over rough terrain and face unknown dangers so that they could see the infant Jesus, that's awesome.

PETE TOWNSEND

Reflective material
(sketches, meditations and poems)

And when it's all over . . .

Baby Jesus, goodbye,
  baby Jesus, goodbye!
We've put him away with the Christmas tree,
  get him out again next year, maybe,
  baby Jesus, goodbye!

But Jesus grew to a man,
  Jesus grew to a man.
He lived and he loved us so much that he died,
  that is why God was crucified,
  Jesus grew to a man.

Baby Jesus is dead,
  baby Jesus is dead.
In fact he was never there at all,
  just a plastic doll in a cattle stall,
  baby Jesus is dead.

But Jesus rose again,
  Jesus rose again.
He's alive and he cares about you,
  he wants you to have eternal life too,
  Jesus rose again.

Baby Jesus is gone,
   baby Jesus is gone.
He goes away with the Christmas cheer,
   and then it's all over – till next year,
   baby Jesus is gone.

But Jesus is coming as King,
   Jesus is coming as King.
He waits for you to invite him in,
   he wants so much your love to win,
   Jesus is coming as King.   MARY HATHAWAY

Meditation of the Magi

Do you know what we gave him –
   that little boy in Bethlehem?
Go on, have a guess!
A rattle?
A toy?
A teddy bear?
No, nothing like that!
In fact, nothing you'd associate with a child at all,
   even if he *was* destined to be a king.
Gold, that's what I brought!
And my companions?
Wait for it!
Frankincense and myrrh!
Yes, I thought you'd be surprised,
   for, to tell the truth
   we're pretty amazed ourselves looking back,
   unable to imagine what on earth possessed us
   to choose such exotic and unusual gifts.
It wasn't so much that they were costly,
   though they were, of course –
   to a family like his they were riches beyond their dreams.
But we could more than afford it –
   little more than small change to men of our means.
No, it wasn't the price that troubled us afterwards,
   but the associations,
   the possible meaning his parents might have read into our presents
   when we'd gone.
Not the gold, there was no problem there –
   a gift fit for a king and designed to say as much, of course.
But frankincense?

Well, the main use his people have for that, as we learned later,
   is to sweeten their sacrifices,
   to pour out on to their burnt offerings
   so that the fragrance might be pleasing to their God.
Hardly the most appropriate gift for a baby.
But compared with myrrh!
Don't tell me you don't know?
It was a drug used to soothe pain,
   either for that or as a spice for embalming –
   more fitting for a funeral than a birth,
   having more to do with suffering and death than celebration!
So what were we thinking of?
What possible significance could gifts like those have for a little child?
Frankly, I have no idea.
Yet at the time the choice seemed as obvious to us
   as following the star,
   as though each were all part of some greater purpose
   which would one day become clear to all.
Were we right?
Well, after all I've said, I rather hope not,
   for if this king was born to die,
   to be offered in sacrifice rather than enthroned in splendour,
   then his must be an unusual kingdom,
   very different from most we come across –
   in fact, you might almost say, not a kingdom of this world at all!

NICK FAWCETT

Ride that camel! Follow that star!

Based on Matthew 2:1-12

Narrator	Melchior, Caspar and Balthazar were three wise men. They used to meet together often to talk about important things, and to look at the stars. They would sit around, very late at night (long after well-behaved children were asleep!) discussing whatever new star they had most recently seen. One evening, Melchior got very excited.
Melchior	Look over there! There's a great big star that I've never seen before. I wonder what it means.
Balthazar	I'll look it up. Let me see, 'Star – extra bright . . .' Hey, it says here that it means a special king has been born, and the star will lead us to him.

Melchior	Then what are we waiting for? Let's go and follow it.
Narrator	Everybody suddenly got very busy, packing the things they would need, and by the next night, when the star appeared again, they were ready to go. How do you think they travelled?

- Would they *ride* on donkeys?
- Would they *drive* in a car?
- Would they *ride* on bicycles?

Of course, they would ride on camels, wouldn't they?

Balthazar	Come on everyone, let's get moving! The three of us will ride ahead and the servants follow behind with all the food and water and camping kit – and I hope you've remembered to pack the kettle.
Narrator	They travelled through the desert for many weeks, moving at night when they could see the star, and sleeping in their tents during the day. Eventually, they saw a big city ahead.
Melchior	Where are we?
Caspar	According to my reckoning that should be Jerusalem.
Balthazar	Good, that's a capital city. Let's find the palace.
Narrator	Now this was definitely a bad idea. The king in Jerusalem was the wicked king Herod – and he got a bit worried when he heard what the wise men wanted.
Herod	(*Aside, to audience*) I'm the king! There's not room for another one. I'd better find him and get rid of him.
Narrator	So Herod did a bit of checking up, and then went back to the wise men.
Herod	I think the king you're looking for is in Bethlehem. When you've found him, would you let me know, so that I can go to see him, as well?
Narrator	So off went the wise men, and Herod turned to his courtiers and started making plans.
Herod	Right! When those silly men come back and tell me where this so-called king is, I'll have him killed. King indeed!

| Narrator | The wise men went to Bethlehem, and found Mary and Joseph with Jesus. They had some presents for the baby. |

- *Gold*, for a king
- *Frankincense*, for God's special king
- *Myrrh*, for his suffering

	Then they went to their tents to sleep. And next morning they got ready to leave for home.
Balthazar	We mustn't forget to stop and tell that nice King Herod where Jesus is.
Melchior	I don't think so. I've found out that 'nice King Herod' as you call him is bad news.
Caspar	I knew it! Shifty character! Don't trust him a millimetre! I vote we give him a miss.
Melchior	Good idea! Let's go home the pretty way.

MICHAEL FORSTER

Lent

Ash Wednesday

Choosing the way of God's Kingdom

Matthew 6:1-6, 16-21

(also Isaiah 58:1-12; Psalm 51:1-18; 2 Corinthians 5:20b-6:10)

A reading from the Gospel of Matthew (6:19-21)

Do not store up for yourself treasure on earth,
   where moth and worm eat things up,
   where thieves break into houses and steal.
Store up for yourself treasure in heaven,
   where no moth or worm eats things up,
   where no thieves break into houses and steal.
For heart and treasure
   go together.

ALAN DALE

Introductory material

The Easter tree

We are very fortunate that in our part of the world the seasonal pattern of nature helps us to a better understanding of the meaning of Lent and Easter. The apparently dead winter trees and bushes are gradually transformed during this period. By Easter Sunday fresh green leaves are showing the rebirth of nature. What was dead, dark and cold is showing life, light and hope. As far as possible, according to where you live, the children's attention needs to be drawn to this annual transformation in nature. Of course, a parallel should be drawn with our own lives as Christians.

The Easter tree is one good way of tying the two together. On a large sheet of white card, or poster board, or perhaps on a surface taken from the inside of a large (empty) cereal packet, draw a simple outline of a tree in winter, including the roots. Cut out the outline (don't make the branches and twigs too detailed otherwise there will be problems) leaving the roots in the ground. Get the children to colour the trunk and branches brown – nothing more, because it is representing an apparently dead tree in winter. Mount the tree on a second piece of board, allowing about a quarter of an inch (or a centimetre) between the two cards. Write the heading 'Easter Tree' above the tree on the backing card. On Ash Wednesday hang the Easter Tree in your kitchen where everyone can see it. On that day get the children to fill a sheet (possibly one each) with little ovals which they colour green. These are to be the leaves and their dimension should be kept in some sort of proportion with the tree.

The tree works alongside the [practical and reasonable] resolutions that have been made by the family for Lent. Each time (perhaps once a day so that they can all be done together) a good turn has been done, or a resolution kept, a green leaf is stuck onto the tree. By the time Easter Sunday comes the tree should be covered in foliage. The roots, which should not have been coloured brown when the trunk was, can be coloured in for each of the Sunday Masses and holy communions of Lent: it is from our Sunday worship together and the reception of the risen Christ in holy communion, that the grace and strength comes to live our lives as children of God. It is from union with Christ and his community that we receive the grace and strength to do good.

On Easter Day the tree will serve as a decoration and lovely memorial of our efforts throughout Lent. On Easter morning, to symbolise the resurrection, little yellow or white bows can be tied between the green leaves around the branches.

TONY CASTLE

Prayers

Approach – Ash Wednesday

Living God,
  on this first day of Lent we come together
    seeking your presence,
    offering our worship,
    and asking for guidance.
  Lord, hear our prayer.

We come, remembering once more
    the temptation of Jesus in the wilderness,
    and his refusal to give way.
  Lord, hear our prayer.

We come remembering those forty days and nights of trial,
    that time of prayer and meditation,
    preparation for the future.
  Lord, hear our prayer.

We come remembering the life,
    the death,
    the resurrection and exaltation that followed.
  Lord, hear our prayer.

Living God,
  help us, learning from his example,
    to use this season wisely,
    making time to hear your voice
    and reflect on your word.
  Lord, hear our prayer.

Help us to honestly examine ourselves,
    carefully and prayerfully searching our hearts.
Lord, hear our prayer.

Help us to see ourselves as we really are,
    and as you would have us be,
    ready to follow you and do your will,
    no matter what the cost.
Lord, hear our prayer.

Help us to know where we are faithful to you
    and where we fail,
    recognising our strengths and also our weaknesses.
Lord, hear our prayer.

Living God,
    give us courage to stand before your searching gaze
        and accept your verdict,
        humility to accept your correction and receive forgiveness,
        wisdom to hear your word and feed on it through faith.
    So in the days ahead may we grow closer to you
        in the likeness of Christ.
    Lord, hear our prayer.
    for we ask it in his name.
    Amen.   Nick Fawcett

Petition – The righteousness of God

Living God,
    you have taught us that we should long to know you better,
        not just to want that
        but to urgently, passionately and wholeheartedly yearn for it,
        striving with all our being
        to understand your will and fulfil your purpose.
    Blessed are those who hunger and thirst after righteousness,
        for they shall be filled.

Teach us the secret of such hunger.
Instead of cluttering our lives with so much that can never satisfy,
    teach us to empty ourselves so that we may be filled by you;
    to desire your kingdom,
    seek your will
    and study your word,
    earnestly,
    eagerly,
    expectantly.

Blessed are those who hunger and thirst after righteousness,
for they shall be filled.

However much we know of your love,
however richly you may have blessed us,
teach us to keep that hunger alive,
to thirst always for a deepening of our faith,
a strengthening of our service
and a greater awareness of your purpose.
Blessed are those who hunger and thirst after righteousness,
for they shall be filled.

Thanks be to God,
through Jesus Christ our Lord.
Amen.   NICK FAWCETT

Intercession – Reconciliation with God

This will involve first admitting our need of God's mercy and forgiveness and then examining our lives in his light to see what needs to be done. God does not simply patch up the bits of us that look bad – he completely renews and restores, giving us the joy and peace of forgiveness.

Let us come before God, our creator and sustainer,
with the needs of the church and of the world.

We bring to your love, O Lord,
all who have committed their lives to your service;
that they may all be one,
bound together by your Holy Spirit.

Silence for prayer

Father of mercy:
hear us with compassion

We bring to your love all the areas of the world
in which there is hostility and unrest;
that new routes to negotiation
and reconciliation may emerge.

Silence for prayer

Father of mercy:
hear us with compassion

We bring to your love
the members of our human families
especially any we find difficult
to get on with or understand;
that our love for one another
may enter a new dimension
of warm and positive caring, seasoned with laughter.

Silence for prayer

Father of mercy:
hear us with compassion.

We bring to your love
all who have become hard and aggressive
through years of festering hate or jealousy;
that their unresolved conflicts
may be brought to your light and healed.

Silence for prayer

Father of mercy:
hear us with compassion.

We bring to your love all those, dear to us,
who are separated from us by death;
may we come, one day, with them
to share the eternal peace and joy of heaven.

Silence for prayer

Father of mercy:
hear us with compassion.

We thank you for all your blessings and patient loving,
and especially for coming to save us from our sin.

Silence for prayer

Merciful Father,
**accept these prayers
for the sake of your Son,
our Saviour Jesus Christ, Amen.**

SUSAN SAYERS

All-age-talk material

Which way now?

Reading

Matthew 7:3-14 (to be read at the end of the talk rather than before it)

Aim

To bring home the fact that following Jesus sometimes involves difficult but important choices on which our future depends.

Preparation

On a large sheet of card, or directly on to a whiteboard, prepare for a game of Hangman by drawing dashes to represent each letter of the following:

- The gate that leads to destruction is wide and the way is easy.
- The gate that leads to life is narrow and the way hard.
- Those who find it are few.

You will also need a marker pen to fill in the missing letters as they are guessed (or to draw the 'hanged man').

Talk

Tell the congregation that you are challenging them to a game of Hangman, only it is a game with a difference! Instead of guessing one word, they have to guess 31 words, which together summarise two verses from the Bible! Invite people to suggest a letter. (Although identifying 31 words sounds difficult, it is actually easier than identifying a single word – the hard part is for you to fill in all the places where a particular letter fits!)

When the game has been completed, explain that it was all about choices – making the right choices! There were 26 letters to choose from, but, of course, not 26 opportunities to choose them, so you had to make a decision as to the best ones to choose. In the same way, it was the need to decide that Jesus was talking about to the crowds in those words we've just uncovered. What he actually said was this:

'Enter through the narrow gate; for the gate is wide and the road is easy that leads to destruction, and there are many who take it. For the gate is narrow and the road is hard that leads to life, and there are few who take it.' (*Matthew 7:13*)

Just as there were many letters to choose from in the game but only a few right ones, so it is with life in general. There are all kinds of choices we can make, but though some may look appealing they lead us nowhere, or, worse, lead us astray. The way that leads to life is the way that Jesus has shown, but it is a way that involves difficult and sometimes costly choices which we may prefer not to make.

Lent reminds us that Jesus was willing to make such difficult choices himself; taking the way of the cross, of suffering and sacrifice, so great was his love for the world. And that example asks each of us, quite simply, which way will we choose: the way of self-interest and self-service, or the way of self-denial and serving others.

Read the complete passage from Matthew's Gospel.   NICK FAWCETT

Reflective material
(sketches, meditations and poems)

Humility

Humility
   is like the snowdrops
   flowering along the bank,
   for they are
   small and white
   and they bloom in purity
   low down
   near the earth.

Humility
   is like the goldfinch
   perched in the tree,
   for though he is
   coloured with joy
   in red, yellow,
   black and white,
   he cannot see
   his own glory.

Humility
   is like the seagull
   soaring in the sky,
   for his wings
   are spread
   in strength
   with an easy grace
   of which he is
   totally unaware.

Humility
   is like the buds
   opening in spring,
   for their
   leaves unfold
   with gladness,
   responding
   instinctively to
   the warmth of love.

Humility
   is like the violet
   growing in the grass,
   for its birth
   is imperceptible
   and yet it is touched by God
   in the beauty
   of its growing.   MARY HATHAWAY

Reading: Luke 4:14-15

Then Jesus, filled with the power of the Spirit, returned to Galilee, and a report about him spread through all the surrounding country. He began to preach and teach in their synagogues and was praised by everyone.

Meditation of John the Baptist

He was back at last!
After countless days of silence,
   no sight nor sound of him,
   suddenly he was back where he belonged
   and taking the world by storm.
It was a relief, believe me,
   for I'd begun to wonder what I'd done,
   whether I'd somehow put my foot in it,
   even got the wrong man.
You see, he'd come to me there in the Jordan,
   and I'd thought immediately, 'This is the one,
   the Saviour God has promised,
   the lamb that takes away the sin of the world!'
And what an honour,
   what a joy for me, John, to baptise him,
   to be there at the beginning of the Messiah's ministry,
   the inauguration of God's kingdom!

Only then he disappeared,
  without trace,
  the last I saw of him making off into the wilderness,
  alone.
What's going on, I wondered?
Where's he off to?
I wanted him back here at the sharp end where he was needed –
  wasn't that what he'd come for –
  to bring light into darkness,
  joy out of sorrow,
  hope in despair?
But he was gone,
  and as the days passed with no word,
  no sign,
  no news,
  so the doubts began to grow.
Had I misunderstood,
  presumed too much?
Had I caused offence,
  given the wrong signals?
I wondered,
  and I worried,
  day after day my confusion growing,
  and I'd all but given up hope,
  ready to write the whole business off as some sad mistake,
  when suddenly he was back,
  the word spreading like fire,
  his name on every tongue –
  Jesus of Nazareth,
  preacher and teacher,
  the talk of the town.
I still don't know what he got up to out there,
  why he needed to spend so long out in the desert,
  but it doesn't matter any more,
  for he's here now where we need him,
  and he's come back stronger and surer,
  almost as though the wilderness
  meant as much to him as his baptism,
  if not more!
Does that make sense to you?
It does to me.

                                             NICK FAWCETT

First Sunday of Lent

Jesus is tempted as we are, yet stays true to his calling,
choosing the way that leads to the cross

Luke 4:1-13

(also Deuteronomy 26:1-11; Psalm 91:1-2, 9-16; Romans 10:8b-13)

A reading from the Gospel of Luke (4:1-13)

Jesus was filled with the Holy Spirit which led him into the desert where he was tempted by the devil for forty days. All that time he had nothing to eat and he was famished.

The devil said to him, 'If you are God's Son, then turn this stone into a tasty loaf of bread.'

Jesus replied, 'Scripture tells us that man does not live on bread alone.'

Then the devil tempted Jesus a second time by showing him a glimpse of all the kingdoms of the world. 'All this belongs to me,' he said, 'but I will give this power and glory to you if you worship me!'

Jesus answered him, 'Scripture tells us to worship the Lord our God and serve him alone.'

Then the devil led Jesus to the Temple in Jerusalem, and on its rooftop he tempted him for a third time. 'If you are indeed the Son of God,' the devil said, 'then throw yourself off, for Scripture says: God has ordered his angels to guard you and they will cradle you in their arms to protect you from any harm.'

Jesus said to the devil, 'Scripture also tells us: do not put the Lord God to the test.'

Finally, the devil gave up trying to tempt Jesus, and he left him alone and waited for his next opportunity.

This is the Gospel of the Lord
Praise to you, Lord Jesus Christ   KATIE THOMPSON

Introductory material

'Examine yourselves to see whether you are living in the faith. Test yourselves.' So wrote the Apostle Paul in his second letter to the Corinthians. And there, in a nutshell, is a perfect summary of what this season of Lent is all about – a time for self-examination, for looking honestly and openly at the state of our Christian lives. Just as Jesus was tested in the wilderness, so we too need to test ourselves. Just as he wrestled with temptation, so we too must wrestle with the things that may destroy our relationship with God. Just as he had to come to terms with what God expected of him, so we too have to seek God's guidance and ask for grace to accept his will.   NICK FAWCETT

Prayers

Thanksgiving – Thanks for forgiveness

Almighty God,
    we thank you that we can come now before you,
        that you are here waiting to meet with us and speak to us.
    We thank you that though we have no claim on your love,
        and no right to expect any mercy,
        you are always reaching out to us,
        eager to forgive and forget.
    Gracious God, open our hearts to your love.

    We thank you that though we repeatedly fail you,
        and though we resist your will,
        you go on wiping the slate clean,
        offering us a new beginning, a fresh start.
    Gracious God, open our hearts to your love.

    We thank you that you love and care about each one of us,
        that for all our faults and weaknesses
        you accept us just as we are.
    Poor though our faith may be,
        you are always ready to guide,
        to help,
        and to bless.
    Gracious God, open our hearts to your love.

Almighty God,
    help us to open our lives to you,
        to be honest with you, ourselves and others.
    Help us to see ourselves as we really are,
        the good and the bad, the strengths and the weaknesses,
        the lovely and the unlovely.
    Help us to recognise our sins and to confess them,
        throwing ourselves upon your mercy.
    Gracious God, open our hearts to your love.

And so may we receive the cleansing,
        the renewal
        and the forgiveness you long to show us.
    Gracious God, open our hearts to your love.
    in the name of Christ.
Amen.

NICK FAWCETT

Intercession

Temptation. Man and woman spoilt God's perfect creation by falling into temptation and disobeying their creator. We are all guilty of sin, but through Christ we are given the strength and grace to resist temptation just as he did.

Trusting not in our weakness but in God's mercy
let us pray to him now.

We pray for Christians whose faith
is being tested by hardship,
spiritual dryness or any outside pressures;
that they may hold fast to you, Lord Christ,
and emerge stronger in the knowledge
of your loyal, sustaining love.

Silence for prayer

Lord you are the rock:
on whom our security rests.

We pray for those involved in advertising,
broadcasting and journalism,
and for all in the entertainment business;
that they may not encourage selfishness or violence,
but discretion and insight.

Silence for prayer

Lord you are the rock:
on whom our security rests.

We pray for the people on either side of us now;
for the families represented here,
and all who live in the same street as we do;
that we may live out the pattern
of Christlike loving in a practical way.

Silence for prayer

Lord you are the rock:
on whom our security rests.

We pray for those blinded by prejudice
or self-centred thinking; for those being dragged down
by a drug or alcohol habit they feel powerless to stop;
that they may be led tenderly to freedom.

Silence for prayer

Lord you are the rock:
on whom our security rests.

We pray for those who,
having worshipped you on earth,
have now passed into eternity;
may they spend eternity in unending love and praise.

Silence for prayer

Lord you are the rock:
on whom our security rests.

Father, we thank you
for showing us the way to abundant life.

Silence for prayer

Merciful Father,
accept these prayers
for the sake of your Son,
our Saviour Jesus Christ, Amen.   SUSAN SAYERS

Short prayer

Loving God,
    you tell us that we will not be tested
    beyond our limit,
    that we shall not be tempted
    beyond what we can withstand.
But you tell us also to examine ourselves,
    to keep on looking at our lives,
    ensuring that we are serving you
    and honouring you as we should.
Loving God,
    all too easily we grow casual in our discipleship,
    dismissing the need for any such soul-searching.
Yet Lent reminds us that even Jesus felt the need
    for such a time,
    spending those forty days and nights
    in the wilderness
    following his baptism.
Help us to recognise what he went through
    and why he went through it,
    and so help us to test ourselves
    and see ourselves as we really are,
    and as we should be.   NICK FAWCETT

All-age-talk material

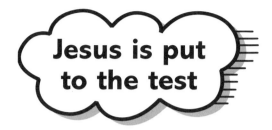

Jesus is put to the test

Today is the
First Sunday of Lent. The word
'Lent' comes from the Old English
word 'lencten'

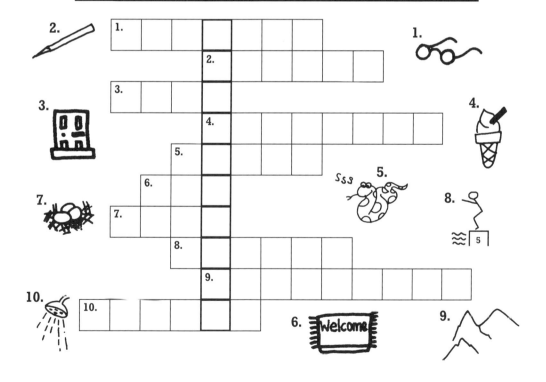

Use the clues to find out what the word Lent means

KATIE THOMPSON

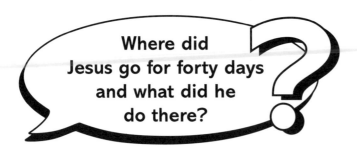

Where did Jesus go for forty days and what did he do there?

Add or subtract letters to crack the code!

A B C D E F G H I J K L M N O P Q R S T U V W X Y Z

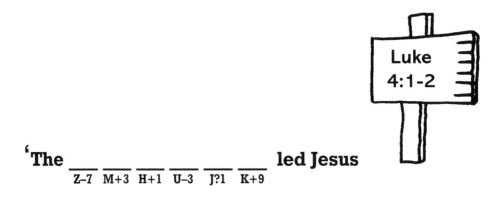

Luke
4:1-2

'The ___ ___ ___ ___ ___ ___ led Jesus
 Z–7 M+3 H+1 U–3 J?1 K+9

through the ___ ___ ___ ___ ___ ___ ___ ___ ___ ___
 R+5 C+6 O–3 R–14 A+4 O?3 M+1 C+2 Y–6 P+3

for ___ ___ ___ ___ ___ days, he
 D+2 J+5 C+15 V–2 X+1

had ___ ___ ___ ___ ___ ___ ___ to ___ ___ ___ there
 L+2 V–7 S+1 B+6 G?2 K+3 N–7   A+4 E–4 L+8

because he was ___ ___ ___ ___ ___ ___ ___ ,
 C+3 B?1 R+1 W–3 Q–8 L+2 J–3

KATIE THOMPSON

Give each member of the group a piece of paper and a pen, and ask them to write three statements about their hopes or desires on the piece of paper (don't write any name or initials which might identify the writer). For example:

1. I want to build a boat.
2. I want to become an actor/actress.
3. I want to travel around the world.

When each group member has finished, collect the statements, shuffle them and then distribute them around the group. Ask one group member to read the three statements and see if the rest of the group can guess who wrote the statements. To add a little bit of mystery, have some statements already prepared which are not specific to anyone in the group. These statements could be based on someone you, or the group, knows or be entirely fictitious. Some of these statements could be totally bizarre!

How well do we know each other? How well do we know ourselves, particularly when we are faced with a really difficult situation?

Take a look at 'He is the Lord' by Kevin Prosch (*The Source*, 159), or 'Is it true today? by Martin Smith (*The Source*, 241).

It isn't always easy to be confident or certain about what we know or believe. It's especially difficult to be positive and self-assured when we are in an awkward situation.   PETE TOWNSEND

Read Luke 4:1-13

Jesus had just been baptised in the River Jordan and a voice from heaven had said: 'You are my own dear Son, and I am pleased with you' (Luke 3:22), when he goes off into the desert for a few days. This was to be a period of preparation for Jesus and he was possibly looking forward to some time on his own before things started to heat up. No sooner had he put a foot in the sand when the devil starts to have a go at him. Possibly Jesus sighed and thought: 'Well, there goes my peace and quiet!' Having just been acknowledged as God's Son and told that his Father was pleased with him, along comes someone to question everything.

The devil started by saying 'If . . .'. It's a question, a seed of doubt, a prod at Jesus' self-assurance. By then Jesus was hot, tired, hungry and thirsty. It certainly wasn't the best time to start fielding difficult questions. Jesus could quite easily have replied, 'Right now isn't a good time to answer questions' or 'Let me sleep on it', but he knew that he'd have to face these challenges sooner or later. His answers were part reply and part reassurance to himself. He needed to respond to the devil with words that not only refuted the devil's 'if', but also reaffirmed what Jesus knew to be true.

It's important to remember that the words Jesus used in his replies were not just some simple quotes that he recalled from his childhood, but were true statements, an underlining of his knowledge of who he was and what he had to do.

It's never very easy to feel confident when we are in a difficult situation and someone asks awkward questions. You know that when a question starts with either: 'I thought that . . .' or 'Are you sure that . . .' it's going to be tough finding the appropriate answer. There are many situations where it's tough for us to feel confident in what we believe and 'if' we are doing the right thing. Ask the group if they can think of any situations which have made them question what they believe or doubt that they are doing the 'right' thing.

Make a list of some of the following statements and see if any relate to the situations discussed:

- I am God's child. (John 1:12)
- I am Christ's friend. (John 15:15)
- I have been bought with a price. I belong to God. (1 Corinthians 6:19-20)
- I am complete in Christ. (Colossians 2:10)
- I have been forgiven. (Colossians 1:14)
- I am born of God and the evil one cannot touch me. (1 John 5:1, 18)
- I have direct access to God through the Holy Spirit. (Ephesians 2:18)
- I have not been given a spirit of fear, but of power, love and a sound mind. (2 Timothy 1:7)
- I may approach God with boldness and confidence. (Ephesians 3:12)
- I am confident that the good work that God has begun in me will be perfected. (Philippians 1:6)
- I cannot be separated from the love of God. (Romans 8:39)

There are many more Bible verses which you might add to the list.

PETE TOWNSEND

Jesus was tempted to use his powers in the wrong way. What were the three tests he had to face?

1

To turn stones into

_ _ _ _ _

Luke 4:3

2

To become
_ _ _ _ _ of the world, and stop worshipping God

Luke 4:5-7

3

To jump off the

_ _ _ _ _ _ _
and let the angels catch him

Luke 4:9

Did Jesus choose God's way?

YES

NO

KATIE THOMPSON

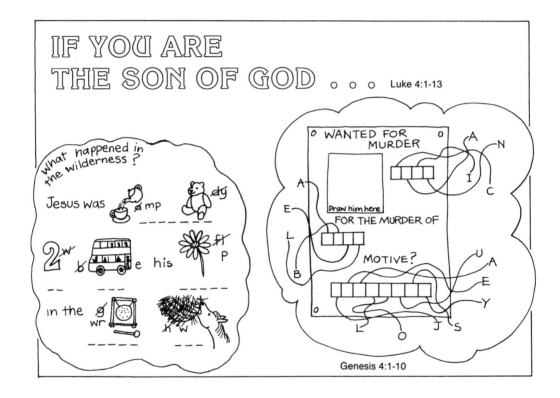

SUSAN SAYERS

It's your choice

Reading

Luke 5:1-11, 27-28

Aim

To illustrate the message that Lent is about choices – not just those Jesus had to make during his temptation in the wilderness, but the choices we have to make every day of our lives.

Preparation

You will need a small selection of sweets, a coin, three or four straws (one shorter than the others), and a dice.

Talk

Tell the congregation that you have a mouth-watering selection of sweets with which to tempt them. Invite volunteers to come forward, and explain that before they can choose a sweet they must first make another simple choice. Make the right decision, and a sweet is theirs.

Choices can be made as follows, or using ideas of your own:

- Conceal a coin in one hand, and ask which hand it's in.
- Hold up your collection of straws, and ask who can draw the short straw.
- Throw the dice, and ask volunteers to guess which number will come up.
- Ask a straightforward true or false question. For example, Luke was a fisherman: true or false?
- Ask a multiple choice question. For example, the other name given in the Bible to Levi is (a) Simon, (b) Matthew or (c) Philip?

What has all this to do with the reading from Luke's Gospel. The answer is simple: in each case it was up to the volunteer to come to their own decision. No one forced them to come forward and take part; no one influenced their choice as they made their decision – it was up to them.

The same was true for Peter, James and John. When Jesus first called them, there was no pressure. He didn't insist on joining them; he asked if he could. He didn't force them to carry on fishing; he encouraged them to throw out their nets one last time. He didn't compel them to become his disciples; he invited them to follow. The final decision was theirs, no one else's.

And so it is with us. God has given us free will. He offers guidance through the Scriptures, he shows us how to live through the example of Jesus, but he never twists our arms. We have a choice: our way or his; to live for ourselves, or live for him; self-interest or self-sacrifice? Lent calls us to think about the choices before us, and to decide which path we will take.   NICK FAWCETT

Multiple choice

Reading
Luke 4:1-12

Aim
To demonstrate that choices are not always easy, and the right way is not always as clear as we would like, but if we seek God's guidance he will help us choose wisely.

Preparation
The only preparation needed is to print the three alternative spellings for 'Commitment' (see below). You may, however, like to print all the questions for visual effect.

Talk
Tell the congregation that you have prepared a simple quiz for Lent, with a mixture of easy and not-so-easy questions. Invite volunteers to suggest answers.

GENERAL KNOWLEDGE

- What is the highest mountain in the world? (Everest)

- How much is 25 divided by 5? (5)

- What colour do you get if you mix yellow and red? (Orange)

- Who won the FA Cup last year? (Make sure you know the answer!)

TRUE OR FALSE:

- A rolling stone gathers no moss (True)

- 4 + 4 = 9 (False)

- Henry VIII had six wives (True)

- You shall love your neighbour as yourself (As Christians, we believe that's true)

MULTIPLE CHOICE

- What is the capital of Canada: (1) Toronto, (2) Ontario, or (3) Ottawa? (Ottawa)

- How many horns does an Indian rhinoceros have: (1) none, (2) one, or (3) two? (Two)

- Which spelling is correct: (1) Committment, (2) Commitment, or (3) Comitment? (Commitment)

- What is the speed of sound: (1) 240 mph, (2) 760 mph, or (3) 980 mph? (760 mph)

There were three different kinds of questions in the quiz: some where the answer was obvious; others which called for a choice between three possible answers; others still where the answer depended on personal convictions about right and wrong! And that mixture of questions was chosen for a purpose, because in life we are faced in much the same way with different kinds of choices. Sometimes a course of action is clearly right or wrong. Sometimes we may be faced with a variety of options, and we have to choose which one is right. And sometimes the choice we make is down to what we believe – a question of faith.

Choices, then, are not always easy, but when we are faced with the need to choose we should look back to the forty days Jesus faced in the wilderness. For at the end of that time he too was faced with difficult choices – the need to choose between good and bad, right and wrong! There were three very different temptations. To bow before Satan – that was clearly wrong. But to turn stones into bread, what was so wrong with that? And as for throwing himself off the temple to test God's purpose, couldn't the Bible itself be used to justify this? Complicated but vital choices at the very start of his ministry, which, for Jesus, would affect not only his own future but ours too.

Lent calls us to take a long and hard look at our lives; to consider the choices we have made, and the choices facing us now. The answers may not be easy to find, but if, like Jesus, we are ready to seek God's guidance and listen to his voice, we will find the wisdom we need to choose between what's right and what's wrong.   NICK FAWCETT

Be watchful

Beforehand make these two traffic signs from card, or draw them on acetates for an OHP.

First ask some volunteers to play a game. One stands at the front holding a stop sign and the others go to the back. They have to get up to the front without being noticed. If the person at the front sees them moving s/he shows the stop sign and they must go and sit down. While the game is being played, keep distracting the person at the front and see what happens! If someone thinks they can be even more vigilant, try the game once more, now that everyone realises you are deliberately trying to distract their attention to prevent them being watchful.

Make the point that sin creeps up on us like this, little by little. It's all the day-to-day acts of meanness, selfishness, unkindness, dishonesty and so on that gradually make us comfortable behaving with cruelty and lack of love, until we're completely bitter, cynical and destructive people. Jesus warns us to be watchful, so we can stop (show the stop sign) bad habits before they get very far.

The trouble is that Satan doesn't like us being watchful and will try to distract us, often in ways which seem very nice and reasonable (as you were doing). So don't be deceived by that. Make a point of learning what is right (show the other sign) by spending time with Jesus in prayer every day; don't let yourself be distracted from being watchful.   SUSAN SAYERS

Reflective material
(sketches, meditations and poems)

Meditation of the devil

I thought I had him.
Not just once but three times
    I thought I'd caught him out,
    stopped him in his tracks before he'd barely had time to get started!
And I was close,
    even *he*, I expect, would give me that.
Oh, he started off well enough –
    sure of his destiny,
    confident of his ability to grasp it.
But then he would have, wouldn't he,
    coming out into the wilderness like that straight after his baptism,
    heart still skipping within him,
    the memory fresh,
    the voice of God ringing in his ears.
But forty days on –
    forty days of gnawing hunger, desert heat and night-time chill –
    and then it was a different story,
    hard then to think of anything but the pain in his belly
    and the simple comforts of home.

So I saw my chance,
   and made my move.
Nothing crude or clumsy –
   no point scaring him off unnecessarily –
   just a subtle whisper,
   a sly suggestion:
   'Turn this stone into bread.'
And he was tempted, don't be fooled.
I could see by the gleam in his eyes and the way he licked his lips
   that, if you'll pardon the expression, he was chewing it over.
It wouldn't have taken much to make him crack, I'm certain of it;
   one whiff of a fresh-baked loaf
   and I'm sure he'd have given in –
   why didn't I think of it!
Only then he remembered those cursed scriptures of his,
   and all my hard work was undone in a moment:
   'One does not live by bread alone.'
It was a setback,
   but I pressed on, confident I was making ground.
And soon after he was up on the mountains,
   the world stretching out before him as far as the eye could see.
'All this is yours!' I whispered.
   'Just forget this Messiah business and grab it while you can.'
Oh, you may sneer with hindsight at my methods,
   but it's worked before,
   many a lofty ideal sacrificed on the altar of ambition.
But not Jesus –
   in fact, this time not even a suggestion of compromise:
   'It is written, "Worship the Lord your God, and serve only him."'
So I took him in his imagination up on to the temple
   and played my trump card:
   'Go on,' I urged him, 'Throw yourself off.
   If you are who you think you are, God will save you,
   for *it is written:*
   "He will command his angels concerning you, to protect you.
   On their hands they will bear you up,
   so that you will not dash your foot against a stone."'
A master-stroke, so I thought,
   quoting his own scriptures at him like that,
   and, let's face it, we all like a little reassurance, don't we,
   however strong our faith;
   the knowledge, should the worst come to the worst,
   that there'll be someone to bail us out when we need them?
'Why should he be any different?' I reasoned –
   he was as human as the next man,

as vulnerable as the rest of your miserable kind.
But, somehow, even then he held firm:
   'It is said,' he answered,
   "Do not put the Lord your God to the test."'
Well, that was it,
   I knew I was beaten.
There was nothing left to throw at him,
   so I slithered away to lick my wounds.
But I'll be back, you mark my words,
   and next time, when it's his whole life in the balance,
   a question of do or die,
   then we'll see what he's really made of, won't we?
Then we'll see which of us is finally the stronger.   NICK FAWCETT

Meditation of Mary, mother of Jesus

He looked awful,
   absolutely drained.
And it's hardly surprising, is it?
Forty days out in the wilderness –
   that's hell enough for anyone,
   but without food – I ask you?
He was lucky to be alive!
Barely was, mind you, when he came staggering back into Nazareth.
A complete wreck he was,
   just about done in!
'Why did you do it?' I asked him.
'What got into you?'
And all he could say was that he had to,
   that everything depended on it.
He was never the same afterwards.
I used to joke the sun had got to him.
But it wasn't the sun, of course,
It was much more than that.
He wrestled out there,
   with himself,
   with the world,
   with all the forces of evil,
   and in some way I don't quite understand,
   he won.
It was a costly time, there's no doubt about that,
   a disturbing, frightening time –
   I could see the pain in his eyes afterwards.
He'd had to struggle,

make painful choices,
   confront life at its darkest.
And though I never told him, I admired him for that.
It takes courage to face reality,
   to ask youself what it's really all about.
Mind you, I always knew he had it in him.
He'd always been such a good boy,
   right from the start;
   too good some said.
Well, perhaps he was in a way –
   look where it got him after all.
Yet it wasn't as easy as many thought.
He was still tempted, all too often,
   and there were times
   when it would have been so easy for him to give in,
   so easy to compromise,
   to bend just the once.
I know that's what he faced out there in the wilderness
   though he never told me what exactly happened.
But he came back stronger, I have to admit it,
   more certain,
   more determined.
Not that he didn't have his moments afterwards –
   don't make that mistake.
It wasn't all plain sailing from then on.
He had to battle like you and I,
   harder if anything,
   for the path he took was so much more demanding.
Oh no, he endured temptation all right,
   as real as any we might face.
The difference is he overcame it,
   right to the end.
That's what made him so special.
That's why people follow him, even now!   NICK FAWCETT

Second Sunday of Lent

The nature of Christ's kingdom and the cost of commitment

Luke 13:31-35

(also Genesis 15:1-12, 17-18; Psalm 27; Philippians 3:17-4:1)

A reading from the Gospel of Luke (13:31-33)

The government is unfriendly

One day, in Galilee, some Jewish Leaders came to Jesus.

'You'd better get out of here,' they said. 'King Herod's after you.'

'This is what I've got to say to that "fox", and you can tell him,' said Jesus. 'I shall go on doing what I have been doing, healing people who are sick in mind or body – today and tomorrow and the day after. I shall finish the work God has given me to do. A man of God is in no danger – outside Jerusalem City.'

ALAN DALE

A reading from the Gospel of Luke (13:34-35a)

Jerusalem

Jerusalem, Jerusalem, killer of God's great men,
   murderer of God's messengers,
   how many times have I longed
   to gather your people together as a family,
   like a bird gathering her brood under her wings;
   you would not have it so.
Look! You've made the Temple your kind of Temple,
   not God's.

ALAN DALE

Alternative reading

A reading from the Gospel of Luke (9:28-36)

With the disciples Peter, James and John, Jesus climbed a mountain to pray. While Jesus prayed, his clothes shone with dazzling white light as radiant as the sun, and his appearance was transformed!

Suddenly, Moses and Elijah appeared in glory next to Jesus and began speaking to him.

Peter and his friends were amazed by everything they saw, and Peter said to Jesus, 'Lord, this is all so wonderful! I could build three shelters, one for each of you!'

At that moment a cloud descended and covered them on the mountain top, and the disciples were afraid. Then a voice from the cloud spoke, 'This is my Son, the chosen one, listen to what he says.'

When the voice fell silent, the disciples found themselves alone with Jesus. The three friends told no one at that time about the wonders they had witnessed that day.

This is the Gospel of the Lord
Praise to you, Lord Jesus Christ   KATIE THOMPSON

Introductory material

'Be still and know that I am God.' How often have we heard those words? But more important, how often do we make time to be still? Like Martha, all too easily we spend our lives rushing around, always aware of something else to do, something else that demands our time and attention. We live in an ever more pressurised world in which time to stop and stare has become an all too rare luxury. But Lent reminds us that we fail to make time for what really matters at our peril. It calls us to pause and reflect. It challenges us to ask what life is ultimately all about. Today then we make a space in our lives, and through music, through words, through slides and through silence, we seek to make sense of it all. 'Be still and know that I am God.'   NICK FAWCETT

Prayers

Thanksgiving and petition – Examining ourselves
Almighty and all-seeing God,
    we thank you for this season of Lent –
        a time to reflect upon our discipleship,
        to consider our calling,
        to test ourselves and see whether we are in the faith.

Almighty God,
    help us for once to be honest with ourselves,
        to see ourselves as we really are,
        with all our weaknesses,
        all our ugliness and sinfulness.

Help us to face all those things
    which we usually prefer to push aside –
        the unpleasant truths we sweep under the carpet,
        pretending they are not there.

All-seeing God,
we can fool ourselves
but we cannot fool you.
We can pretend all is well
but cannot conceal our inner pain.
We can deny our need of you
but cannot disguise our emptiness without you.
We can seek fulfilment in this world
but will never find real peace outside your love.

Almighty and all-seeing God,
we claim to be in the faith
but sometimes that faith is skin-deep.
We claim to love you
but often that love is flawed.
We claim to serve you
but all too frequently we serve self first.
Search us and help us to search ourselves,
control us, and help us to control ourselves,
and give us grace to grow strong in faith
and whole in Christ,
for in his name we ask it.
Amen.

NICK FAWCETT

Intercession (1)

Conflict between right and wrong. We need discernment to recognise God's will on our journey through an often confusing and disturbing world. Following Jesus demands both trust and calm, and level-headed assessment of anyone setting him or herself up as a prophet or spiritual leader. If we learn to look with the eyes of Christ, we shall not be led astray.

Followers of the Way of Christ,
let us bring to the Lord the needs of our times.

Father, we pray for your blessing
on all who confess belief in you;
that they may witness powerfully
to your unselfish love and humility
by the way they act and the lives they lead.

Silence for prayer

Father, lead us:
free us from all that is evil.

Father, we pray for your blessing
on all who administer justice;
those working in Law Courts and serving on juries,
and those who make laws;
that they may be given insight and integrity.

Silence for prayer

Father, lead us:
free us from all that is evil.

Father, we pray for your blessing on us during this Lent
as we examine our lives and draw closer to you;
that through our self-discipline and prayer
we may enter your stillness and know your will for us.

Silence for prayer

Father, lead us:
free us from all that is evil.

Father, we pray for your blessing on all in prison
or on probation; on those living in acute poverty
or in refugee camps; on all who work among them
to heal, redirect, support and encourage.

Silence for prayer

Father, lead us:
free us from all that is evil.

Father, we pray for your blessing
on those who have passed through death, especially . . .
may we one day share with them
eternal life in your presence.

Silence for prayer

Father, lead us:
free us from all that is evil.

In silence, Father, we bring to you
our individual concerns and joys.

Silence for prayer

Merciful Father,
accept these prayers
for the sake of your Son,
our Saviour Jesus Christ, Amen.

SUSAN SAYERS

Intercession (2)

Lord Jesus Christ,
    we pray, week in, week out, that your kingdom will come
      and your will be done.
    It's easy to say the words,
      far harder to mean them,
      for they are concerned finally not just with you but with us.
    Help us to understand that your kingdom is not just in the future,
      but something that begins within us, here and now,
      and so help us to recognise our role in bringing it nearer,
      through the love we show,
      the care we display
      and the service we offer.
    Your kingdom come, your will be done,
      on earth as it is in heaven.

So now we pray for our world
    and for an end to all that frustrates your purpose.
We think of those in countries racked by conflict,
    famine, disease and poverty;
    of those who face repression and discrimination,
    persecuted for what they believe or for who they are;
    and of those who are victims of crime, violence and war.
Your kingdom come, your will be done,
    on earth as it is in heaven.

We pray for the unemployed and homeless,
    the sick and suffering,
    the lonely and unloved,
    the disabled and disadvantaged.
Your kingdom come, your will be done,
    on earth as it is in heaven.

We pray for those who work
    to build a more just and loving world,
    all who strive to bring help and healing to those in need –
    pastors, preachers, missionaries and evangelists,
    doctors, nurses, psychiatrists, counsellors.
Your kingdom come, your will be done,
    on earth as it is in heaven.

We think, too, of aid agencies,
    pressure groups, charities, churches,
    politicians, police and members of the armed forces –
    these and so many others who, in different ways,
    contribute to the fulfilment of your purpose.
Your kingdom come, your will be done,
    on earth as it is in heaven.

Lord Jesus Christ,
    we look forward to that day when you will rule in splendour,
        when you will establish justice between the nations
        and there will be an end to sorrow,
        suffering, darkness and death.
    Until then,
        help us to commit ourselves to your service
        and to work for your glory,
    so that we may honestly say and truly mean:
    Your kingdom come, your will be done,
        on earth as it is in heaven.
    In your name we pray.
    Amen.   NICK FAWCETT

Short prayers

God of peace,
    quieten our hearts
    and help us to be still in your presence.
We find this so hard to do,
    for our lives are full of noise and confusion,
    a host of demands and responsibilities
    seeming to press in upon us from every side,
    consuming our time and sapping our energy.
We run here and there,
    doing this and that,
    always something else to think about,
    another pressing matter
    demanding our attention –
    and then suddenly,
    in the middle of it all,
    we stop and realise we have forgotten you,
    the one we depend on to give us strength
    and calm our spirits.

God of peace,
    we offer you now this little space we have made
    in the frantic scramble of life.
Meet with us,
    so that we may return to our daily routine
    with a new perspective,
    an inner tranquillity,
    and a resolve to make time for you regularly,
    so that we may use all our time more effectively
    in the service of your kingdom;
    through Jesus Christ our Lord.
Amen.   NICK FAWCETT

Loving God,
    we do not know all there is to know,
    or understand all there is to understand,
    but one thing we are sure of:
    that in Jesus Christ we have met with you,
    experiencing your love,
    rejoicing in your mercy,
    receiving your guidance,
    thrilling to your blessing.
There is much still to learn
    and much that will always be beyond us,
    but we have seen and heard enough
    to convince us of your grace,
    and we have tasted sufficient of your goodness
    to know that nothing can ever separate us
    from your love revealed in Christ.
Help us to live as he taught us,
    to love as he urged us,
    to serve as he showed us
    and to trust as he told us.
So may we live in him and he live in us,
    to the glory of your name.
Amen.   NICK FAWCETT

All-age-talk material

KATIE THOMPSON

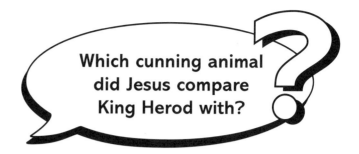

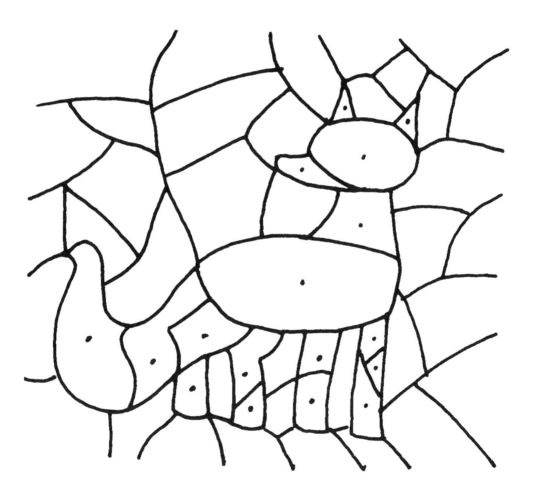

A ___ ___ ___

KATIE THOMPSON

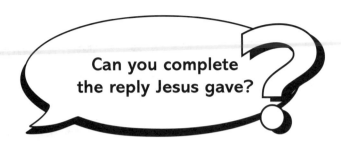

Can you complete the reply Jesus gave?

Use the numbered letters on the clock face to finish his words

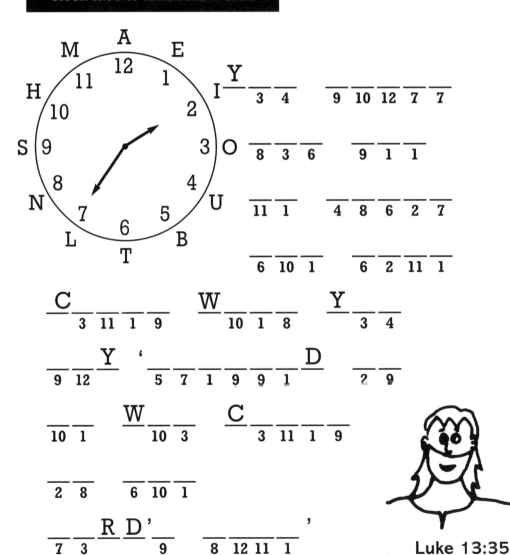

Luke 13:35

KATIE THOMPSON

Divide the group into three categories: Grabbers, Givers and Goodies. Distribute the clip-on clothes pegs so that every group member has the same number of pegs and ask everyone to put the pegs anywhere on their clothes as long as they are visible (the more pegs each member has the better).

At a given signal, the three groups go around and behave as their name implies. The 'Grabbers' try and take as many pegs as they can and put them onto their clothing, the 'Givers' simply offer their pegs to anyone and the 'Goodies' try and take the pegs that the 'Grabbers' have taken and give them back to the original owner!

It might be advisable to suggest that you are not liable for any torn clothing!

Sometimes, feelings of anger, frustration or confusion can distract us from our intended aim or destination. It can be difficult to keep going when everything seems to be against you.

How would we react if what we were doing provoked a threat on our lives? Would we decide that it might be better to live a while longer and take a rain-check on our actions or would we shrug our shoulders and get on with what we intended to do?   PETE TOWNSEND

Read Luke 13:31-35

Jesus and the Pharisees had not seen eye to eye during the past few months. Some of them had bad-mouthed Jesus and he'd had a few choice words to say about them and their 'religious' behaviour.

The Jews themselves had defined seven behavioural categories of Pharisee. They called one category the 'Shoulder' Pharisees, because whatever good deed or act of kindness that they did, they made sure everyone knew about it. There were the 'Hang on a minute' Pharisees who played the game of 'put it off' whenever it came to helping someone or parting with money. Another category were the 'Bruised' Pharisees who thought that looking at a woman was sinful and so closed their eyes whenever they saw a female. Walking into solid objects was a very frequent occurrence! One category always walked as if they were carrying a huge weight on their shoulders. They believed that walking with a stoop was a sign of humility; other people thought they were just plain stupid.

One group of Pharisees kept a diary of their good deeds and used this as a sort of bargaining account with God. Perhaps it went something like: 'God, I've done three good deeds this week and now it's my turn, OK?' Another category were those Pharisees who believed that at any moment God would get really angry with them and so they went around continually looking behind them (that category is the 'Timid' Pharisees). And finally, there were those Pharisees who genuinely believed that doing acts of charity and being honest with God was the best way to follow and worship God.

So, when some Pharisees came to Jesus and warned him of Herod's threat to kill him, it could have been difficult to try and guess what the Pharisees were up to. Were they really concerned about the threat to Jesus, or did they think they were doing a good deed by warning him? Did it count as a 'tick' in the 'act of kindness' box, or did they see Herod's threat as part of God's anger for some reason? Jesus could have spent all day trying to sort out why, and for whose benefit, these Pharisees had come to warn him. But rather than waste time, he decided that he had a task to complete and nothing was going to stop him. Even though Jesus knew for certain that he was going to his death, he was determined to do things his way (which was God's way) and it didn't matter what people might say or do.   PETE TOWNSEND

God's way or ours?

Start by showing everyone how you have spoilt something by using it to do what it wasn't designed for – such as a knife for a screwdriver, or scissors as wire cutters. As we are made like God, and God is loving, we only feel that deep-down sense of peace and rightness when we are using our bodies, minds and spirits in the way they were designed to be used.

Now arrange two teams of three people (mixed in age and character) rather like a quiz show. Have each team holding their team name: THE GOD SQUAD and THE SELF SET. Ask a volunteer to be a Christian in the street, on his journey through life. He walks from the back to the front, and every so often you tell him to stop to sort out a problem. Have the first problem read out clearly, then ask each team what their advice would be. The Christian then decides which to accept, and the congregation can express their approval or not by clapping or groaning. Then he continues on his journey until the next problem and so on. It will be best if you think up situations pertinent to your congregation, but here are some suggestions to get you going:

1 The TV news shows a famine and you have just received your pay packet.

2 Your brother/sister has messed up your favourite tape.

3 The grass needs cutting but your friends are round.

4 You're gasping for a drink, and find a purse lying on the pavement.

In conclusion, make the point that if we say we're Christians it must affect the way be behave, but that even if we choose wrongly sometimes, God can still bring some good from the resulting situation.   SUSAN SAYERS

Reflective material
(sketches, meditations and poems)

Meditation of Peter

I wanted to hold on to that moment for ever,
    to keep things just as they were for the rest of eternity,
    for I feared life would never be so special again.
It was just the four of us –
    well, six if you count Moses and Elijah, but I'm not sure you can do that –
    the four of us sharing a blessed moment of peace and quiet;
    no crowds pleading for a miracle,
    no lepers begging for healing,
    no Pharisees baying for his blood,
    no Sadducees spoiling for a fight.
Just us,
    together,
    as we'd all too rarely been.
And we knew it couldn't last;
    he'd made that perfectly clear when I dared suggest otherwise.
There was trouble round the corner,
    his enemies waiting to pounce,
    and he knew it was only a matter of time before they got him.
Not much of a prospect, was it –
    rejection, suffering, death?
I don't know how he stuck it, I really don't.
But we didn't want to think about such things,
    not then anyway,
    and up there on the mountain it all seemed a million miles away,
    out of sight, out of mind.
Can you blame me for wanting to stay,
    for wanting to hang on to the moment for as long as possible?
Only I couldn't, of course.
You can't stop the clock, can you, and make the world stand still?
You can't store those golden moments safely away,
    untarnished by the march of time.
Life goes on, as they say,
    and you have to go with it,
    like it or not.
It was hard to accept that,
    hard to go back to the daily round
    with its familiar demands and expectations.
Yet as I spoke to Jesus, coming down the mountain,
    I realised suddenly it had to be;

that there was no other way –
   going back, I mean.
Without that there would have been no point,
   those sacred moments an empty illusion.
He knew that,
   and slowly, very slowly, I came to know it too.
It was a vital time, a special time,
   one that gave him new strength,
   new resolve,
   the inspiration he needed to face the future and fulfil his destiny.
But it was as much for us as for him
   a moment we could look back upon,
   so that afterwards we might keep on looking forward.   NICK FAWCETT

Third Sunday of Lent

The grace of God, and the folly of rejecting it,
is portrayed in the parable of the vineyard

Luke 13:1-9

(also Isaiah 55:1-9; Psalm 63:1-9; 1 Corinthians 10:1-13)

A reading from the Gospel of Luke (Luke 13:1-9)

Some of the people told Jesus about the Galileans who had been killed by Pilate while offering sacrifices to God.

Jesus said to them, 'Just because they were killed doesn't mean that they were worse sinners than anyone else. Think of the eighteen people in Siloam who died when the tower fell on them. Do you think that proves that they were guiltier than anyone else in Jerusalem? Indeed, it does not! And I tell you that you will all come to the same end unless you turn away from your sins.'

Then he told them a parable:

A man went to check how many fruits were growing on a fig tree in his vineyard, but he found there was none. So he sent for his gardener and told him, 'This tree has grown no fruit for the last three years. Cut it down and make space for another.'

But the gardener said to him, 'Master, give the tree one more year so I have time to feed and care for it. If it still has no fruit on it, then cut it down.'

This is the Gospel of the Lord
Praise to you, Lord Jesus Christ   KATIE THOMPSON

Prayers

Approach

Lord of all,
  in reverence and humility,
    awe and wonder,
    we come to worship you.
  Meet with us now,
    be with us always.

We step aside from the busy routine of our lives –
    a few moments away from our daily activities
    and humdrum concerns;
    an opportunity to bring them

quietly and prayerfully before you,
and to place them in your hands.
Meet with us now,
  be with us always.

We bring ourselves –
  our strengths and weaknesses,
  our faith and doubts,
  our hopes and fears.
Meet with us now,
  be with us always.

We bring our families, our friends and neighbours –
  those we love,
  those we know,
  and those we simply pass in the street.
Meet with us now,
  be with us always.

We bring our community, our town, our country
  and our world –
  places near and far,
  integral to our lives
  or far removed from our experience.
Meet with us now,
  be with us always.

In quiet confidence we entrust all into your care,
  knowing that your love is more powerful
  and your power more loving
  than we can ever know or imagine.
Meet with us now,
  be with us always.

Lord of all,
  we come to worship you,
    bringing ourselves,
    bringing our loved ones,
    bringing our all.
  Meet with us now,
    be with us always.
    Amen.
                                                    NICK FAWCETT

Confession

Merciful God,
   we have failed you again in so much,
     in the things we have done
     and the things we have not done –
     our faith weak,
     our discipleship hesitant,
     our commitment poor –
     and yet still you accept us.
  For your unfailing pardon,
    receive our thanks.

We have not worshipped you as we should,
   or served you as you desire,
   or obeyed you as you command,
   and yet still you care.
For your unfailing pardon,
    receive our thanks.

We have created you in our own image,
   forsaking you for our own interests,
   losing sight of your kingdom,
   and yet still we have a place in your purpose.
For your unfailing pardon,
    receive our thanks.

We have not loved you with heart and soul and mind,
   we have not loved our brothers and sisters in Christ,
   we have not loved our neighbours as ourselves,
   and yet still *you love us.*
For your unfailing pardon,
    receive our thanks.

We have failed to take up our cross to follow Christ,
   we have denied your Spirit freedom to move within us,
   we have sinned against you and others
   in thought and word and deed,
   and yet still you call us your children.
For your unfailing pardon,
    receive our thanks.

Merciful God,
  forgive us,
    cleanse us,
    restore and renew us.

Assure us once more of your forgiveness,
   for we are truly sorry,
   and send us out in newness of life,
   to live and work to your glory.
For your unfailing pardon,
   receive our thanks.

In the name of Christ.
Amen.   NICK FAWCETT

Intercession

Father, we lean on your love as we pray
for your church – collectively,
and as a mixed bag of individuals,
with needs, disappointments and fears.

Silence for prayer

In all things, Father:
we pray your kingdom in

We lean on your wisdom as we pray
for local, national and international leaders,
subject to pressures and conflicting values.

Silence for prayer

In all things, Father:
we pray your kingdom in

We lean on your affectionate understanding
as we pray for our homes and all homes in this area,
with their expectations and misunderstandings,
their security and insecurity.

Silence for prayer

In all things, Father:
we pray your kingdom in

We lean on your compassion as we pray
for all who are hurting in body, mind or spirit.

Silence for prayer

In all things, Father:
we pray your kingdom in

We lean on your faithfulness as we pray
for those who have died, and those who mourn.

Silence for prayer

In all things, Father:
we pray your kingdom in

We lean on your accepting love as we pray
in thankfulness for all you are doing in our lives,
and all you have in mind for us in the future.

Silence for prayer

Merciful Father,
accept these prayers
for the sake of your Son,
our Saviour Jesus Christ, Amen.   SUSAN SAYERS

Short prayer

Lord,
I've gone through every emotion in the dictionary.
I've shouted until my throat hurts.
My head aches with the thoughts
    of senseless violence,
    of mindless actions
    that have robbed people
    of their hopes, their dreams, their lives.
I can't pretend to understand
    or find an answer
    to the jigsaw of events
    that froze a moment in time
    for ever.
Tears sometimes say more
    than mere words can express.
A cry from the heart
    speaks more wisdom
    than a thousand wise men.
But all I can say is
    I don't understand, Lord.
All I can pray is
    that somehow,
    for all those involved,
    you would bring peace
    and understanding,
    while I place my life
    in your hands.
Keep me safe, keep me willing
    to hear your voice and your heart.   PETE TOWNSEND

All-age-talk material

God gives us another chance

These pictures telling the story of the fruitless fig tree are in the wrong order. Put the letters of the pictures in the correct order on the lines below

SEE Luke 13:6-9

A

It produced no fruit
for three years

B

The owner came
to cut it down

C

A fig tree grew
in a vineyard

D

The gardener gave it
special care. If fruit
still would not grow
then he would cut
it down

The
Fig-tree
parable

E

The gardener asked
him to give it a
chance

___ ___ ___ ___ ___

KATIE THOMPSON

God is
always ready to give us
another chance to
try again

Colour the pictures below

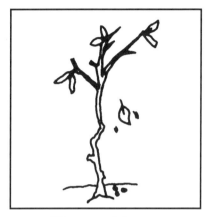

Another
chance

**Diseased tree
with no fruit**

**Healthy tree,
lots of fruit**

Another
chance

**A selfish and
unkind person**

**A kind and
loving person**

KATIE THOMPSON

Hardly a day goes by without some news which shocks us and causes us to question someone's behaviour.

Read Luke 13:1-9

Jesus is brought news of an atrocity carried out by the Roman soldiers acting on the orders of Pilate. It was almost as if he were being asked, 'How much more evidence do you need before you condemn the Romans for what they do?'

To the Jews, the whole concept of the 'Messiah' or 'Saviour' was that God would establish his kingdom on earth. Many believed that Jesus was going to force the Romans out of Israel and a new order, or government, would take their place. The Essenes, in particular, trained for the day when God's kingdom would be established by force. Another collection of groups was known as the Zealots, who thought that God might need a bit of a hand when it came to sorting out the Romans. Several other small groups existed, including one called the Sicarii (dagger men), who carried out assassinations and really wound the Roman authorities up.

So the people were expecting Jesus to say, 'Yeah, let's give those Romans a real hiding'. Instead of inciting them to action, Jesus suggested that the people look at the situation from another perspective. Firstly, he wanted everyone to understand that the people who had been killed were not being punished by God for being dodgy characters. And secondly, he wanted to get across the idea that everyone is capable of behaving in a way or committing acts that some other people would find horrifying.

In Luke 13:5, Jesus puts forward the view that the people should hate the sin, or crime, but not hate the person involved. The story of the fig tree is one way of suggesting that we need to be patient and give a person time to regret what they've done and turn to God. Forgiveness is an easy word to say but an extremely difficult thing to do. Jesus is warning against creating a 'goodies' and 'baddies' list because everyone is capable of doing the wrong thing. Change is a heart attitude and not an act of revenge.

Ask the group if they have heard of any news or events recently which have made them feel angry or powerless. Discuss some of the atrocities or natural disasters which have occurred in various parts of the world.

- What do the group feel about these situations?
- Is anyone to blame?
- What should happen to the people involved?

Discuss some local or personal issues which cause the group to feel similar emotions to those provoked by what they've just discussed. Why did these events happen? Could they have been avoided?

Give each member of the group a piece of paper and a pen. Ask each of them to write a sentence or two about a situation which they feel strongly about or one in which they may have been involved. When they have finished, fold the pieces of paper and place them in a pile in the centre of the room.

PETE TOWNSEND

Jesus will help us to bear the fruits of God's love in our lives

Cross out each 'FRUIT' and copy the hidden words on to the tree below

**KIFRUITNDNESS   LFRUITOVE   FORFRUITGIVENESS
GENEFRUITROSITY   HONEFRUITSTY   SHFRUITARING**

KATIE THOMPSON

All-age exploration of the Word

Isaiah 55:1-9; Psalm 63:1-8; 1 Corinthians 10:1-13; Luke 13:1-9

Strength for the journey

Regular spiritual feeding gives us the strength to resist temptation and grow in holiness.

1. Suitable for younger children

Before the service (advance preparation)

- Copy the activity sheet and prepare the work area. You will need a jug of water and some plastic cups, scissors, crayons and glue.
- Get the children (especially young ones) to make paper cups, using the activity sheet.

During the service

After the Gospel, gather the group in their work area.

Teaching

Place the jug and cups down in the centre of the group and remind them of the person who was drinking during the reading from Isaiah. Give the children a drink of water, and talk about how good it is to drink when we are really thirsty.

God invites us to come to him and drink a different kind of water. It isn't just our bodies which get thirsty and need a drink. Our souls, which live for ever, need spiritual food and drink as well. We get that from spending time with God, talking and listening to him in prayer, reading the Bible and coming to church with our Christian brothers and sisters to worship God and meet him in Communion.

All together

During the All-age talk the children will show the cups they have made, and remind everyone of how God invites us to drink his water of life.

SUSAN SAYERS

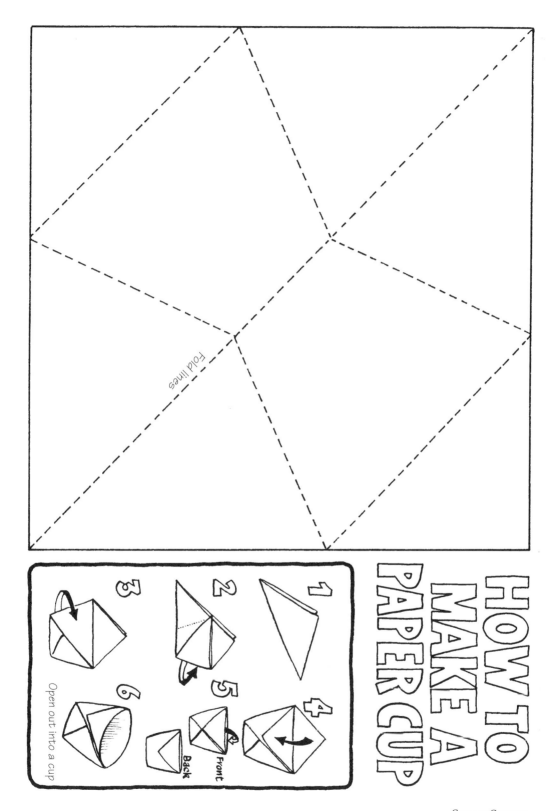

Fold lines

HOW TO MAKE A PAPER CUP

1

2

3

4

Front

Back

5

6

Open out into a cup

SUSAN SAYERS

2. Suitable for older children

Before the service (advance preparation)
- Copy the activity sheet and prepare the work area. Bring a pot plant which is not thriving very well, a bigger pot, some more earth and some water.
- Cut some blue and green lengths of crêpe paper for the children to wave during some of the hymns.

During the service
- After the Gospel, gather the group in their work area.

Teaching

Place down the pot plant and remind them of the Gospel, with the gardener and the fig tree. The gardener didn't want the tree to be thrown out until he had given it lots of good nourishing food and water to help it grow strong. Talk over with them what you could do with your pot plant to help it grow better, and let them help you give this plant what it needs.

When it is looking happier in its new pot, talk about the way we need feeding too, not just our bodies but our souls as well. When we come to Communion, Jesus is feeding us spiritual food and drink, to make us strong and healthy, and resistant to evil. We need that feeding or we get weak and can't fight off the dragons of temptation! God has the supplies of strength we need to stand up for what is right and good and honest and fair. It doesn't cost anything to get them, either – God offers them to us for free.*

As we share the bread and wine at Communion or receive God's blessing there at the altar, what happens is that invisibly our souls are being fed all the power and goodness they need to make us strong in the battle.

All together

During the All-age talk the children will share some of their ideas about God's invisible feeding.

- At the offertory and dismissal hymns the children wave their streamers.

* The idea of fighting off evil needs to be handled with sensitivity. It certainly is a battle and we need to prepare children for this, but we are not encouraging them to use violence as a way of solving problems. I have deliberately chosen the dragon image to place the battle in the land of story, so they can understand it as a symbol. Stress the real weapons against evil as courage, prayer, truth, hope and God's power of love.

As we SHARE the BREAD and WINE

invisibly

our SOULS are being FED all the POWER and GOODNESS they need to make us STRONG in the BATTLE against EVIL

Take whatever you need.

GOD'S POWER

HOPE

Strength TRUTH

Strength PRAYER

Strength COURAGE

Draw you fighting the dragon of evil and temptation!

Reflective material
(sketches, meditations and poems)

Meditation of Saul, convert and apostle

What would you have done, had it been you,
    had you come to that fig tree you'd planted
    and found, yet again, no sign of fruit on it,
    nothing to justify the time and expense spent on its cultivation?
Would you have waited another year,
    given it one more chance to blossom despite your disappointment,
    or would you have abandoned it as a bad job,
    ordered it to be dug up to make room for a better specimen,
    one more likely to reward your investment?
Remember, this wasn't a first-year planting –
    it should have been yielding a plentiful harvest years back,
    and the likelihood is that no fruit one year
    means no fruit the next,
    what reason to expect any change?
Only, of course, it wasn't finally a fig tree Jesus was talking about here –
    it was you and me,
    people like us,
    and the harvest we produce in our lives,
    or, at least, the harvest we're meant to produce.
Sadly, it's all too often a different story –
    despite the care and attention God has lavished on us,
    the patient preparation and dedicated nurture,
    there's precious little to show for it,
    no harvest worthy of the name.
Why bother with us any further?
What reason to expect any sentiment from God,
    any chance to atone for past failures?
None at all.
And yet . . . don't despair,
    for, while we shouldn't take it for granted,
    the wonderful thing is this:
    year after year Jesus goes on asking we be given one more chance
    and year after year God continues to grant that request.   NICK FAWCETT

Order of Service

Things to do and people to do them

Suggested order of service

The people and the priest:

greet each other in the Lord's name

    (this includes an introduction to the teaching Eucharist and any practical details)

confess their sins and are assured of God's forgiveness

    (today this focuses on the way we have given in to temptation)

keep silence and pray a Collect

proclaim and respond to the Word of God

- Isaiah 55:1-9 – this reading is spoken in the context of a street vendor
- 1 Corinthians 10:1-13 – this passage has an accompanying action
- Luke 13:1-9 – the second part of the Gospel is acted out
- After the Gospel, children and adults respond to the Word in their own teaching, in different parts of the church
- All-age talk gathers these responses together

pray for the Church and the world

    (using the whole building as a holy space)

exchange the Peace

prepare the table

    (the older children help with this)

pray the Eucharistic Prayer

    (the younger children are gathered around the altar so that they can see what is going on)

receive Communion

depart with God's blessing

Susan Sayers

Time of Confession and Forgiveness

Invite everyone to remember the times they have been tempted, and in their own strength have been too weak to stop themselves falling into sin. Have some recorded music playing quietly as people are given the space to bring these occasions to mind in penitence.

> Empowering God,
> we confess that we have failed to hold fast to you in times of testing,
> and in that weakness we have fallen into temptation.
> We are very sorry, and repent of our sin.

The words of forgiveness are proclaimed.

Old Testament reading – Isaiah 55:1-9

The reader starts at the back of the church and shouts the first two verses as s/he walks up to the front, carrying a picnic hamper or cool box, and a large water container with cup attached. When they reach the front they pour out some water and drink a few sips before continuing with verse 3. They hold the water and sip from it from time to time as the rest of the passage is read, coaxing the people to try this godly life as a street vendor might encourage us to try a product. The water, cup and hamper are left near the altar to remind people of God's offer as they come to receive the bread and wine at Communion.

New Testament reading – 1 Corinthians 10:1-13

Just before the passage is read, someone does a balancing act, such as standing on a wobble board or standing in a one-legged position. The president draws attention to the way they have to concentrate hard to avoid falling, which is what Paul is talking about in this letter to the Corinthians. Whether you are reading the whole passage or just verses 12-13, the balancing continues throughout as people listen to the words.

Gospel – Luke 13:1-9

At verse 6 a gardener with his spade pretends to be digging and the garden owner walks up to the front, looking at various plants and examining them, till he joins the gardener at the front and examines his fig tree. He says verse 7 either learnt by heart or using his own words, and the gardener, obviously fond of the tree, replies in the same way.

Intercessions

As recorded music plays, people move around the building on a prayer trail, using it as a metaphor to help their prayer focus. At the different parts of the building they can pray in the words provided or in their own words. Here are some suggested points of prayer, though your own trail will naturally use your own building. People walk around in pairs or threes, adults with children, older children with younger ones, so that all are involved at their own level.

- *At a clear window:*
  Pray for the light of God's wisdom to make things clear to those who are confused or doubtful.

- *At a stained glass window*:
  Thank God for colour and light in our lives, and ask for the church to be full of Christians who let God's light shine through them.

- *At a main door*:
  Pray for all who come and go here. Pray for those who are new to the faith, and those who have stopped believing. Pray for those who feel shut out of life.

- *At the altar or holy table:*
  Thank God for his strengthening food and pray for the Holy Spirit to fill us with love like Jesus' costly love.

- *At the lectern*:
  Pray that the Word of God may take root in our lives so that we grow up strongly in Christ, bearing fruit.

- *At the pews:*
  Pray for the world, and our calling to go out in the power of the Spirit, bringing God's healing and love.   SUSAN SAYERS

Fourth Sunday of Lent

The love of God is portrayed through the parable of the Prodigal Son.
God loves us as a mother loves her children

Luke 15:1-3, 11-32

(also Joshua 5:9-12; Psalm 32; 2 Corinthians 5:16-21)

A reading from the Gospel of Luke (Luke 15:1-3, 11-32)

A crowd of tax collectors and other sinners had gathered around Jesus, much to the anger and disdain of the scribes and Pharisees. When Jesus overheard them complaining, he told them a parable:

> There was a man who had two sons and the younger one came to his father and said, 'Father, give me everything that will one day belong to me, so I can enjoy my riches now.'
>
> The father did this, and the son set off to look for adventure. He travelled to a distant land and spent all his money enjoying himself.
>
> There was a famine in that land, and the young man found himself penniless and hungry. 'If I stay here I will surely starve,' he thought, so he decided to return to his father and ask for his forgiveness.
>
> The father saw his son coming and ran to welcome him. As he hugged him, the young man said, 'Father, I am so sorry. I no longer deserve to be called your son.'
>
> But the father told his servants to prepare a feast and to bring the finest clothes, and they began to celebrate.
>
> When the man's other son returned home from working in the fields, he asked the servants, 'What is the reason for such a celebration?'
>
> When he heard their explanation, he was filled with anger and refused to join the party. So his father came looking for him, and the son said to him, 'I have been hard-working and loyal, and never once did you throw such a party for me. Yet you are happy to do so for my brother who has been greedy and selfish and treated you very badly.'
>
> The father answered his son, 'You are always with me, and everything I have belongs to you. Your brother who was lost has been found. He is not dead after all, but alive, and it is only right that we should celebrate his return with joy!'

This is the Gospel of the Lord
Praise to you, Lord Jesus Christ   KATIE THOMPSON

Alternative translation – God, the prodigal father; Luke 15:11-32

An Arab bishop has assured me that no Palestinian father would ever demean himself to the extent that this father does. But God is even more prodigal than his spendthrift children, and forgives them unconditionally in a most irrational way, despite their worst excesses. And if the resentment of the elder brother finds an echo in our own hearts, we are even more lost and distant from God than the younger son had been. Luther said that if we had nothing of the New Testament except this parable, we would have the complete Gospel.

A farmer had two sons.
One day, the younger one said,
'Dad, if only you'd die,
so that I could have my share of the estate!'
Instead of exploding with anger at such impertinence,
the farmer generously sold part of the farm,
and gave him his share.
That done, the boy packed his things and went abroad.
There he had a wild time, spending his money like water.

At last his pockets were empty.
Then the harvest failed right across the country,
and he was left with no money and no food.
So he took a job with a local farmer
who put him in charge of feeding the pigs (imagine!).
He could have joined the pigs at their trough,
he was so hungry,
but no one lifted a hand to help him.

Finally he came to his senses.
'Back at home,' he said to himself,
'there's not a farmhand who hasn't got more than he can eat.
And here's me starving to death.
I'm going back.'
And he turned over in his head
the sort of apology he ought to make.
'Dad,' he would say,
'I've wronged God, and I've wronged you.
I don't deserve to be called a son of yours any more.
Will you take me on as a farmhand?'
So he set off home.
While he was still some way off,
he could see his father out on the road,
looking for his return.
Full of pity, the father did the unthinkable.
He went running down the road to meet the boy,
and threw his arms round his neck and hugged him.

The son began to say his piece:
'Dad,' he said, 'I've wronged God and I've wronged you.
I don't deserve to be called a son of yours any more . . .'
But the father cut him short.
'Quick,' he called out to the servants,
'Go and get his best clothes out;
put the family ring on his finger,
and find some shoes for his bare feet.
And kill that calf we've been fattening!
Tonight we'll have a barbecue for the whole village.
My boy was lost and he's been found.
He was dead and he's come back to life.'
So the celebrations started.

During all this,
the elder son had been working on the farm.
As he was on his way home,
he'd almost reached the farmhouse
when he heard bagpipes and dancing.
'What's going on?' he asked a farmhand.
'Your brother's back,' the man said.
'And you dad is roasting the calf we've been fattening
because he's safe and sound.'
The elder brother was furious,
and wouldn't even go inside the house.

So again the father came running out
and begged him to come in and join the party.
'Never!' the son replied.
I've slaved for you all these years,
and always done everything you told me to do.
And what payment do I get?
Not a sausage! No parties with *my* friends!
But this son of yours can throw all your money away on girls!
Then he comes home,
and you go and kill the fattened calf for him!'
'Son,' said the father,
'you've always been close to me, as I have to you.
All the farm is yours – you know that.
But we *had* to have a party tonight.
It's your *brother* who was lost and has been found,
it's your *brother* who was dead and has come back to life.'

God is like that.

H. J. RICHARDS

Introductory material

Mothering Sunday or a celebration of the family

Few Christian festivals can have undergone as many changes in recent years as Mothering Sunday. Its original emphasis on motherhood and 'mother church' eventually broadened into a celebration of Christian families, but family life today is quite different even from fifty years ago. Working mothers, single parents and restructured families are almost becoming the norm, while traditional patterns of family life have largely disintegrated under the weight of information technology, media influence and ease of travel. The Church has always championed the family as part of God's created order, but many people experience family life as anything but positive or joyful. Inevitably they feel uncomfortable or even offended if the liturgy rejoices in what they have found to be painful, or if it seems to exclude them because they cannot share the happy experiences of others. Any Christian celebration of the family, whether on Mothering Sunday or at some other time, must therefore be very sensitive to those who have suffered through family or marital breakdown, abusive treatment, inadequate parenting, or bereavement – and not least those who, to their great sadness, are unable to have children.

Outside Local Ecumenical Projects Mothering Sunday may not be the easiest of Sundays on which to share worship with those of other traditions, though most would share the same concerns. An evening service may enable Churches to join together more easily, though this is likely to exclude younger children. Alternatively, it might be possible to organise a united service which focuses on the Christian concept of family without ignoring those who do not fit neatly into that framework, for whatever reason. This also provides an opportunity to emphasise the nurturing role of the local Church. The material in this outline service is based on Mothering Sunday, but could be used on any similar occasion and adapted to specific circumstances as required.   STUART THOMAS

If there's one thing most of us find hard, it's saying sorry after we've made a mistake. To do that means swallowing our pride, overcoming our embarrassment and laying ourselves open to a possible rebuff. It's far easier, though far less satisfactory, to keep our head down and wait for the hurt to subside. But if 'Sorry' can be the hardest word to *say*, there are three words, directly related, which can be even more difficult to *mean*: the words 'I forgive you'. We may be happy enough to say that; we may want to mean it and genuinely believe that we do; but to really forgive someone in the true sense of the word is a rare gift indeed. All too often a past mistake is dredged up again in the heat of anger; an error which we considered long-since forgotten suddenly thrown back in our face. And probably each of us is as guilty of doing that as any. With God, it is different. When we confess our sins and are truly sorry, they are put behind us, over and done with, dealt with once and for all. No going back to them later; it is as if they never were. That's the good news. The bad news is this: God wants us to show that same level of forgiveness to others. It's a lot to ask and we will probably always finally fail, but if we are serious about discipleship, we need to try. If God can forgive us, who are we not to forgive in turn?   NICK FAWCETT

Prayers

Petition – The love of God

Gracious God,
  we praise you that you are, above all else, a God of love,
    not of judgement, anger or vengeance,
    but of constant and total love.
  You have given your all for us:
    teach us to give freely in turn.

Though we fail you again and again,
    caring more about ourselves than you,
    and more about ourselves than others,
    still you go on loving us,
    fiercely and wholeheartedly.
  You have given your all for us:
    teach us to give freely in turn.

Though we turn away from you,
    wilfully rejecting your guidance
    and repeatedly betraying your trust,
    still you long to take us back,
    to restore a living, loving relationship.
  You have given your all for us:
    teach us to give freely in turn.

Though our relationship with you is so often one-sided,
    our commitment in such contrast to your faithfulness,
    our response so feeble beside your grace,
    still you go on blessing us,
    your generosity inexhaustible.
  You have given your all for us:
    teach us to give freely in turn.

Though we fail to love others,
   divorcing faith from our daily relationships,
   allowing divisions to come between us,
   and forgetful of our responsibilities towards the wider world,
   still you have time for us,
   patiently seeking to deepen our commitment
   and broaden our horizons.
You have given your all for us:
   teach us to give freely in turn.

Gracious God,
   help us so to know you that your love flows through us,
      reaching upwards in worship,
      inwards in fellowship
      and outwards in service,
      to the glory of your name.
You have given your all for us:
   teach us to give freely in turn.

In the name of Christ.
Amen.   NICK FAWCETT

Thanksgiving – The servant of God

Lord Jesus Christ,
   you entered our world,
      taking on our humanity,
      identifying yourself totally with us.
   For your astonishing love,
      we thank you.

You came to lead us out of darkness into your marvellous light,
   to set us free from everything that separates us
   from one another and from you,
   to bring us life in all its fullness.
For your astonishing love,
   we thank you.

You came as the Word made flesh,
   as King of kings and Lord of lords,
   as the Prince of Peace,
   as the Son of God.
For your astonishing love,
   we thank you.

And yet you came taking the form of a servant,
    humbling yourself even to death on a cross,
    offering your life for many,
    taking the way of costly sacrifice.
For your astonishing love,
    we thank you.

You could have served yourself,
    looked to your own glory,
    but you resisted temptation,
    your thoughts only for us.
For your astonishing love,
    we thank you.

You give us the privilege of sharing in the work of your kingdom,
    offering our service in turn,
    giving of ourselves without reserve,
    putting our own interests second
    to the needs of those around us.
For your astonishing love,
    we thank you.

Lord Jesus Christ,
    teach us to show our gratitude in all we do,
    all we say,
    all we think
    and all we are.
For your astonishing love,
    we thank you.
Amen.   NICK FAWCETT

Confession – The grace of God

Loving God,
    once more we have failed you,
        once more we seek your pardon.
    Through your grace,
        have mercy.

Forgive us that, like your people across the ages,
    we are all too human –
    our spirits willing but our flesh weak,
    our intentions good but our living up to them poor,
    our commitment real but our discipleship all too often false.
Through your grace,
    have mercy.

Forgive us that though you speak to us day by day,
   though you challenge us through your word,
   though your voice is there for all ready to hear it,
   repeatedly we have been slow to listen.
Through your grace,
   have mercy.

Forgive us that though you have tried to lead us back to you,
   disciplining us in love,
   gently correcting our mistakes,
   we have wilfully rejected your guidance.
Through your grace,
   have mercy.

Forgive us that though you have always been faithful,
   never letting us down,
   constant in your care,
   we have been unfaithful in so much.
Through your grace,
   have mercy.

Forgive us that though you are worthy of all praise,
   though you and you alone hold the key to life,
   and though each day you draw near to us,
   many times we have not made time for you.
Through your grace,
   have mercy.

Loving God,
   help us to recognise our faults
   and, with your help, to turn from them,
   so that we may be the people you would have us be.
Through your grace,
   have mercy.

In the name of Christ.
Amen.

NICK FAWCETT

Intercession – The forgiveness of God

Merciful God,
   we pray for those who walk through life with a sense of guilt,
   burdened by past mistakes,
   overwhelmed by a sense of failure,
   troubled by feelings of shame,
   depressed by the knowledge of their own weakness.

Help them to understand that in you
    they can find true forgiveness
    and a new beginning.
In your mercy,
    hear us.

We pray for those who commit evil
    with no sense of wrong-doing,
    no concept of sin,
    no hint of remorse,
    no sign of scruples.
Help them to glimpse what is right and good,
    and to be touched by the renewing, transforming grace of Christ.
In your mercy,
    hear us.

We pray for those who have been wronged by others;
    hurt,
    deceived,
    betrayed,
    let down.
Help them to be ready to forgive others
    as you have forgiven them.
In your mercy,
    hear us.

We pray for those whose relationships are being tested –
    with family and friends,
    with those at work or in their place of leisure,
    with other Christians,
    even in their own fellowship.
Help them to understand the cause of division between them
    and to work towards the healing of all such rifts,
    forgiving and seeking forgiveness.
In your mercy,
    hear us.

Merciful God,
    help all those who are burdened by past mistakes
        to discover the forgiveness you so freely offer,
        and to show that mercy themselves.
    In your mercy,
        hear us.
    Amen.   NICK FAWCETT

Short prayers

Lord,
   it's often difficult
   to know who's right and who's wrong.
Just as it takes two to argue,
   it takes two to agree
   to build the bridge
   which will join two islands
   that have been separated
   by an ocean of misunderstanding.
Please help us to learn
   how to build bridges,
   no matter how far
   or how wide
   the gap.
Help us to be willing
   to realise the loneliness
   of anger, of hurt and of damaged pride,
   so that we can be a continent of hope
   and not a cluster of islands in a raging sea.   PETE TOWNSEND

Gracious God,
   we have no reason to expect your mercy,
   for though we say we are sorry
   we go on letting you down time after time,
   making the same mistakes we have always made,
   ignoring your will,
   even wilfully rejecting your guidance.
And yet you go on forgiving us,
   always ready to receive us back
   and to help us start again.
We praise you for the wonder of your love,
   your goodness which can never be exhausted.
Help us, who have been forgiven so much,
   to forgive others, who owe us so little.
Give us a generous heart
   and a gracious spirit;
   the ability not just to speak of forgiveness
   but to display the truth of it in our lives.
Teach us to give those who have wronged us
   the opportunity to begin afresh,
   the past forgotten
   and the slate wiped clean.
Through Jesus Christ our Lord.
Amen.   NICK FAWCETT

All-age-talk material

Building bridges takes a lot of effort and can often prove to be more difficult than we ever imagined.

Read Luke 15:1-3, 11-32

Jesus gives us a story-line any soap opera would be proud of. Under Jewish law the eldest son was entitled to two thirds of his father's property and the youngest son was given a third. Sometimes the father could give his sons their inheritance early if he wanted to retire from running his affairs and take it easy. But in this instance, the younger son actually says, 'I wish you were dead'. Things must have been pretty rough for the son to feel like this. Perhaps, as the younger son, he felt he wasn't given enough respect or responsibility. He might even have been jealous of the fact that his elder brother was going to get twice as much of the inheritance as he was. There are many reasons why families argue, fall out and say things they later wish they hadn't.

In the story, the young son allowed the money to slip through his hands and he was left hoping that the pigs would leave him a few crumbs to eat. For a Jew, the pig was about as welcome as a chocolate gâteau at a weight-watchers' convention.

The younger son soon realised that he had lost more than he had ever gained by turning his back on his father and decided to go home and ask to become one of his father's farm workers. As soon as his father saw him coming, he ran to meet him (the father running from his property to greet his son wasn't a normal action in Jewish society).

Once back home the young son was treated far differently from what he had expected. He was given a robe, which meant the same as giving someone honour and respect. Then he was given a ring, which signified authority. Next he was given shoes, which were a symbol of freedom and finally, a feast was prepared. Father and son were reconciled, brought back together, not back to where they were when the argument began, but to a new place, a position where the son was given more than he could ever hope for.

In contrast, the elder brother lost the plot completely. He was annoyed at his father's actions, and refused to be reconciled to his brother. Everyone within the family had been affected by the young son's actions but the father had chosen to welcome his son back with open arms. Perhaps if the father (God) decides to throw a party we should all take part in the celebration and not question his judgement. In other words, if God forgives, who are we to argue?

Ask the group to suggest situations that they've experienced where arguments have caused people to feel separated from those they once felt close to.

- How did it happen?
- What were the causes?
- Have the people concerned dealt with the problem?
- How was it resolved?

You might have to be sensitive to some of the issues or the fact that some of the group may feel too awkward or shy to talk personally. It may prove easier to discuss ways of avoiding conflict within a group or family. Ask group members to suggest a list of recommended actions or behaviour which either avoid conflict or bring people back together.   PETE TOWNSEND

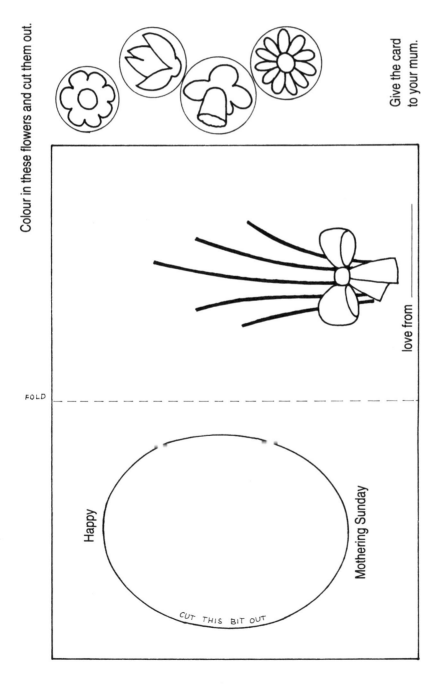

SUSAN SAYERS

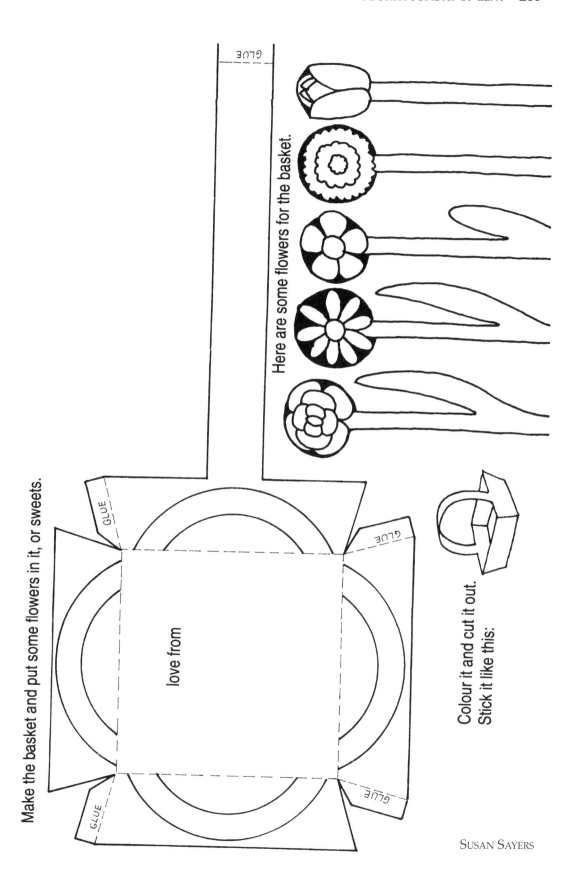

Make the basket and put some flowers in it, or sweets.

Here are some flowers for the basket.

love from

Colour it and cut it out.
Stick it like this:

SUSAN SAYERS

Block out the wrong words to see what he decided

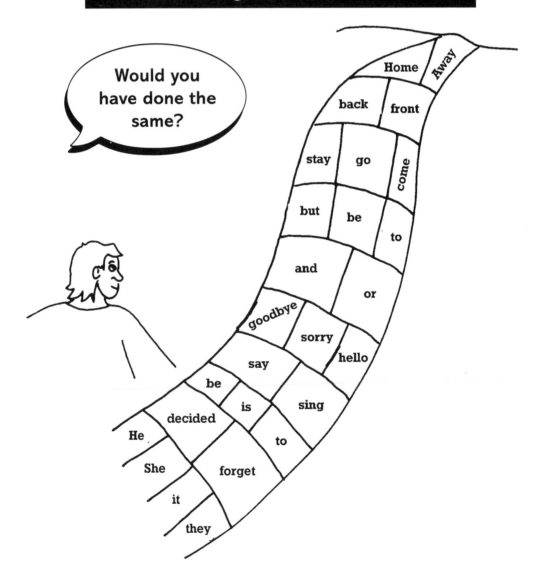

KATIE THOMPSON

When the father saw his son coming he ran to greet him

Use the code to find out what the father said to his son

A B D E F H I L N O S T U V W
1 2 3 4 5 6 78 9 10 11 12 13 14 15

'

___ ___   ___ ___ ___   ___ ___ ___ ___   ___ ___ ___
6   4   15 1 11   3   4   1   3   2   13 12

___ ___ ___   ___ ___   ___ ___   ___ ___ ___ ___ ___ !
9 10 15   6   4   7 11   1   8   7 14   4

___ ___   ___ ___ ___
6   4   15 1 11

___ ___ ___ ___   ___ ___ ___
8 10 11 12   2 13 12

___ ___ ___   ___ ___   ___ ___
9 10 15   6   4   7 11
               ,
___ ___ ___ ___ ___   Luke 15:24
5 10 13 9   3

Father forgive me

Katie Thompson

The son who came back

Luke 16:11b-32

The story of the prodigal son is a very well-known parable

Choose words from the list below to complete the story

**FATHER   SAD   PENNILESS   FORTUNE
MONEY   HOME   SONS**

A man had two _____ . The younger son asked

his _____ for his share of the father's

_____ . The son left _____ and his father

was very _____ . The son spent all his

_____ enjoying himself and soon he was

_____ and hungry. 'What should I do?' he

asked himself.

KATIE THOMPSON

Reflective material
(sketches, meditations and poems)

Meditation of a lapsed Christian returned to faith

Lost and found!
It wasn't the first parable he'd told on that theme,
   but to me it was the best;
    those words of his, when I heard them read,
    falling like music on my ears,
    for though the message was much the same as before,
    the implications were so very different.
I was just like that young man, you see,
    the second of the two sons,
    not simply lost but having wilfully gone astray.
I'd known and understood the Father's love,
    what it was to be part of his family,
    and I'd gone and frittered it all away,
    preferring my way to his,
    squandering the riches he'd given me,
    living with no thought of his will or guidance.
It was my own doing, no one else's.
I'd plumbed the depths of despair,
    sunk until I could sink no lower,
    and it was all down to me;
    a self-made humiliation.
That's what frightened me the most:
    to be lost is one thing –
    anyone can make a mistake –
    but to be the knowing instrument of your own destruction,
    to recognise the error of your ways
    and carry on regardless,
    can God forgive that?
I thought he'd washed his hands of me,
    that if I dared approach him he'd shake his head
    and tell me, 'I told you so',
    so I kept my distance
    and lived with my shame as best I could.
Only, suddenly, here was Jesus speaking not just of forgiveness
    but joyful acceptance,
    a love reaching out to meet me,
    celebrating my return,
    welcoming me home,
    and it dawned on me that the mercy of God
    is greater than I'd ever begun to contemplate.

I'd walked away,
   thrown his gifts back into his face,
   and I'd assumed there could be no return.
But I was wrong,
   for he was there waiting,
   longing to receive me back,
   arms outstretched to hold me close.
I was lost,
   and now I'm found!

NICK FAWCETT

The prodigal daughter

The message

Based on the parable of the prodigal son.

Characters

1 = father/narrator
2 = daughter

Setting the scene

The narrator starts the story. The daughter stands with her back to the audience until her first line.

Script

1   This is the story of a young woman . . .

2   *(The daughter turns around)* I'm a young woman.

1   . . . who was really stubborn and selfish and she always wanted her own way.

2   That sounds like me.

1   Yes. One day she went to her father and said . . .

2   Dad?

1   Yes.

2   I want all my money now.

1   All of it?

2   All of it.

1   That's a lot of money.

2   I know.

1   Because the father loved his daughter he gave her everything she asked for. He gave her . . .

2   Yes?

1   . . . her pocket money.
(Father puts his hand in his pocket, acts out giving money to his daughter)
He gave her her birthday money too.
(Father acts out giving daughter birthday money)
And he even gave her her Christmas money as well.
(Father acts out dragging large heavy sack of money and passes it into his daughter's hands for her to drag away)
The daughter staggered off to spend it all. First she went to the sweet shop and bought lots and lots of sweets to eat.

2   Hmm . . . I want some of those, and some of those, and some of those . . .

1   She ate them and she ate them and she ate so many she felt really sick.

2   *(Makes sound of throwing up)*

1   Arrgh! Next she went to the computer store to buy lots of games to play. She played them and she played them until she couldn't see straight any more. *(Daughter makes appropriate noises)* Then she went to the fairground to go on all the different rides.

2   Wow, Oohh . . . etc.

1   Suddenly she realised she had no more money left. No money meant she couldn't buy anything to eat or drink. She had no more friends. She was really sad and very miserable.

2   I'm really sad and miserable. Nobody wants to be my friend now that I haven't got any money left.

1   Then she remembered her father.

2   Daddy. *(Said hopefully. Pause)* No, he certainly wouldn't want to see me.

1   Why not? I'm sure your dad still loves you even though you've done all these wrong things. If you went home now I'm sure he'd welcome you back.

2   You don't understand. You see, I've been really stubborn and selfish and greedy.

1   I'm sure he'd want to see you. Please, why not go home and see? Go home to your dad. He would want to see you.

(Next line said to the audience)

2   Oh no he wouldn't.

(The audience are encouraged to join in with the narrator)

1   Oh yes he would.

2   Oh no he wouldn't.

1   Oh yes he would.

2   Oh no he wouldn't.

1   Oh yes he would.

2   O . . . K then.

1   So the daughter set off home wondering if her father would still love her. After all, she had been naughty and selfish and stubborn and greedy. The father stood looking day after day for his daughter's return. One day, in the distance, he could see her walking towards his house. The father ran to the front door, burst it open and charged down the garden path to greet her.

2   Daddy *(Pause)*, I've been really stupid, selfish, greedy and stubborn but I'm really sorry now. Will you forgive me?

1   Daughter, I forgive you. Come home now. We'll have a really big party. You can invite all your friends and we'll play your favourite games. Come on.

Application

A daughter and not a son, but the same story Jesus told and the same message too. A story of how we have all gone our own way, turned our backs on our Father God. How we need to come to our senses and turn back to him and when we do – what a response! God loves us to bits and will welcome us with open arms.

Discussion starters

• What was the father's response to the son? What does that teach us about God?
• Where are we right now in our relationship with God?

Bible verses

• Luke 15:11-32
• John 3:3-16

TONY BOWER

'All my love, Mum'

My big brother and I both went to the same boarding school, starting in a preparatory school at the age of 11, then going to the senior school at 12. He had been in the senior school three years already before I arrived, and in the early days he used to keep me company some time each day, to make sure I was settling in.

We were together when the first letters from our mother were delivered, the first ones of that term, the first ones to come one each when we were both at the same school. That was a comfort in itself. It could have been that now we were together, one letter would have been thought to be enough, to be shared between us. Instead, we got a letter each.

I can still recall how the long stone corridor felt as we read our letters. At the end of my letter, Mum signed off, 'All my love, Mum.' Panic stations! Why did she go and write a thing like that, with my brother right beside me? My brother got to the end of his letter, and then suggested we swap, to see if there was extra news in the letter we hadn't read yet. My heart sank, but I couldn't refuse.

So I read his letter, and there at the end of it was the solution, so simple. It read, 'All my love, Mum.' Such is the wonder of a mother's love, she can give all of it to every child she has. And as Isaiah says, even if a human mother changed her mind, God won't. Each of us can be the beloved disciple of Jesus, each of us the beloved child of God. There is plenty of room. GERALD O'MAHONY

Touch of love

Leader   Snowdrops and catkins are almost over
   and crocuses grow gold, purple and white.
  Bluebell leaves are showing
   and the yellow coltsfoot smiles up at the sky.

  Winter is over, the world has been reborn:
All   at the touch of your love it's young once again.

Leader   Buds on the trees are swelling
   and daffodils are almost in bloom.
  Birds flash their spring colours
   and lambs can be seen in the fields.

  Winter is over, the world has been reborn:
All   at the touch of your love it's young once again.

Leader   The sun sparkles on the water
   and warms the river bank.
  Old branches send forth new shoots
   and flowers blossom on the bare earth.

  Winter is over, the world has been reborn:
All   at the touch of your love it's young once again.

Leader   Everything is full of new life
   and the promise of beauty to come.
  It's your world, Lord, and you made it
   and all the birds are singing for joy.

  Winter is over, the world has been reborn:
All   at the touch of your love it's young once again.   MARY HATHAWAY

'We are merely servants'

Jesus has many stories about servants and slaves. He even saw himself as being the Servant prophesied by Isaiah. Some of the servant stories told by Jesus involve rewards for doing well, but there is one story or parable which makes us think twice about whether servants may expect to be rewarded. This is the one in Luke's gospel (17:7-10) about whether the master will make a fuss of the servant when he comes in from working in the fields, saying, 'Draw up a chair, join me at the table for supper.' (I am paraphrasing, of course.) Does not the master say, 'Get my supper and serve it to me, and when I have finished, you can have yours'? Servants should not expect thanks for doing what they were supposed to do. So, too, we as followers of Jesus should not expect thanks from God, but should dub ourselves 'worthless servants' and admit that at best we have only done what we were told to do. That is the line of this particular servant story.

What can we deduce from this? The prodigal son coming home had his head filled with the notion of being a servant, and paying his way. Jesus would say this is not the point: his parable does not allow the son to make the request but shows him cut off, before he could make it, by the father's generous welcome.

We are welcomed home to God because we are children of God and loved as such. Our service to God is what we do freely in gratitude for God's love given and promised for ever. We cannot expect the giver to be grateful for our gratitude. If we expect thanks for saying 'Thank you' we are likely to be disappointed. We would be unwise to limit God's love that way.   GERALD O'MAHONY

Order of Service

1. Mothering Sunday

Opening response

We kneel in worship before our Father
**Every family in heaven and on earth
takes its name from him.**

We pray that he will strengthen us
through his Spirit,
**that Christ may dwell in our hearts
through faith.**

We pray that we may be rooted
and established in love,
**that with all the saints
we may grasp the full extent of Christ's love.**

To the one who can do infinitely more
than we could ever imagine,
to him be given glory
in the Church and in Jesus Christ to every generation.

Hymn

For the beauty of the earth (HON 137)*

Prayer of thanksgiving

We give God thanks
for his gift of relationships and community,
saying, 'Lord, we give you thanks',
and praise your holy name.

For parental love and care,
which enfolds us in our early years,
Lord, we give you thanks,
and praise your holy name.

For a mother's love,
which nurtures and protects her children,
Lord, we give you thanks,
and praise your holy name.

For a father's care,
which supports and provides for his family,
Lord, we give you thanks,
and praise your holy name.

For the affection of brothers and sisters,
with whom childhood experiences are shared,
Lord, we give you thanks,
and praise your holy name.

For the support of wider family,
who share in joys and sorrows
and bring new horizons,
Lord, we give you thanks,
and praise your holy name.

For the loyalty and fellowship of friends,
who stay by us in good times and bad,
Lord, we give you thanks,
and praise your holy name.

* *Hymns Old and New* (Kevin Mayhew)

For the Christian family,
with whom we share faith in Christ
and the hope of heaven,
Lord, we give you thanks,
and praise your holy name,
the glory of Jesus Christ,
our Saviour and friend. Amen.

Hymn
O Lord, all the world (HON 378)

Confession and absolution
Lord, we are sorry for the times
when we have failed to respect our parents
or encourage our families.
Lord, forgive our sin,
and help us to do your will.

We are sorry for the unkind words
and selfish actions
which spoil family life and love.
Lord, forgive our sin,
and help us to do your will.

We are sorry for the uncaring attitudes
and unfair judgements
which create unhappiness and resentment.
Lord, forgive our sin,
and help us to do your will.

We are sorry for the ingratitude
and self-centredness
which takes for granted
all that we have and enjoy.
Lord, forgive our sin,
and help us to do your will,
to the honour and glory of your Son,
our Saviour Jesus Christ. Amen.

Almighty God, merciful and forgiving Father,
pardon all our sin, in thought, word and deed,
and restore us to a right relationship
with you and with one another,
through Jesus Christ our Lord. Amen.

Song

Lord, we come to ask your healing (HON 319)

First reading

Exodus 2:1-10 or 1 Samuel 1:20-28

Anthem

'Father of all' (Tambling) *Anthems Old and New*

Second reading

Colossians 3:12-17 or Luke 2:39-52

Hymn

For Mary, mother of our Lord (HON 136) or Jesus put this song into our hearts (HON 275)

Address

Response

To enable the congregation to express their common membership of God's family, invite them in advance to bring to the service a symbol of the practical care they show to someone else, or would be willing to show. For children, a bottle of washing-up liquid or shoe-cleaning wax would illustrate ways they could show care for a parent or older person – the sort of task for which badges are awarded by uniformed organisations such as Cubs and Brownies. However, adults should not be let off the hook! DIY tools and aids, gardening implements, kitchen utensils or an iron come readily to mind as symbols of practical ways of showing Christian care. For those not blessed with practical skills, care might mean help with finances, transport, childminding, dog walking, sitting with an elderly person for a couple of hours to relieve a carer, or getting involved with local concerns such as road safety – a bit of creative thought will soon identify an appropriate symbol for any of these. Everyone who brings something should be invited at this point to bring them up to a focal point (ideally, though not necessarily, an altar or communion table).

Intercession

We bring to God our prayers
and concerns for families;
for those who find family life
to be a source of unhappiness and tension,
and for those who have no family.
Lord of love,
receive this prayer.

For families on the verge of breakdown,
unsure where to find relief
or a way out of their difficulties . . .
May they know your guidance and wisdom
to find an outcome
which brings peace to their hearts.
Lord of love,
receive this prayer.

For children who are frightened and insecure,
neglected or abused
by those they trust and rely on . . .
May they know your loving hand
on their lives,
and find in you a friend who is always faithful.
Lord of love,
receive this prayer.

For those whose family life is overshadowed
by addiction or violence,
who live with the consequences of alcohol
or drug abuse . . .
May they know your peace
and encouragement
in helping those unable to help themselves.
Lord of love,
receive this prayer.

For families without a home
or adequate resources,
whose life is a struggle for survival . . .
May they know the hope you alone can give,
and trust you to bring them
through their troubles.
Lord of love,
receive this prayer.

For those without family or friends,
who experience the pain of loneliness
as a result of bereavement, divorce
or the absence of friendship . . .
May they know your eternal presence
alongside,
reassuring and comforting them.

Lord of love,
receive this prayer,
which we ask in the name of your Son,
Jesus Christ our Lord. Amen.

Our Father . . .

Song

A new commandment (HON 4) *or* Let there be love (HON 298)

Final prayer

Lord, bless the homes we now go to;
make them open and welcoming
in your name.

Lord, bless the families we now return to;
make them signs of your love and care.

Lord, bless the lives we now continue with;
make them worthy of your kingdom.

Lord, bless and guide us,
whatever we do, wherever we go.
Go before us, watch over us
and keep us in your love,
for the sake of Jesus Christ, our Lord. Amen.

Hymn

Bind us together (HON 60) *or* Now thank we all our God (HON 354)

Blessing   STUART THOMAS

2. Lenten journey

Focus

A large crucifix or simple cross made from two wooden cross-pieces bound together and placed on a background piece of purple fabric; a Bible opened at Matthew 16:24; a large candle; a tray filled with damp sand and the impression of two footprints.

Introduction

The season of Lent begins on Ash Wednesday when ashes are traditionally blessed and used as a sign of repentance and a reminder of the dust from which we are created and to which we will one day return. It should not be a time of doom and gloom, which we only associate with hardship and misery as we try to think of ways to give up some of our pleasures in life. It should be a season of renewal, of new beginnings and fresh opportunities for drawing closer to God. It should be a special time when we open ourselves up to God's grace, and walk closely beside him as we make our Lenten journey towards Easter and the joyful celebration of Christ's resurrection.

Penitential reflection

Peter asked Jesus this question, 'Lord, if someone sins against me again and again, how many times should I forgive that person? As many as seven times?' In reply Jesus said, 'Not just seven times, Peter, but seventy-seven times.' (Matthew 18:21-22)

For the times
when we harden our hearts
and are unforgiving towards one another:
Lord, have mercy.
Lord, have mercy.

For the times
when we are quick to point out the faults of others,
without recognising our own:
Christ, have mercy.
Christ, have mercy.

For the times
when we allow selfish words and actions
to lead us away from God's love and friendship:
Lord, have mercy.
Lord, have mercy.

Scripture

Old Testament reading – adapted from 1 Kings 19:4-8

Elijah had walked through the wilderness for a whole day, until finally he slumped exhausted beneath the shade of a small bush and tried to escape from the heat of the fearsome sun. He was totally fed-up. 'Lord, take my life,' he pleaded. 'I would rather die now than take another wretched step,' he muttered, before falling into a deep sleep.

Some time later he was wakened by an angel sent from God. 'Elijah get up and have something to eat and drink,' the angel said, and Elijah discovered a freshly baked scone and a jar of water had appeared beside him. So he ate and drank before falling asleep once again. Then the angel returned for a second time, and again encouraged Elijah to have something to eat and drink. 'Unless you eat and drink you will not have enough strength for your journey,' the angel told him. So Elijah did as the angel had said, and feeling refreshed and strengthened, he set off to complete his long journey to Mount Horeb.

New Testament reading – adapted from Ephesians 4:25-26, 32-5:20

From now on, be honest and tell no lies to one another, because, after all, we each belong to the one body of Christ. If someone makes you angry, sort out your argument with them before the end of the day when the sun sets, so that the anger you feel is not carried in your heart to spoil another day. Be kind and understanding towards one another, and ready to forgive as willingly as God forgives you. Above all, as God's children, follow his example of goodness and try to love one another as much as he loves you.

Gospel – adapted from Matthew 26:37-39 and Luke 22:41-44

When they had finished eating supper together, Jesus and his disciples made their way to the Garden of Gethsemane, where Jesus was overwhelmed by fear and dread. His heart was almost crushed by the sadness he felt, and he was seized by a terrible fear of the suffering which lay ahead of him. In his despair he cried aloud, 'Father, if it is possible, take this cup of suffering away from me!' But then he added, 'Let everything happen according to your will and not mine.' As he continued to pray, his sweat fell to the ground like droplets of blood, and an angel from God appeared to comfort and strengthen him for what lay ahead.

Reflection

Jesus and Elijah had a great deal in common. Both were filled with despair at the thought of the journeys God wanted them to make. Sometimes, as we begin our Lenten journey, the thought of six weeks of special effort and self-denial can fill us with a certain amount of despair and reluctance too! Neither of them wanted to take the next step along the road they were expected to follow, and in their desperation they both turned to God for consolation. God heard their cries for help and responded with the support and strength which they needed at that particular moment. For Elijah that meant feeding him so that he would be sufficiently revived and refreshed to carry on his way. God feeds and nourishes us too, not just as we make our journey through Lent, but as we each make our own personal journey through life. Jesus said, 'I am the living bread which has come down from heaven.' By feeding us at the table of his Word and the table of the Eucharist, he helps us to know and love him more in our everyday lives.

So ask yourself: this Lent will I make a special effort to spend time reading or listening to God's Word? Will I try to meet the person of Jesus more often through the sacraments of Reconciliation and Holy Communion?

In the agony in the garden, we perhaps see Jesus at his most human and vulnerable. The Son of God made man, whose only 'crime' was to love and be loved, knew what suffering awaited him on his journey to the cross on Calvary, and he was afraid. We all know how it feels to anticipate something which we dread. It might be something we must do in public, perhaps an exam or an operation, or it may be something as simple as a visit to the dentist! Although our fear cannot compare with Christ's agony in the garden, we too will often find ourselves calling on God in prayer to help us get through our moment of difficulty.

So ask yourself: this Lent will I make an extra effort to spend more time getting to know God through prayer? Will I be prepared to try out new ways of praying?

Sometimes we need to remind ourselves that although God always hears our prayers and responds to help us, that response is often apparent not so much in the extraordinary but in the ordinary events and people around us, as this little story illustrates so well!

There was once a man who loved God and had complete faith in him. When it began to rain so hard that the basement of his house filled with water, he was not unduly concerned. 'God will save me if the floods continue to rise,' he told himself as he moved his belongings upstairs. The rain continued to fall night and day, and as the water steadily rose a man in a canoe came by and offered to rescue the man from his flooded house. 'There's no need,' he replied. 'I know that God will save me.' As the water rose still further, the man in the house retreated upstairs to the next floor. Another boat came past, and again its occupants offered to rescue him from his house, which by this time was rapidly disappearing beneath the water. But again he refused, as he cheerfully declared, 'God will save me!' Finally the man was forced to take shelter on the roof of his house, but when a helicopter flew by and offered to pluck him to safety – yes, you've already guessed – the man refused their help and decided to wait for God to save him.

Eventually the flood water swept him away and the poor man drowned! When he arrived still dripping at heaven's pearly gates, he was ready to give God a piece of his mind. 'I had complete faith in you,' he told God angrily. 'I believed that you would save me and yet you let me drown!' God said to him, 'I tried to rescue you three times – first by canoe, then by boat, and when you still refused to listen, I even sent a helicopter.'

Unlike the man in the story, we must be open to recognising the fact that God often answers our prayers through the actions and words of those around us. In times of need, it is our giving and our reaction which forms God's response to the prayers of others in need. In times of difficulty and disaster, he answers their cries for help by working through us and our generous donations and efforts to ease their suffering. He depends on ordinary people working in ordinary ways to achieve the extraordinary.

So, finally, ask yourself: this Lent will I make a special effort to give generously to others? Can I find new ways to ease the suffering of others?

Intercession

United in love,
we gather as brothers and sisters in Christ
to pray for our own needs
and the needs of the world:

We pray for the Church and all her Christian people;
may we be guided on our journey through life
by the light of faith
towards Christ our Saviour.

Silence

Loving Father:
lead us.

We pray for those
who proclaim the Good News to the world
by word and deed;
may the Holy Spirit guide them
on their journey through life,
as they share their faith with the world.

Silence

Loving Father:
lead us.

We pray for people
forced to leave their homes and families
because of war, fear or disaster;
may they be guided
on their journey of uncertainty and suffering
by our loving support
and efforts to bring them comfort and hope.

Silence

Loving Father:
lead us.

We pray for people
wandering in the wilderness of doubt
as they search for God in their lives;
may our loving Father,
who searches for everyone who is lost,
guide them on their journey of discovery.

Silence

Loving Father:
lead us.

We pray for anyone
who has wandered far from God's love;
may they be guided on a journey
of friendship and reconciliation,
as they discover the forgiveness and healing
of our heavenly Father who never stops loving them.

Silence

Loving Father:
lead us.

Knowing that our heavenly Father is listening,
in the silence of our hearts
let us share our own unspoken prayers with him.

Silence

Heavenly Father,
as we journey through Lent,
keep us close to your love
and mould us in the image of Christ your loving Son.
We ask this in the name of Jesus our Lord.
Amen.

Activities and ideas

- Decide on a charity which the children would particularly like to support during the season of Lent. Help them to gather information about its work and aims, and produce a visual display. Encourage them to think of different ways in which they can raise funds both individually and as a group to support their chosen cause, and help them to plan and run events to achieve their aims.

- Give each child a small card cut-out in the shape of a cross with the following verse from Matthew's Gospel written or printed on one side: 'If anyone wants to come with me, he must forget himself, take up his cross and follow me' (Matthew 16:24). Help the children to reflect about, and then write down on the other side of their cross, their private goals for their own journey through Lent. Invite them to come forward individually and touch the focal crucifix with their own crosses. They should keep these carefully as a reminder to themselves of their aims for Lent.   KATIE THOMPSON

Fifth Sunday of Lent

Mary anoints Jesus' feet: a costly response denoting his yet costlier sacrifice

John 12:1-8

(also Isaiah 43:16-21; Psalm 126; Philippians 3:4b-14; John 12:1-8)

A reading from the Gospel of John (John 12:1-8)

Six days before the Passover Jesus came to Bethany, the home of Lazarus, whom he had raised from the dead. There they gave a dinner for him. Martha served, and Lazarus was one of those at the table with him. Mary took a pound of costly perfume made of pure nard, anointed Jesus' feet, and wiped them with her hair. The house was filled with the fragrance of the perfume. But Judas Iscariot, one of his disciples (the one who was about to betray him), said, 'Why was this perfume not sold for three hundred denarii and the money given to the poor?' (He said this not because he cared about the poor, but because he was a thief; he kept the common purse and used to steal what was put into it.) Jesus said, 'Leave her alone. She bought it so that she might keep it for the day of my burial. You always have the poor with you, but you do not always have me.'

NEW REVISED STANDARD VERSION

Alternative reading from the Gospel of John (John 8:1-11)

Jesus was teaching in the Temple when the Pharisees brought a woman to stand before him. 'This woman has been caught doing something wrong, and the law says that she should be stoned. What do you think?' they asked, because they wanted to trick Jesus.

After a few moments Jesus stood up and said, 'Let the person who has never done anything wrong throw the first stone at her.'

The crowd that had gathered began to leave one by one, until Jesus and the woman stood alone. Jesus said to her, 'Has anyone thrown a stone at you?'

'No, sir,' she answered.

'Then I have forgiven you,' he said. 'Now go and sin no more.'

This is the Gospel of the Lord
Praise to you, Lord Jesus Christ
KATIE THOMPSON

Prayers

Praise

Merciful God,
   we remember today how you reached out
      through the ministry of Christ,
      welcoming those whom society had rejected,
      accepting those whom the world considered unacceptable.
   You have time for us, just as we are:
      Lord, we praise you.

We remember how you called Matthew, the tax collector,
      how you dined with Zacchaeus,
      how you touched the lepers,
      and how you showed mercy to the woman caught in adultery,
      time and again, breaking the mould,
      offering us, through his faithfulness,
      forgiveness and new life.
   You have time for us, just as we are:
      Lord, we praise you.

We remember that you forgave rather than condemned,
      built up rather than pulled down,
      encouraged rather than criticised,
      drew near rather than kept your distance.
   You have time for us, just as we are:
      Lord, we praise you.

Merciful God,
   we rejoice that you accept us today,
      not for any actions on our part,
      nor through anything we may one day do,
      but simply by your grace.
   You have time for us, just as we are:
      Lord, we praise you.

We rejoice that you value us
      despite our many weaknesses and our repeated faults,
      your nature always to have mercy,
      your grace inexhaustible.
   You have time for us, just as we are:
      Lord, we praise you.

Help us to express our worship
    through receiving the love you so freely offer,
    and celebrating your gift of new life.
You have time for us, just as we are:
    Lord, we praise you.

In the name of Christ.
Amen.
                                                NICK FAWCETT

Petition – The peace of God

Gracious God,
    you have promised to all who love you
        a peace that passes understanding.
Forgive us that we have failed to make that our own.
Teach us to be still,
    and to know that you are God.

We rush about, our minds preoccupied by many things,
    filling our days with frantic activity,
    cramming ever more into every moment,
    our lives dominated by a sense of the unforgiving minute.
We strive and hanker after that which is finally unimportant,
    unable to satisfy.
We brood and worry over problems that we cannot change,
    magnifying little things out of all proportion.
Teach us to be still,
    and to know that you are God.

Speak to us through the example of Jesus –
    the way he made time for quietness
    so that he could speak with you,
    the need he recognised for space and silence
    in which to seek your guidance
    and to reflect on your will.
Teach us to be still,
    and to know that you are God.

Gracious God,
    forgive us that for all our busyness
        we so often forget the one thing needful,
        the one thing that really matters –
        the knowledge of your love.
    Help us to live each day,
        each moment,
        with that foremost in our minds,
        and so may we find your peace,
        the rest for our souls that you have promised.
    Teach us to be still
        and to know that you are God.

Through Jesus Christ our Lord.
Amen.   NICK FAWCETT

Intercession – Where there seems no hope of change

Loving God,
    there are times when we look at people's lives
        and find it hard to believe things can ever
        change for the better –
        we see them racked by illness,
        weighed down by anxiety,
        tormented by depression,
        crippled by debt,
        broken by alcohol,
        destroyed by drugs,
        scarred by bereavement,
        shattered through unemployment,
        and we wonder what their prospects really are,
        what hope we can realistically offer them,
        what help we can possibly give.
    Transforming God,
        may your light shine where there is darkness.

We pray for such people known to us now –
    family,
    friends,
    members of our fellowship,
    colleagues at work,
    neighbours,
    acquaintances;
    as well as the countless people unknown to us,
    each struggling under their own particular burdens.
    Transforming God,
        may your light shine where there is darkness.

We pray for our world –
　　for those many people who face suffering,
　　injustice,
　　hardship,
　　and death.
　Transforming God,
　　may your light shine where there is darkness.

Reach out to all who are in despair, we pray,
　　all who long for change
　　but see only hopelessness stretching before them.
　Touch their lives,
　　and bring help, hope, healing, and wholeness.
　Transforming God,
　　may your light shine where there is darkness.

Loving God,
　it is hard sometimes to believe those around us,
　　still less the world around,
　　can ever change for the better.
　We see countries broken by war,
　　people consumed by hatred,
　　thousands living in fear,
　　nations turned against nation,
　　multitudes made homeless by disaster,
　　continents facing famine,
　　and again we wonder what the prospects really are,
　　what hope anyone can offer,
　　what help can possibly be given.
　Transforming God,
　　may your light shine where there is darkness.

Help us to see beneath the surface,
　　recognising you are at work
　　and that things can change.
Help us to see beyond appearances,
　　recognising you are a God able to transform
　　even the most hopeless of situations.
Give to us and to all people the assurance
　　that there is no one and no situation
　　unable to be transformed by your power.
Transforming God,
　　may your light shine where there is darkness,
　　through Jesus Christ, our Lord.
Amen.   NICK FAWCETT

All-age-talk material

Read John 12:1-8

Jesus had gone to Bethany, to the house of Simon the Leper, for a meal. Martha, Mary and Lazarus were most likely the children of Simon. The meal was to be a leisurely dinner, a time to enjoy eating, drinking and good company.

The meal had been prepared especially for Jesus after his extremely busy time teaching and healing all around the area. The sight of Lazarus at the table would have made the meal a special occasion. Lazarus (formerly known as dead Lazarus!) was a close friend and Jesus must have taken real pleasure in raising him from the dead.

Everyone would have known that the meal was a special occasion but not everyone would have been able to say why it was so special. Jesus knew that these were his last few days of freedom and being with his disciples and close friends would have been particularly important for him. The disciples would have known that things were 'hotting up' but even they might not have been able to say precisely what was going to happen. To Mary, Martha and Lazarus it was enough to have their close friend spend some time with them.

Martha seems to have been the practical person, the one who knew how to make people feel comfortable and catered for. She offered her skills in the kitchen as an expression of her love towards Jesus. Mary expressed her love in a different way.

The washing of feet was a normal courtesy before a meal. Mary's actions were significant for three reasons. First, the perfume that Mary poured on Jesus' feet was expensive and quite probably irreplaceable, given the cost. Second, it was usually traditional, and a sign of honour, to use oil or perfume to anoint someone's head. By anointing Jesus' feet Mary was showing her humility by not claiming the honour of anointing Jesus' head. And third, Mary wiped Jesus' feet with her hair. At the time, no respectable woman would appear in public with her hair loose. By using her hair to wipe the feet of Jesus, Mary was setting aside tradition and respectability in her desire to express her love for Jesus, regardless of what people thought of her.

In their different ways both Mary and Martha gave Jesus an expression of their love. No one objected to Martha's gift of food as everyone would have shared in the meal and enjoyed the food. Mary's gift was personal and only for Jesus.

We each have our own, individual ways of expressing how we feel and what we consider precious. Every expression is relevant and special. Just because some acts are highly visible and make an impact immediately doesn't mean that other forms of expression are less important or meaningful. Each of us is unique and important to God. The most important thing is the expression of our hearts, not what other people think of us.   PETE TOWNSEND

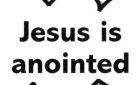

Jesus is anointed

Jesus went to Bethany, and met three good friends. Who were they?

Write the first letter of each object on the line above to spell out their names

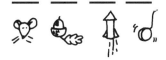

KATIE THOMPSON

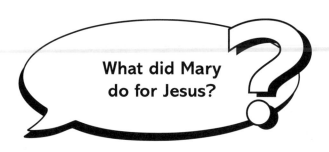

What did Mary
do for Jesus?

Use the code to find out !

♥	S	H	A	N	I
♦	R	U	E	D	W
✿	F	T	P	M	O
	A	B	C	D	E

♥A ♥B ♦C

♥C ♥D ✿E ♥E ♥D ✿B ♦C ♦D

♥B ♥E ♥A   ✿A ♦C ♦C ✿B   ♦E ♥E ✿B ♥B

✿C ♦B ♦A ♦C   ♥D ♥C ♦A ♦D

♥C ♥D ♦D   ♦E ♥E ✿C ♦C ♦D   ✿B ♥B ♦C ✿D

♦E ♥E ✿B ♥B   ♥B ♦C ♦A

♥B ♥C ♥E ♦A

John 12:3

KATIE THOMPSON

Judas was angry...

'This money could have been spent on the poor!'

He really wanted the money for himself

Colour the numbers below to read what Jesus said to Judas

1 You
2 SO
3 WILL
4 BUT
5 ALWAYS
6 ME
7 THEN
8 HAVE
9 BE
10 THE
11 SEE
12 POOR
13 BUT
14 RICH
15 YOU
16 DO
17 WILL
18 NOT
19 ALWAYS
20 MY
21 BE
22 HAVE
23 LOVE
24 ME

1, 3, 5, 8, 10, 12, 13, 15, 17, 18, 19, 22, 24

John 12:8

KATIE THOMPSON

Reflective material
(sketches, meditations and poems)

Sacrificial scent

Soldier   See what I mean, Sir. Spending a whole year's wages on a jar of perfume. I don't let my wife spend a cent on scent. Waste of money.

Official   Yes, I had noticed your wife's . . . aroma.

Soldier   The woman was off her trolley, out of her mind, on another planet, in La La Land.

Official   Thank you, soldier. I get the picture, I don't need you to keep colouring it in.

Soldier   A complete balm pot!

Official   Soldier!

Soldier   Yes, Sir.

Official   Some people may look upon her act as one of supreme sacrifice. Giving all she had on one item.

Soldier   That's not sacrifice, Sir, that's stupidity. A sacrifice is when you lay down your life for your empire, standing on the front line, facing the enemy.

Official   Yes, that is sacrifice.

The official looks at the report.

Soldier   Sir, what are you reading?

The official looks up.

Official   It's the report of the crucifixion.

Soldier   Ah.

Official   You were there. You remember what happened?

Soldier   Yes, Sir. It's all written down.

Song: Tonight

Tonight

For lyrics and music see next page.

Mary and John walk slowly to centre stage. They stand looking forward as the song is sung. John comforts Mary as they look at the cross. The stage lighting needs to be soft lights on Mary and John and begin turning to a red light to show Jesus' death and then complete darkness as Mary and John leave the stage.

Or alternatively . . .

The Cross

The stage is set in darkness. Two forlorn figures move slowly to the centre. It's Mary and John. As they stand looking forward there is the sound of a hammer hitting a nail. There is a pause between each blow. John puts his arm around Mary who buries her head into John's chest, unable to look. After a number of hammer-blows there is absolute silence. Mary turns to look at the cross. John and Mary hold their positions for a while; there is the sound of thunder before John leads Mary away.

Stage Directions: A soft light on Mary and John would work well. If possible the white light turning to red after the sound of the hammer to depict Jesus' death. At the sound of the thunderclap the stage falls into darkness. The sound of the hammer and nail and the thunderclap would probably work best on tape coming over the PA. The scene needs to be played slowly to allow for the dramatic tension and drama that is unfolding.   TONY BOWER

Tonight

1. To - night,   when the world rests on your shoul - ders, oh, to - night,   a
2.   day,   when your dreams are liv - ing night - mares, oh, to - day,   does

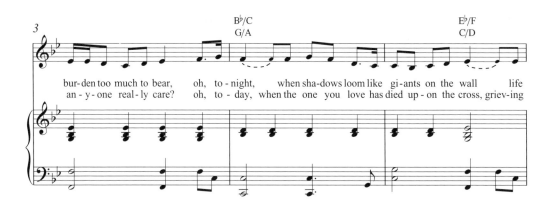

bur - den too much to bear, oh, to - night,   when sha - dows loom like gi - ants on the wall   life
an - y - one real - ly care? oh, to - day,   when the one you love has died up - on the cross, griev - ing

makes no sense at all. But   like   an   o - a - sis,
hearts, the pain the loss.

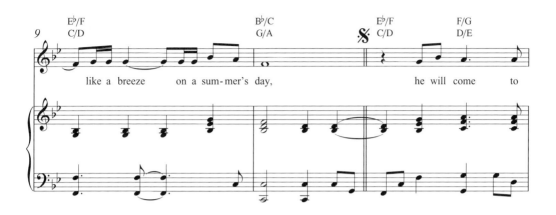

Holy Week

Palm Sunday*

Joy and sorrow as Jesus enters Jerusalem

Luke 19:28-40

(Liturgy of the Psalms: Psalm 118:1, 2, 19-29; Luke 19:28-40; Liturgy of the Passion: Isaiah 50:4-9a; Psalm 31:9-16; Philippians 2:5-11; Luke 22:14-23:56 or 23:1-49)

A reading from the Gospel of Luke (Luke 19:28-40)

Jesus made his way to Jerusalem, and when he reached the Mount of Olives, he sent two of his disciples to fetch a young colt from a nearby village.

'If anyone asks, tell them that the master needs it,' Jesus said, and they did as he had explained.

They brought the colt to Jesus, and laid a cloak on it, before helping him on to its back.

Crowds of people had lined the road to Jerusalem, and were waiting to welcome Jesus when he came. As he approached, they threw cloaks on the road before him and sang out in greeting: 'Blessed is the King who comes in the Lord's name! Peace and glory in the highest heavens!'

Hearing this, some of the Pharisees urged Jesus to quieten the crowd, but Jesus said to them, 'The very stones will cry out if their voices are silenced.'

This is the Gospel of the Lord
Praise to you, Lord Jesus Christ   KATIE THOMPSON

Introductory material

'Blessed is the king who comes in the name of the Lord. Peace in heaven and glory in highest heaven.' The joyful cries of the crowd that assembled outside Jerusalem to welcome Jesus into the Holy City. Words for us tinged with sadness and irony, because those same cries were all too quickly to turn to shouts of 'Crucify! We have no king but Caesar!' Yet if the welcome was to be short-lived, it gives us nonetheless a fleeting glimpse of the welcome Jesus shall one day receive; the rejoicing, the praise, the celebration there will be when finally, in the fullness of time, he returns to establish his kingdom. In our service today, we remember what has been and look forward to what shall be, in awe and wonder offering our praise.   NICK FAWCETT

*For resources on Passion of Christ see Maundy Thursday and Good Friday

Prayers

Praise

Loving God,
   we join this day in glad and joyful praise.
   We welcome Christ once more
     as our King, Lord, and Saviour –
     we promise him our loyalty,
     we bring him our love,
     we bow to him in worship,
     we greet him with wonder.
   Hosanna to the Son of David,
     glory in the highest heaven.

Loving God,
   come to us again through Christ this day.
   Speak to us as we read familiar words,
     as we sing familiar songs,
     as we recall his triumphal entry into Jerusalem long ago,
     as we remember all it meant and all it cost.
   Hosanna to the Son of David,
     glory in the highest heaven.

   Help us to see that it was not only in the welcome of Palm Sunday,
     but in the rejection which followed
     that Jesus revealed your glory,
     and so help us to offer him our service in the days ahead,
     through the good times and the bad.
   Hosanna to the Son of David,
     glory in the highest heaven,
     now and for evermore.
   Amen.

NICK FAWCETT

Confession

Lord Jesus Christ,
   we welcome and praise you this day.
   We lift up our voices in glad hosannas.
   We joyfully acknowledge you as King of kings
     and Lord of lords.
   Yet we know in our hearts, even as we greet you,
     sincere though we may be,

that our worship and commitment is sometimes
as weak and shallow as that which greeted you
as you entered Jerusalem long ago.
Son of David,
  have mercy upon us.

Lord Jesus Christ,
  forgive us that we go on making
    the same mistakes made on that first Palm Sunday.
  We profess to follow you
    but in our hearts follow our own inclinations.
  We are self-centred in our discipleship,
    looking as much for what we can receive as give.
  We are preoccupied with appearances,
    our external show disguising an inner poverty
    which only you can see.
  We are ready to serve when life is good,
    but reluctant when it involves the way of sacrifice.
  Son of David,
    have mercy upon us.

Lord Jesus Christ,
  you knew, as you entered Jerusalem,
    that the welcome of the crowd would turn to rejection,
    yet still you came and still you died for them.
  We praise you for that truth,
    and we thank you that still you come to us,
    inviting us to respond and share in your kingdom.
  Son of David,
    have mercy upon us.

Come again now into our hearts,
    cleansing us of all that is evil,
    all that is impure and unworthy,
    all that keeps us from you.
  Son of David,
    have mercy upon us.

Come to your Church,
    filling it with love,
    harmony,
    humility,
    and faith.
  Son of David,
    have mercy upon us.

Come to your world,
  blessing it with peace,
  justice,
  freedom,
  and hope.
Son of David,
  have mercy upon us.

Lord Jesus Christ,
  we welcome you today
    as the Prince of Peace,
    the King of kings,
    the Servant of all,
    the Lord of all,
    all in all!
Son of David,
  have mercy upon us,
  for your name's sake.
Amen.   NICK FAWCETT

Petition and intercession – The Prince of Peace

Lord Jesus Christ,
  you came not as a king mighty in battle,
    but as the Prince of Peace,
    the promised deliverer,
    sent to heal and restore our broken world.
  So now we pray for peace and unity between nations.
  Your kingdom come,
  your will be done.

We thank you for signs of hope in the world today –
  for the desire to make this planet a safer place,
  for initiatives that have been taken
  to reduce nuclear and conventional arms,
  for the breaking down of seemingly insurmountable barriers,
  and for a willingness to engage in genuine dialogue
  rather than empty rhetoric.
Prosper all such efforts,
  and grant that a spirit of trust and co-operation
  may develop among all.
Your kingdom come,
  your will be done.

We pray for those places where tension continues –
　where there is still hatred,
　division,
　violence
　and slaughter.
We pray for all those caught up in the awfulness of war –
　those maimed and injured,
　those who have lost loved ones,
　those for whom life will never be the same again.
Break down the barriers which keep people apart –
　the prejudice and intolerance,
greed and envy,
　injustice and exploitation which continue to scar our world.
May your Spirit of love overcome all that causes people
　to take up arms against one another.
Your kingdom come,
　your will be done.

Lord Jesus Christ,
　Prince of Peace,
　　come again to our world
　　and bring the unity that you alone can bring.
　May the day come when swords shall be beaten into ploughshares,
　　and spears turned into pruning hooks;
　　when nation shall not lift sword against nation,
　　neither learn war any more;
　　a day when no one will hurt or destroy
　　on all your holy mountain.
　Your kingdom come,
　　your will be done.

For your name's sake.
Amen.   NICK FAWCETT

Intercession

The King of glory rides on a donkey into Jerusalem

We pray for the church, the body of Christ,
longing for its healing, strengthening
and openness to your will.

Silence for prayer

The Lord is among us:
his Spirit prays through ours

We pray for the world and all the nations,
longing for peace and tranquillity,
justice, mercy and forgiveness.

Silence for prayer

The Lord is among us:
his Spirit prays through ours

We pray for all our relatives
and the family life of our country,
longing for the grace to love and honour
one another,
to trust and to persevere.

Silence for prayer

The Lord is among us:
his Spirit prays through ours

We pray for those who are ill or in distress,
longing for your comfort, healing and refreshment.

Silence for prayer

The Lord is among us:
his Spirit prays through ours

We pray for those who are passing
through the gate of death,
longing for your merciful love.

Silence for prayer

The Lord is among us:
his Spirit prays through ours

We praise you and worship you
for all your blessings,
but especially for your generous saving love
and faithful presence with us.

Silence for prayer

Merciful Father,
accept these prayers
for the sake of your Son,
our Saviour Jesus Christ, Amen.

SUSAN SAYERS

Short prayer

Lord Jesus Christ,
    you entered Jerusalem on a wave of enthusiasm,
    greeted by your joyful people,
    shouts of praise and protestations of loyalty
    on every side.
Yet you knew that the bubble would soon burst,
    that the welcome was only skin-deep.
Lord Jesus Christ,
    we come today to worship you
    with equal gladness,
    but conscious that our commitment too
    may not be as strong as it should be,
    our faith fickle if put to the test.
Help us to learn from the first Palm Sunday,
    so that our hosannas may ring out
    as loudly tomorrow
    as they do today.   NICK FAWCETT

Reflecting

During the week reflect on Luke 19:28-40.

The climactic moment. Three long years of living closely with this extraordinary man had welded them heart and soul to him. They had hung on his teaching, wondered at his healings, been ignited by his passion, drunk from his wisdom, adored his presence. Now he was to enter the Holy City to claim his kingdom – not in secret as so often before, but openly, at the time of Passover. They were ecstatic. The devotion in them burst like a dam, but they had no idea of the failure, tragedy and disaster that was about to engulf them as they danced and bellowed their praises.

Faith needs its ecstatic beginnings but is not truly born until it has faced the dark night of loss.   PATRICK WOODHOUSE

All-age-talk material

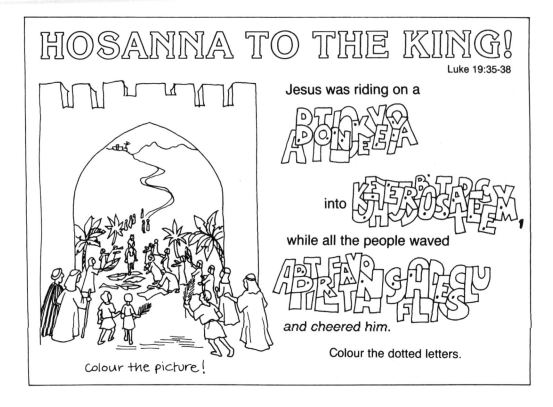

SUSAN SAYERS

Behold your King. (Zechariah 9:9)

The donkey is hiding. Colour in the dotted shapes to find him.

G	N	I	D	I	R	J	E	S	U	J I
P	H	A	R	I	S	Y	E	K	N	O D
D	I	S	C	I	P	L	E	S	X	Y R
W	O	L	A	O	C	L	B	J	U	E S
O	R	S	E	H	L	E	N	E	P	S E
R	O	W	W	D	T	T	V	R	H	I E
C	S	R	O	H	B	O	J	U	A	S S
L	O	V	A	O	L	R	E	S	R	C I
K	I	N	G	R	P	I	R	A	I	I R
X	Y	R	O	S	O	D	U	L	S	P A
D	I	S	C	E	Y	U	S	E	E	L H
H	E	A	R	T	S	N	A	M	F	E P

WORDSEARCH

Find the following words in the grid:

PHARISEE, DONKEY, DISCIPLES, BETHANY, JESUS, JERUSALEM, CROWD, KING, LOVE, RIDING, JOY, HORSE, COLT, HEARTS.

MICHAEL FORSTER

Discovering the kingdom

Reading
Luke 19:29-40

Aim
To show that Jesus is a different type of king, ruling over a different kind of kingdom.

Preparation
From silver or gold card, make thirteen simple crowns, and on the front of each one stick a large label with the name of one of the following:

Tutankhamen
Nebuchadnezzar
Julius Caesar
James VI
Henry V
Louis XIV
Philip II
Genghis Khan
Frederick the Great
Montezuma
Nicholas
Boadicea
Jesus

Now, on coloured pieces of card or paper, cut out thirteen large contoured shapes, representing countries. On each of these write the name of one of the following countries:

Egypt
Babylon
Rome
Scotland
England
France
Spain
Mongolia
Prussia
Aztecs (Mexico)
Russia
Iceni

Using Blu-Tack, stick these 'countries' around the front of the church, on walls, the lectern and choir stalls.

Talk

Ask the congregation if they have ever wondered what it must be like to be a king? Tell them that, for a few lucky volunteers, today is their opportunity to find out, because for five minutes you are going to give them the chance to rule a country. Ask for thirteen volunteers, give each one a crown to wear, and then ask each 'king' to discover their kingdom and hold it up for all to see. The correct countries are:

Tutankhamen	Egypt
Nebuchadnezzar	Babylon
Julius Caesar	Rome
James VI	Scotland
Henry V	England
Louis XIV	France
Philip II	Spain
Genghis Khan	Mongolia
Frederick the Great	Prussia
Montezuma	Aztecs (Mexico)
Nicholas	Russia
Boadicea	Iceni
Jesus	?

All of your 'kings' should quickly be able to find their kingdoms except for the one whose crown bears the name 'Jesus'. Arrange the 'kings' in a line with 'Jesus' on one end; then starting at the other end announce the name on each volunteer's crown and country, and ask whether these have been paired correctly (exchange if necessary). Continue along the line until you reach the volunteer wearing the crown with the name 'Jesus'. Why has no country been found to match?

When Jesus entered Jerusalem on what today we call Palm Sunday, it was to be welcomed as king by the crowds who had gathered there to greet him.

'Blessed is the king who comes in the name of the Lord!', they shouted. *(Luke 19:38)*

So what kind of king was Jesus; and where was, or is, his kingdom? The obvious answer, of course, is that he was king of the Jews, or the king of Israel. And that is exactly what many people at the time hoped he had come to be, what others feared he intended to be, and what the Roman authorities suspected he claimed to be.

Then Pilate asked him, 'Are you the king of the Jews?' *(Luke 23:3)*

But the answer Jesus gave was very different.

'My kingdom is not from this world. If my kingdom were from this world, my followers would be fighting to keep me from being handed over to the Jews. But as it is, my kingdom is not from here.' *(John 18:36)*

And those are words we need to remind ourselves of today. When we talk about Jesus being our king, when we sing hymns with words like 'You are the King of Glory', 'Majesty', or 'Rejoice, the Lord is King', we are not saying he is a king like any of these others we have looked at today. For Jesus was not a king in the sense of ruling a single country many years ago. Rather he came as the servant of all, the one who laid down his life for his people, the one who put others before himself, yet the one raised up by God as ruler over all, the King of kings and Lord of lords, now and for all eternity. It is in that example that we glimpse the kind of kingdom God has in store for us and all his people; and here that we see the kind of king who will rule over us. In the words of the hymn, 'This is our God, the servant king'.

Finish with the hymn 'From heaven you came' *(The Servant King)*.

NICK FAWCETT

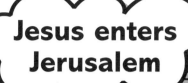

Jesus sent his disciples off to find a colt for him to ride

Which colt hasn't been ridden yet?

Luke 19:29

KATIE THOMPSON

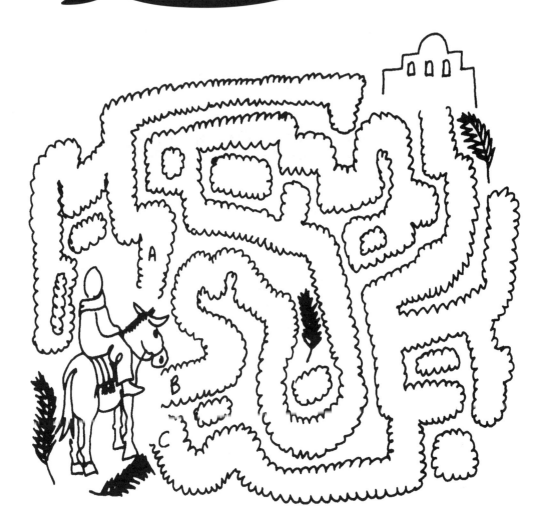

Find the way to Jerusalem. Choose A, B or C

KATIE THOMPSON

The difference a week makes!

Reading

Luke 19:28-40

Aim

To demonstrate the contrast between the fickleness of human nature and the faithfulness of God, each so powerfully displayed in the events from Palm Sunday to Easter Sunday.

Preparation

You will need a large sheet of paper pinned to a board, or a whiteboard, and a marker pen. Across the top of the board write the following:

LOVE   CHEER   WAVE   JOY   PALM   KING

Talk

Tell the congregation that you want to talk about change, and to help illustrate what you mean you need their help. Show them the letters at the top of your display board, and tell them that you want to change the words in as few stages as possible to very different words: 'Love' to 'Hate'; 'Cheer' to 'Cross'; 'Wave' to 'Mock'; 'Joy' to 'Woe'; 'Palm' to 'Harm'; and 'King' to 'Kill'. Invite suggestions as how best to do this, and write these down beneath the relevant word until the change has successfully been made. If the ways below are faster (or if you can do better!), demonstrate afterwards.

LOVE	CHEER	WAVE	JOY	PALM	KING
COVE	CHEEP	RAVE	TOY	PALE	PING
CAVE	CHEAP	RACE	TOE	HALE	PINT
HAVE	CHEAT	RACK	WOE	HARE	TINT
HATE	CHEST	ROCK		HARM	TILT
	CREST	MOCK			KILT
	CRESS				KILL
	CROSS				

Point out that in a relatively short time it was possible to change the word you started with into a word very different in meaning. But if changing the words so easily seems remarkable, more remarkable still is the fact that the changes you have made actually happened. What day is it? Palm Sunday. What day will it be next Friday? Good Friday.

Palm Sunday and Good Friday: two very different days reminding us of very different events, yet there is less than a week between them. In less than a week love changed to hate, cheering changed to a cross, the joyful waving of crowds changed to mockery, the joyful hurling of palm branches turned to the hurling of insults and attempts to harm Jesus, the shouts welcoming him as King turned to shouts demanding he should be killed; a day of joy turned to a day of woe. In just a few days, each of these changes took place.

An astonishing turnaround; but thankfully there was to be another more astonishing still, for on Easter Day Jesus was to change it all back again! Hate was replaced by love, the tears after the cross were replaced by cheers following the Resurrection, the mocking of the crowds gave way to waves of happiness, woe was replaced by joy, the one who had been killed was worshipped as Lord of lords and King of kings!

Palm Sunday reminds us how quickly people can change, ourselves included; how short-lived our love and faithfulness can be. But it reminds us also that the love of God shown in Christ never changes; that whatever may fight against his will, and however faithless we may be, his love and purpose will endure for ever!   NICK FAWCETT

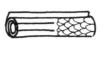

How to make a palm tree

1. Colour the tree green and brown on both sides.

2. Cut down the lines.

3. Roll the tree up like this and stick it in place.

4. Pull the green parts down so the palm tree looks like this.

COLOUR THIS PART GREEN   COLOUR THIS PART BROWN

CUT DOWN THE LINES

Susan Sayers

The people welcomed Jesus with shouts of adoration

Solve the maths problem and use the code to find the missing letters

A B C D E F G H I J K L M N O P Q R S T U V W X Y Z
1 2 3 4 5 6 7 8 9 10 11 12 13 14 15 16 17 18 19 20 21 22 23 24 25 26

2	6	3	20	17	10	2		4	7
−0	×2	+2	−1	+2	−5	×2		×2	−2

' ___ ___ ___ ___ ___ ___ ___ ___   IS   ___ ___

19	5	10		3	20	7	8	11
+4	+3	+5		×1	−5	+6	−3	+8

___ ___ ___   ___ ___ ___ ___ ___   IN

6	22	12	2	12		2	10	11	15
+6	7	+0	×2	+1		×7	−9	+2	−10

THE   ___ ___ ___ ___ , ___   ___ ___ ___ ___ ,

Luke 19:38

KATIE THOMPSON

Read Luke 22:14-23

The Passover meal was a celebration of the release of the Israelites from slavery in Egypt (see Exodus 12-13). Jesus brought his disciples together to share in his last Passover meal, which the disciples understood was a special meal because everyone in Jerusalem, and many visitors to the city, celebrated the Passover. For Jesus, this meal held more significance than the disciples appreciated.

The relationship between Jesus and the religious authorities had become tense. He had challenged their traditions and thinking and they were worried he was becoming too popular. The disciples were also aware of the tension but they seemed confident that Jesus had everything under control. Jesus did have everything under control, but not in the way the disciples thought.

On the night of the original 'Passover' the angel of death killed every first-born son but *passed over* the homes where the lintels of the doors had been smeared with the blood of a lamb. Jesus had already been referred to as the 'Lamb of God' (see John 1:29).

During his meal with the disciples, Jesus took the unleavened bread (made without yeast as a reminder of how the Israelites had to escape from Egypt as quickly as possible – there hadn't been any time to wait for the dough to rise). The bread was a symbol, recalling a significant event. Jesus took the bread, broke it and told his disciples that the bread represented his body, to be broken as a sacrifice. Next, Jesus took the wine, another symbol, and drank it. The wine was to act as a reminder of Jesus' blood, which again represented a sacrifice.

The death and sacrifice of Jesus was the only way in which a relationship with God could be restored. The symbols of the bread and the wine are constant reminders that we have continuous access to God because of the sacrifice of Jesus.   PETE TOWNSEND

Equipment:

pack of playing cards

Select sufficient cards for each member of the group to have *one* card. Make sure you include either the Queen of Clubs or the Queen of Spades, but not both. Shuffle the cards and distribute one card to each member of the group. The group must not show their card to any other member of the group. The game is simple. The holder of the black queen has to eliminate the other members of the group by winking at them once. The person winked at counts to ten, then places their card in front of them and say 'I'm out'. They must not identify the person who winked at them. If a member of the group thinks they know who's 'winking' then they are allowed to accuse them. If they are wrong, the accuser is out of the game. The game continues until everyone is 'out' or the eliminator is discovered.

It's infuriating trying to sort out the innocent and the guilty.   PETE TOWNSEND

Reflective material
(sketches, meditations and poems)

Meditation of James the Apostle

Why did he have to spoil it all?
That's what I want to know.
It was all going so well,
   way beyond our expectations,
   until he went and ruined it.
All right, so maybe he had to do something,
   maybe they were abusing the temple,
   making a mockery of what it was meant to be,
   but couldn't he have been more careful,
   more conciliatory,
   more diplomatic?
A quiet word in the right ears, surely that was the best way?
Perhaps a gesture of disapproval to get the point home,
   even a scathing condemnation, though preferably out of earshot.
But this –
   overturning their tables in a fit of rage,
   smashing their stalls,
   driving out their livestock,
   lashing out in fury;
   it was asking for it,
   guaranteed to make enemies,
   and let's face it, hardly good for his image.
A troublemaker they called him after that,
and can you blame them?
Why couldn't he have left things as they were?
They were right behind him,
   ready to do whatever he asked,
   dancing for joy in the streets,
   tearing down branches to greet him.
Oh, I know a few might still have turned against him,
   once they realised what he was saying,
   and what he wasn't –
   there would still have been some determined to do him in, I realise that.
But why did he make it easy for them?
Why invite hostility?
Why refuse to compromise?
I'm trying to understand, I really am, but it's hard.
If it had been me I'd have taken the easy way, despite my convictions –
   toned things down,

avoided confrontation,
   kept in with those who mattered.
That's why I'm still alive today and he's not.
Yet, deep down, I realise he had no other choice,
   not if he was going to be true to himself.
And he always was, I have to give him that.
That's what made him so special,
   that's why I followed him.
   that's why I still do, even now.

NICK FAWCETT

Meditation of one of the owners of the colt

Hello, I thought, what's going on here?
And you can hardly blame me,
   for there I was, minding my own business,
   when suddenly these fellows I've never clapped eyes on
   appeared from nowhere
   and, cool as you like, started to make off with our donkey!
In broad daylight, too, that's what I couldn't get over –
   bold as brass,
   without so much as a by-your-leave!
Well, you can imagine my surprise, can't you?
Hardly the kind of goings-on you expect in a quiet village like ours.
So I asked them straight, 'What's your game?'
And that's when they spoke those special words:
   'The Lord needs it.'
Not the fullest of explanations, admittedly,
   but it was all I needed,
   for straightaway it all came flooding back –
   that day when Jesus came by
   and for a wonderful few moments I met him face to face.
No, you won't have heard about it,
   for it wasn't the sort of encounter to hit the headlines –
   no stunning healing or unforgettable miracle needed in my case,
   but he touched my life as surely and wonderfully as any,
   offering a new direction,
   a fresh start from which I've never looked back.
Quite simply, he changed my life,
   and though I'm not the sort to shout it from the rooftops
   I wanted to respond nonetheless,
   to show Jesus how much he meant to me,
   how much I valued what he'd done.
This was it,
   the chance I'd been waiting for,
   my opportunity to give something back at last.

Hardly earth-shattering stuff, I grant you –
   the loan of a donkey –
   but that didn't matter;
   the fact was that Jesus had need of me
   it was all I needed to know.
He arrived soon after, and I followed him to Jerusalem,
   where the crowds were waiting to greet him,
   wild with excitement,
   shouting their praises,
   throwing down their cloaks in welcome –
   and, small though it had been, I knew I'd done my bit
   to make that great day possible.
Never forget that, whoever you are,
   however little you think you have to offer,
   for some day, some time, your moment will come –
   a day when your contribution to his kingdom
   will be requested in those lovely words:
   'The Lord needs it.'   NICK FAWCETT

Meditation of Simon the Zealot

What a day it was,
   a day I shall never forget –
   the voices raised in jubilation,
   the arms outstretched in welcome,
   the crowds lining the streets,
   waving their palm branches,
   hurling down their cloaks,
   welcoming their king,
   the Son of David,
   the one who came in the name of the Lord.
They believed that at long last the waiting was over,
   the Messiah finally come to set them free.
We believed it too, come to that.
After all his talk of suffering and death we dared to hope he'd got it wrong,
   and for a moment as I watched him I wondered if he felt the same –
   the way he responded to the cheers,
   laughter playing on his lips,
   a smile on his face,
   a twinkle in his eyes.
He was enjoying himself, I'm sure of that,
   determined to savour the moment.

But then I noticed it,
    as we drew near to Jerusalem,
    a tear in the corner of his eye –
    so unexpected.
Not a tear of joy but of sorrow,
    trickling slowly down his face,
    silent testimony to his pain.
He wasn't fooled by it all,
    not like the rest of us.
He knew what they wanted,
    how they would change.
He knew they would offer the cross if he rejected their crown,
    but still he continued, resolute to the end;
    that's the extraordinary thing.
It was a day to remember,
    a day on which they welcomed their king.
But none imagined, least of all I,
    that the crown would be made of thorns,
    and the throne reached via a cross.

NICK FAWCETT

A king on a borrowed donkey

Thinking about it

What's the point?

Jesus' entry into Jerusalem was seen as a challenge to the authorities. Perhaps, though, we could also see it as a challenge to the people's idea of what a king should be.

Doing it

Prayer

Lord Jesus,
thank you for being so special to us.
Please be with us in the things we do today,
and help us to learn to love you more. Amen.

From the known to the unknown

Have the children got bikes? What kinds? What kind of bike do they think the Queen rides? They will almost certainly have seen the Queen on television getting out of very expensive cars and the idea of her riding a bike may seem quite ludicrous to them. Yet, that's the equivalent of Jesus riding a donkey into Jerusalem!

Tell the story: Luke 19:28-40

(See page 272 for a dramatised version of this story.)

He's king in a different way

Jesus was on his way to Jerusalem – and his friends were getting excited.

'This is it,' said John to his brother James. 'He's going to take over – show them he's in charge.'

'Well, about time too,' said James. 'We've been waiting long enough – it's about time for that King Herod to find out who the real king is around here.'

'King of people's hearts is what I want to be,' Jesus reminded them, 'not the kind that bosses everyone about.' But they were so excited about the 'king' bit they never heard any of the rest.

'If you really want to do something important,' said Jesus, 'you can go and get me something to ride on when we get to Jerusalem.'

'A horse!' shouted John, gleefully. 'A big, white horse with its own armour and a proper saddle with one of those little things to put your spear in.'

'Well, a donkey actually,' Jesus answered. 'In fact, a young donkey that no one's ever ridden before.'

James was surprised. 'I know we're poor,' he said, 'but this is your one big chance. You've got to make an impression.'

'Oh, I'm going to make an impression, all right,' Jesus assured him, 'but if you think I'm going into Jerusalem done up like some kind of warlord, you've got me all wrong. Just go and get the colt for me. You'll find it just inside the village. If anyone asks you why you're taking it, just say that I need it.'

So off went James and John. 'I know what it is!' exclaimed James. 'He's playing it clever – going to sneak up on them and then strike when they're not ready.'

As he spoke, they arrived on the outskirts of Bethany where Jesus was well known. They found the colt and untied it – the owner stopped objecting when they told him who it was for – and they brought it to Jesus.

'Couldn't you have found something better than this!' scoffed Peter. 'I'm surprised it's not wearing a nappy!'

'It hasn't even got a saddle!' exclaimed Bart. 'Here, Jesus – you'd better sit on my coat.'

Some of the other disciples also put their coats on the donkey's back, and Jesus sat down. As they set out for Jerusalem there was a feeling of excitement among the disciples. They were sure this must be the big moment when God was going to give them the power to rule over everybody else.

As they got near Jerusalem, people came running to spread their coats on the road – that was their way of welcoming a great leader. On and on they travelled, with the noise growing louder all the time. People started shouting to one another about the great things they knew Jesus had done.

'He healed my daughter,' said one.

'He helped me not to feel guilty all the time,' said another.

'He cured me of a horrible disease,' a third chipped in.

'I know,' came the reply. 'If he hadn't I wouldn't be standing anywhere near to you!'

There were some people in the crowd, though, who weren't enjoying it one little bit.

Simon, the Pharisee, turned to his friend Nick and said, 'If this racket goes on, the Governor will think there's a revolution starting – and he'll blame us for it. We've got to find a way to shut this crowd up.'

'I agree,' Nick answered, 'but what can we do about it? No one's going to listen to us – they're all far too excited for that.'

'I just don't get it,' Simon grumbled. 'We look the part – all the right clothes and everything – and we're supposed to be the respected leaders around here – and no one listens to us. But give them a scruffy carpenter who hasn't combed his hair, and they're all over him.'

'Well, you must admit, he's a nice guy,' Nick pointed out, 'and he really does love people.'

'I'm getting worried about you,' Simon said, threateningly. 'You wouldn't be falling for his patter as well, would you? Anyway, love's got nothing to do with it. Religion's about good behaviour – not love.' With that, Simon pushed through the crowd to get to Jesus. 'Here,' he shouted. 'Are you going to shut these people up before some trouble starts?'

Jesus smiled at Simon. 'Shut them up?' he said. 'There's so much happiness around today that if they didn't shout the stones probably would!'

Later, as James and John returned the donkey to its owner, they were puzzled. 'What was all that about?' James wondered aloud. 'All that fuss, and he didn't make himself king. Nothing's changed.'

'Oh, I don't know,' John replied. 'I know he's not got a throne or a crown or anything, but perhaps he's our king in a different way.'

Respond to the story

Discussion

What kind of king did Jesus want to be?

- The kind that bosses people about?
- The kind that really loves people?
- One who is protected and kept separate?
- One the people can get close to?

Song

One or more of the following songs might be used here:
I will wave my hands
Jesus rode a donkey into town
Sing hosanna
There was one, there were two (The children's band)
We have a king who rides a donkey

Art and craft

Get the children to make a display of different types of transport. You could come to the session prepared with pictures for them to paste onto a large sheet of card or paper, or you could bring a selection of magazines, newspapers, catalogues, etc., and ask them to find and cut out the pictures themselves. Either way, try and get a varied selection: helicopter, limousine, family hatchback, bicycle, milk float, delivery van – and include an obviously royal coach of some kind. Then get the children to think of the kinds of people who would use these different forms of transport, and write them on cards: rock singer, king/queen, company director, newspaper deliverer, etc. Ensure that the children understand the connection between this and the story. Jesus, being a king, might have been expected to choose something a little more majestic than a common donkey, but because his is the power of love, not force, he chose something simple – because it would show the people what kind of king he wanted to be.

Draw or paint a picture of Jesus on the donkey. This is the key picture, but you might want to do others in addition to it, such as:

- The disciples untying the donkey from the wall
- People waving branches, etc.
- Pharisees plotting together   MICHAEL FORSTER

He's king in a different way – Based on Luke 19:28-40

Narrator	Jesus was on his way to Jerusalem – and his friends James and John were getting excited.
John	This is it, James. He's going to take over.
James	Well, about time too. We've been waiting long enough – it's time for that King Herod to find out who the real king is around here.
Narrator	Jesus was sad to hear them talking like that.
Jesus	King of people's hearts is what I want to be – not the kind that bosses everyone about. If you really want to do something important, go and get me something to ride on.
John	(*Gleefully*) A horse! A big, white horse with its own armour and a proper saddle with one of those leather things to put your spear in.
Jesus	Well, a donkey actually. A *young* one no one's ever ridden before.
James	I know we're poor, but this is your chance to make an impression.
Jesus	Oh, I'm going to make an impression all right, but not by going into Jerusalem done up like some kind of warlord. Go and get the colt. It's just inside the village. If anyone asks, just say I need it.
Narrator	So off they went. James thought he knew what Jesus was up to.

James   I know what it is! He's playing it clever – going to sneak up on them and then strike when they're not ready.

Narrator   As James spoke, they arrived on the outskirts of Bethany where Jesus was well known. They found the colt and untied it – the owner stopped objecting when they told him who it was for – and they brought it to Jesus. Peter wasn't impressed at all.

Peter   (*Scoffing*) Couldn't you have found something better than this? Look, Bart – I'm surprised it's not wearing a nappy!

Bart   It hasn't even got a saddle! Here, Jesus – sit on my coat.

Narrator   Some of the other disciples also put their coats on the donkey's back, and Jesus sat down. As they set out for Jerusalem there was a feeling of excitement. The disciples were sure this must be the big moment when God was going to give them the power to rule over everybody else. As they got near Jerusalem, people came running to spread their coats on the road – that was their way of welcoming a great leader. On and on they travelled, with the noise growing louder all the time. People started shouting to one another about the great things they knew Jesus had done.

Bystander 1[*] (He healed my daughter, etc.)

Bystander 2   (He set me free, etc.)

Bystander 3   (He made me clean, etc.)

Narrator   There were some people in the crowd, though, who weren't enjoying it one little bit: Simon the Pharisee and his friend Nick.

Simon   If this racket goes on, the Governor will think there's a revolution starting – and he'll blame us for it. We must find a way to shut this crowd up.

Nick   I agree, but what can we do about it? No one's going to listen to us – they're all far too excited for that.

Simon   I just don't get it. We look the part – all the right clothes and everything – and we're supposed to be the respected leaders

---

[*] Can the children think of examples, and add them to the dialogue? (Have as many bystanders as you like.)

Simon	around here – and no one listens to us. But give them a scruffy carpenter who hasn't combed his hair, and they're all over him.
Nick	Well, you must admit, he's a nice guy, and he really loves people.
Simon	(*Threateningly*) I'm getting worried about you. You wouldn't be falling for his patter as well, would you? Anyway, love has nothing to do with it. Religion's about good behaviour – not love.
Narrator	With that, Simon pushed through the crowd to get to Jesus.
Simon	Are you going to shut these people up before trouble starts?
Jesus	(*Smiling*) Shut them up? There's so much happiness around today that if they didn't shout the stones probably would!
Narrator	Later, as James and John returned the donkey to its owner, they were puzzled.
James	What was all that about? All that fuss, and he didn't make himself king. Nothing's changed.
John	Oh, I don't know . . . I know he hasn't got a throne or a crown or anything, but perhaps he's our king in a different way.

MICHAEL FORSTER

A Prayer for Jerusalem – Najwa Farah

Our heavenly Father,
    who allowed us to live in this city
    where your beloved Son was crucified and raised from the dead,
    make us worthy of its heavenly message.
We pray that the holy places will turn us
    to the things that deepen our faith
    and renew in us the hope of everlasting life.

We beseech you, Lord,
    who know what the people of all faiths in this holy city
    have suffered, and are suffering:
    uprootedness, lostness,
    the pain of being torn apart in separation,
    the pain of unsettlement, the pain of death.
We beseech you, Lord, to give this holy city
    peace built on justice.

We beseech you, Lord, to give the people of this city
   calm in their souls and courage in their hearts.
Strengthen, O God, the hearts of those of all faiths
   who work to bring justice.
Help us, God, as we pass through difficult trials,
   that we may grow to know your truth
   and that we may witness to you by our lives.

May the way of the cross be the one that we choose
   for ourselves,
   that each of us may carry his cross to follow you,
   Shepherd of our souls.
Amen.

From *Sharing Ways and Wisdoms*,
Barbara Butler

The donkey's day out – Luke 19:29-40

Donkey   Well, there I was, munching on a mouthful of hay – because that's what donkeys do – when along came these two men and started to untie me from the wall. I suppose some donkeys would have been pleased but I wasn't very keen. Besides, my mother always told me not to go off with strangers. So I dug my hooves in and refused to budge! You should have seen them trying to move me!

- They *pulled me from the front*
- They *pushed me from behind*
- They *got cross* and *waved their arms about*

And they used some words which well-brought-up religious people shouldn't even have known! Then, just as it was getting really interesting, my owner came out and spoilt it.

Owner   Hey! What do you think you're doing with my donkey?

Thomas   The master needs it.

Owner   All right. Now you stop mucking about, and go with these people!

Donkey   'Mucking about' indeed! I nearly said, 'You ain't seen nothing yet!' But I remembered some advice my mum gave me. 'Never talk to humans,' she'd said. 'It upsets them – they like to think they're the only ones who can do it.' So, off we went, and I had the time of my life!

When we got near Jerusalem, we met up with Jesus and his friends. Jesus sat on my back, and we set off into the town. What a racket! People were singing, dancing and spreading their clothes on the road for me to walk on.

I was getting a bit worried in case there was trouble. Some of the important leaders came over and gave Thomas a message for Jesus.

Thomas   Er, Jesus, some of the lawyers have asked if you can shut the people up.

Jesus   Shut them up? Impossible! There's so much joy around today that if the people didn't shout, the stones probably would!

Donkey   That told them! Mind you, it was a bit scary. I thought for a minute that Jesus was actually going to take over, and revolutions aren't really my thing. But he just went to the temple and caused a bit of a scene, while I was tied up outside. It turned out that Jesus didn't like the traders selling things in the temple, and so he threw them out – jolly good thing too! Then Thomas and Andrew took me home. I didn't think much of their conversation.

Thomas   It's strange – why didn't he ride a horse, like a real king – instead of this scruffy old donkey?

Donkey   I tell you, I nearly refused to go another step! 'Scruffy donkey,' indeed! But my mum always said, 'Never cut off your nose to spite your face,' so as we were going home, and I was tired, I pretended I hadn't heard.

Andrew   Jesus doesn't want to be the kind of king everyone's afraid of. He loves the people and he wants them to love him. So he didn't want anything impressive – just an ordinary mule.

Donkey   It got worse! 'Ordinary'! and 'Mule'! I bet I've got a better pedigree than either of those two fellows had! They will never know how close they came to being in real trouble. But we were nearly home, so I just kept on going.

I liked Jesus – he seemed different. And he treated me well. Yes, I like Jesus. But his friends – oh dear! I'm afraid they've got an awful lot to learn!

MICHAEL FORSTER

Order of Service – Holy Communion

Liturgy of the Passion

Preparation

This worship could be simple and without trimmings.
It would be most fitting for this service to be conducted in the round where possible. The altar or Communion table would be situated in the centre of the congregation and the worship should be led and directed also from within the circle. A table low to the floor could be used for Communion and the congregation could also sit on the floor instead of chairs. Cushions could be used and some chairs placed around the outer circle for those who need them. For the Eucharist the president could kneel. At the distribution members of the congregation could kneel around the table and informally offer one another the bread and wine. Instead of silverware, pottery cups and plates could be used. An unleavened loaf and red wine should make up the meal. For visual inspiration, a bowl or basin and towel could be placed next to the Communion table. For easy access to the words of the worship it would be best to use a service sheet. Sung worship and music should be simple and sensitive. Perhaps unaccompanied singing or simple harmony would be appropriate.

Order of Service

Directions

1 *Welcome and Notices*

Warm and inviting. Visitors and newcomers should be made particularly welcome.

2 *Introduction to the Service and Theme*

SHORT PAUSE

Grace, mercy and peace
from God our Father
and the Lord Jesus Christ
be with you
and also with you.

3 *Extended Time of Sung Worship*

Move directly into sung worship.

Stand

Songs

Songs may be linked together with instrumental music.

We bow down (*The Source 2*)
I bow my knee before your throne (*The Source*)
Every knee shall bow (*The Bridge*)

4 *Open Worship*

(Open to God, open prayer or praise, reflecting, sharing gifts)

The congregation may be encouraged to reflect, express gifts of the Spirit or pray out loud. It is important for the worship leader to direct sensitively at this point.

5 *Silence*

6 *Preparation and Confession*

Let us sit or kneel as we pray together:

Almighty God,
to whom all hearts are open,
all desires known,
and from whom no secrets are hidden:
cleanse the thoughts of our hearts
by the inspiration of your Holy Spirit,
that we may perfectly love you,
and worthily magnify your holy name;
through Christ our Lord. Amen.

God shows his love for us
in that, while we were still sinners,
Christ died for us.
Let us then show our love for him
by confessing our sins in penitence and faith.

We pray together:

Most merciful God,
Father of our Lord Jesus Christ,
we confess that we have sinned
in thought, word and deed.
We have not loved you with our whole heart.
We have not loved our neighbours as ourselves.
In your mercy
forgive what we have been,
help us to amend what we are,
and direct what we shall be;
that we may do justly,
love mercy,
and walk humbly with you, our God.
Amen.

Almighty God,
who forgives all who truly repent,
have mercy upon *you*,
pardon and deliver *you* from all *your* sins,
confirm and strengthen *you* in all goodness,
and keep *you* in life eternal;
through Jesus Christ our Lord.
Amen.

Collect

Almighty and everlasting God,
who in your tender love towards the human race
sent your Son our Saviour Jesus Christ
to take upon him our flesh
and to suffer death upon the cross:
grant that we may follow the example
of his patience and humility,
and also be made partakers of his resurrection;
through Jesus Christ your Son our Lord,
who is alive and reigns with you,
in the unity of the Holy Spirit,
one God, now and for ever. **Amen.**

7 *The Liturgy of the Word*

Reading

Short time of silence

No announcement of the readings. Should be an unbroken time of listening and reflecting.

Gospel Reading

Short time of silence

Sermon

Sermon linked to theme and readings. Informative but also challenging and affirming. Should lead people to point of response or action encouraging them on their journey of discipleship.

8 *Silence*

For reflection and prayerful response

Worship leader should initiate and guide people's response during silence.

9 *Prayers*

If we have any encouragement
from being united with Christ,
if any comfort from his love,
if any fellowship from the Spirit,
if any tenderness or compassion,
then let us be like minded, having the same love,
being one in Spirit and purpose.
Let us do nothing out of selfish ambition
or vain conceit,
but in humility consider others better
than ourselves.
Each of us should look not only to our own
interests,
but also to the interests of others.
Our attitude should be the same as that of
Christ Jesus.
Grant us, Lord, **your servant heart. Amen.**

The prayers follow the silence unannounced.

Lord, you are in very nature God.
You made yourself nothing
and took the very nature of a servant,
being made in human likeness.
You humbled yourself and became obedient
to death – even death on a cross!
Help all our leaders in government and
in the church to reflect in some small way
the same humility and self-denial.
By putting the lives of others first
and sacrificing their own interests
they will lead by the best of examples
and reflect you, the servant king
who made humility a way of life.

Silence

Grant us, Lord, **your servant heart. Amen.**

Master, God exalted you to the highest place
and gave you the name that is above every name.
That at the name of Jesus every knee should bow,
in heaven and on earth and under the earth,
and every tongue confess that you are Lord,
to the glory of God the Father.

PAUSE

We pray that your name will be exalted
in all the earth,
that the people of this nation will know
    you are Lord,
that this church will be a place
where people meet with you,
and that we will make you visible wherever we go.

Silence

Jesus, as Lord of all we ask you to be near to those
in need – the sick, the grieving, the lonely
    and the poor.

Silence

Lord, you have the power to heal and to save
and we ask you to bring healing and wholeness
where there is pain and suffering.
We ask too that you will empower us
    with your Spirit
and send us out to serve people
with your love.

Grant us, Lord, **your servant heart. Amen.**

O God, help us to carry on working out our
salvation with fear and trembling,
for it is you who works in us
to will and to act according to your good purpose.
May we shine like stars in the heavens
as we hold out the word of life
and each day join with all the saints
and all of creation to honour and exalt you.

Grant us, Lord, **your servant heart. Amen.**

The Creed

Let us stand to say the Creed:

We believe in one God,
the Father, the Almighty,
maker of heaven and earth,
of all that is,
seen and unseen.

We believe in one Lord, Jesus Christ,
the only Son of God,
eternally begotten of the Father,
God from God, Light from Light,
true God from true God,
begotten, not made,
of one Being with the Father;
through him all things were made.
For us and for our salvation
he came down from heaven,
was incarnate from the Holy Spirit
and the Virgin Mary
and was made man.
For our sake he was crucified under Pontius Pilate;
he suffered death and was buried.
On the third day he rose again
in accordance with the Scriptures;
he ascended into heaven
and is seated at the right hand of the Father.
He will come again in glory
to judge the living and the dead,
and his kingdom will have no end.

We believe in the Holy Spirit,
the Lord, the giver of life,
who proceeds from the Father and the Son,

who with the Father and the Son
is worshipped and glorified,
who has spoken through the prophets.
**We believe in one holy, catholic and apostolic
    Church.
We acknowledge one baptism
for the forgiveness of sins.
We look for the resurrection of the dead,
and the life of the world to come. Amen.**

10 *The Peace*

Once we were far off,
but now in union with Christ Jesus
we have been brought near
through the shedding of Christ's blood,
for he is our peace.
The peace of the Lord be always with you
and also with you.
Let us offer one another a sign of peace.

All may exchange a sign of peace.

All may sit.

Song to minister
At the foot of the cross (*The Source*)

11 *The Eucharistic Prayer (A)*

The Lord is here.
His Spirit is with us.

Lift up your hearts.
We lift them to the Lord.

Let us give thanks to the Lord our God.
It is right to give thanks and praise.

It is indeed right,
it is our duty and our joy,
at all times and in all places
to give you thanks and praise,
holy Father, heavenly King,
almighty and eternal God,
through Jesus Christ your Son our Lord.

And now we give you thanks
because, for our salvation,
he was obedient even to death on the cross.

Encourage the congregation to
share the Peace with one another in
the centre of the circle.

This song should be sung for the
congregation to help prepare their
hearts for Communion. Encourage
them to meditate on the words.

The tree of shame was made the tree of glory;
and where life was lost, there life has been
restored.

Therefore with angels and archangels,
and with all the company of heaven,
we proclaim your great and glorious name,
for ever praising you and *saying*:

Holy, holy, holy Lord,
God of power and might,
heaven and earth are full of your glory.
Hosanna in the highest.

Accept our praises, heavenly Father,
through your Son our Saviour Jesus Christ,
and as we follow his example and obey
    his command,
grant that by the power of your Holy Spirit
these gifts of bread and wine
may be to us his body and his blood;

who, in the same night that he was betrayed,
took bread and gave you thanks;
he broke it and gave it to his disciples, saying:
Take, eat; this is my body which is given for you;
do this in remembrance of me.

To you be glory and praise for ever.

In the same way, after supper
he took the cup and gave you thanks;
he gave it to them saying:
Drink this, all of you;
this is my blood of the new covenant,
which is shed for you and for many
for the forgiveness of sins.
Do this, as often as you drink it,
in remembrance of me.

To you be glory and praise for ever.

Therefore, heavenly Father,
we remember his offering of himself
made once for all upon the cross;
we proclaim his mighty resurrection
and glorious ascension;

we look for the coming of your kingdom,
and with this bread and this cup
we make the memorial of Christ your Son
    our Lord.

Jesus Christ is Lord:
**Lord, by your cross and resurrection
you have set us free.
You are the Saviour of the world.**

Accept through him, our great high priest,
this our sacrifice of thanks and praise,
and as we eat and drink these holy gifts
in the presence of your divine majesty,
renew us by your Spirit,
inspire us with your love
and unite us in the body of your Son,
Jesus Christ our Lord.

To you be glory and praise for ever.

Through him, and with him, and in him,
in the unity of the Holy Spirit,
with all who stand before you in earth
    and heaven,
we worship you, Father almighty,
in songs of everlasting praise:

**Blessing and honour and glory and power
be yours for ever and ever. Amen.**

12 *The Lord's Prayer*

Let us pray for the coming of God's kingdom
in the words our Saviour taught us.
**Our Father in heaven,
hallowed be your name,
your kingdom come,
your will be done,
on earth as in heaven.
Give us today our daily bread.
Forgive us our sins
as we forgive those who sin against us.
Lead us not into temptation
but deliver us from evil.**

For the kingdom, the power,
and the glory are yours
now and for ever. Amen.

13 *Breaking of the Bread*

The president breaks the consecrated bread.
Come, take this bread, this is his body.
Eat and think of him, this is our saving grace.
Take, this his cup, blood shed for many.
Drink and think of him, this is our saving grace.

We do not presume
to come to this your table, merciful Lord,
trusting in our own righteousness,
but in your manifold and great mercies.
We are not worthy
so much as to gather up the crumbs
under your table.
But you are the same Lord
whose nature is always to have mercy.
Grant us, therefore, gracious Lord,
so to eat the flesh of your dear Son Jesus Christ
and to drink his blood,
that our sinful bodies may be made clean
by his body
and our souls washed
  through his most precious blood,
and that we may evermore dwell in him,
and he in us.
Amen.

The president and people receive Communion.

Encourage the congregation to
approach the table informally,
kneel if possible and offer one
another Communion. Enough cups
and plates should be used so that
people are not lingering too long.
Prayer ministry could be available.

Songs
What kind of love is this (*The Source*)
How deep the Father's love for us (*The Source*)
Here is love (*The Source*)

Sung worship should be gentle and
sensitive. Perhaps solo singing
would be appropriate.
Instrumental music linking the
songs would be effective and help
create an environment of reflection
and prayer. Towards the
conclusion of Communion the
music ends.

14 *Silence*

15 *Prayer after Communion*

Lord Jesus Christ,
you humbled yourself in taking the form
  of a servant,
and in obedience died on the cross for our salvation:
give us the mind to follow you

and to proclaim you as Lord and King,
to the glory of God the Father.

Almighty God,
we thank you for feeding us
with the body and blood of your Son Jesus Christ.
Through him we offer you our souls and bodies
to be a living sacrifice.
Send us out in the power of your Spirit
to live and work to your praise and glory. Amen.

Before the Blessing offer the opportunity for prayer after the service. Perhaps the worship highlighted a need for response, healing or advice.

16 *The Blessing and Dismissal*

The Lord bless you and keep you;
the Lord make his face shine upon you
and be gracious to you;
the Lord turn his face toward you
and give you peace. (Numbers 6:24-26)

Go in peace to love and serve the Lord.
In the name of Christ. Amen.

17 *Prayer Ministry*

(Continues as needed)

Soft worship music could be played as people leave and whilst prayer continues.

TIM LOMAX

Maundy Thursday

The Last Supper and the anguish of Gethsemane

John 13:1-17, 31b-35

(also Exodus 12:1-4(5-10), 11-14; Psalm 116:1-2, 12-19; 1 Corinthians 11:23-26)

A reading from the Gospel of John 13:33-38

'I shall not be with you much longer,' said Jesus to his friends after Judas had gone out of the room. 'Love one another – this is my "new commandment". Love one another in the same way as I have loved you. This will be the mark by which everybody will recognise that you are my friends – the way in which you love one another.'

'Sir,' said Peter, 'where are you going?'

'You cannot go with me now where I am going,' said Jesus. 'You will go with me later on.'

'Sir,' said Peter, 'why can't I go with you now? I'll die in your defence.'

'You'll die in my defence?' said Jesus. 'Believe me, before the cock crows, you will say three times that you are no friend of mine.'   ALAN DALE

Introductory material

Tonight we find ourselves very far from the buoyant mood of Palm Sunday. We recall how Jesus shared a last supper with his friends – and we share in our turn, in remembrance of him. We recall his anguish in Gethsemane as the time of his death drew near. This evening reminds us, as few other days can, of the sheer human cost of the love shown to us in Jesus Christ.   NICK FAWCETT

Prayers

Praise – The broken Christ

Lord God, almighty and omnipotent,
    for your love that goes on creating,
        your power that goes on strengthening,
        your mercy that goes on forgiving,
        your purpose that goes on working,
        and your goodness that goes on giving:
    Receive our praise.

Lord Jesus Christ,
    revealer of the Father's love,
        proof of his power,
        instrument of his forgiveness,
        fulfiller of his purpose,
        agent of his goodness:
    Receive our praise.

Loving God,
    in the name of Christ we worship you,
        we welcome you,
        we acknowledge your greatness,
        we celebrate your goodness.
    Receive our praise.

Lord Jesus Christ,
    once despised and rejected,
        broken and beaten,
        condemned and crucified,
        we welcome you as our risen Lord;
        the King of love,
        the Prince of Peace,
        the Lord of lords,
        the bringer of life.
    Receive our praise.

Loving God,
    you showed us through Christ
        that what seemed to be weakness was strength,
        what appeared to be defeat was victory.
        what appeared to be the end was a new beginning.
    Receive our praise.

Forgive us for so easily being deceived by appearances,
    for measuring success by our own flawed standards.
Teach us to recognise that it is
    not only in the risen Christ but the broken Christ,
    not only in the victorious Christ but the crucified Christ,
    not only in the living Christ but the dying Christ,
    that we see your purposes fulfilled
    and your will being done.
Receive our praise,
    in his name.
Amen.   NICK FAWCETT

Confession – Broken by us

Lord Jesus Christ,
    we are happy to remember that you were broken *for* us,
        less willing to acknowledge that you were broken *by* us;
        yet that is the inescapable truth.
    You took on *our* punishment,
        suffered for *our* sin,
        paid the price for *our* mistakes,
        so that we might receive mercy and discover new life.
    For all the ways we continue to break your body,
        gracious Saviour, forgive us.

You call us to break bread and share wine
    in remembrance of you,
    but, though outwardly we obey,
    inwardly it is a different story,
    our lack of love,
    timid witness,
    stunted vision
    and half-hearted commitment,
    each revealing our forgetfulness of your love.
For all the ways we continue to break your body,
    gracious Saviour, forgive us.

You call us to live as your people,
    a family testifying to your grace
    through the love we show for one another
    and the unity we share,
    but all too often we demonstrate division,
    mistrust,
    intolerance,
    even hatred.
For all the ways we continue to break your body,
    gracious Saviour, forgive us.

You call us to minister in your name,
    to express your care for all through word and deed,
    but day after day we let you down.
Through the compassion we fail to show,
    the love we fail to express
    and the justice we fail to fight for;
    through the hungry we fail to feed,
    the sick we fail to visit
    and the needy we fail to clothe;
    through the truths we distort,
    the hurt we cause

and the selfishness we indulge in,
we inflict more pain upon you,
driving the nails once more through your hands and feet,
hanging you once again upon your cross.
For all the ways we continue to break your body,
gracious Saviour, forgive us.

Lord Jesus Christ,
broken *for* us,
broken *by* us,
you owe us nothing,
we owe you everything,
for you gave your all to set us free,
and yet still we fail you,
time after time,
day after day.
For all the ways we continue to break your body,
gracious Saviour, forgive us.

Cleanse us,
renew us
and restore us
for your name's sake.
Amen.   NICK FAWCETT

Petition – A challenging prospect

Lord Jesus Christ,
we want to follow you,
to walk where you would lead
and travel the road of faithful discipleship,
but, though that desire is real,
sometimes the way is hard and the path uncertain,
such that we wonder if we can see the journey through.
We look to you for guidance:
lead us forward in faith.

Despite all our talk of commitment,
our service is weak and our faith is poor.
We are afraid of the unknown,
nervous of anything that involves risk
and the possibility of sacrifice.
We want to be sure of our ground,
clear as to what is being asked of us.
We look to you for guidance:
lead us forward in faith.

Like the disciples before us,
  we seek some guarantee it will all be worth it.
Teach us today, through the example you gave,
  to walk by faith and not by sight.
We look to you for guidance:
  lead us forward in faith.

Remind us that our trust is in things unseen,
  that you hold in store for us things too wonderful
  for words ever to express.
Inspire us with the prospect of your eternal kingdom
  in which there will be no more pain or sorrow,
  no more darkness or death,
  but where we will be one with you and all your people
  for all eternity.
We look to you for guidance:
  lead us forward in faith.

Remind us that, for the joy set before you,
  you endured the cross,
  disregarding its shame,
  and that you sit now at the right hand of the throne of God.
Teach us to trust in you, the pioneer and perfecter of our faith,
  and so let us lay aside everything that holds us back
  and run with perseverance the race that is set before us.
We look to you for guidance:
  lead us forward in faith.

For your name's sake.
Amen.   NICK FAWCETT

Intercession

The new Covenant between God and his people. The passover feast was an annual celebration of God freeing his people from slavery. The blood of the lamb protected them, and was both a sacrifice and food before their journey. Now Christ offers himself in the bread and wine and in the washing of feet. His sacrifice frees us from sin's slavery.

We belong to the body of Christ.
In his name let us pray to the Father
for the Church and for the world.

We commend to your care and protection
all who are abused, imprisoned or insulted
because of their faith.

Silence for prayer

Lord, by your example:
teach us all to love.

We commend to your light and truth
all governments and committees,
every head of state, and all leaders.

Silence for prayer

Lord, by your example:
teach us all to love.

We commend to your longsuffering patience
and compassion, ourselves,
with our frequent misuse of your blessings
and failure to serve.

Silence for prayer

Lord, by your example:
teach us all to love.

We commend to your healing and wholeness
all who are ill or injured;
those undergoing surgery
and those nearing death.

Silence for prayer

Lord, by your example:
teach us all to love.

We commend to your light and lasting peace
all those who have died, especially . . .

Silence for prayer

We thank you, Lord,
for all your guidance and loving care;
fulfil our needs in the way which is best for us
in the context of eternity.

Silence for prayer

Merciful Father,
**accept these prayers
for the sake of your Son,
our Saviour Jesus Christ, Amen.**

SUSAN SAYERS

Short prayers

Lord Jesus Christ,
    you broke bread with your disciples
    and shared wine,
    and told them to go on doing likewise
    in memory of you.
For countless years,
    across countless generations,
    your people have done just that.
And so now we come,
    to share in your supper,
    and to remember.
Lord Jesus Christ,
    this night of all nights reminds us
    of the great truths of the Gospel –
    of who you were, of what you did,
    of why you came, of when you shall come again.   NICK FAWCETT

Lord Jesus Christ,
    we praise you for your love
    which knows no bounds,
    your grace which was prepared to suffer so much
    for our sakes.
Forgive us that we forget sometimes
    how much it all cost you,
    the inner turmoil, the sorrow,
    the pain you endured to make us whole.
Speak to us afresh through all we share
    this evening,
    and help us to show our response
    not just through these few moments' worship
    but through lives offered in service to you.
In your name we pray.
Amen.   NICK FAWCETT

All-age-talk material

Jesus' friends are hiding because they're afraid. Can you spot them in the picture?

I am with you always. (Matthew 28:20)

```
A E T S S E N K R A D O
O B E D I E F S I L W B
B G A R D L A A C H A H
E D A R K N E P I A T O
D R A Y L W E N R T C P
T G E F E A R B C A H E
S I L E N J E S U E Y T
W A A T N E I D E B O H
G E T W H S E M A N E D
T R S T S U R T R U S E
I G E T H S E M A N E M
N E W L I F E D A R K A
```

WORDSEARCH

Find the following words in the grid:

GETHSEMANE, JESUS, DARKNESS, WATCH, WAIT, PRAY, SILENCE, FAITH, OBEDIENT, GARDEN, FEAR, TRUST, HOPE, NEW LIFE.

Reflective material
(sketches, meditations and poems)

Denial

Lord, forgive us,
   that, like Peter,
   we can swear we do not know you
   even louder than we swore
   when we said we'd never leave you.

Lord, forgive us:
Lord, forgive us.

   Lord, forgive us
   when our courage
   is a thing of bluff and bluster,
   which, when someone calls our bluff,
   soon dissolves in tears and fluster.

Lord, forgive us:
Lord, forgive us.

Lord, forgive us
   when we praise you
   with our lips, but not our action;
   may the cock-crow wake us up
   from our blind self-satisfaction.

Lord, forgive us:
Lord, forgive us.

Lord, redeem us
   when we fail you
   not just three times, but more often;
   may our conscience not grow hard,
   lest it grow too hard to soften.

Lord, redeem us:
Lord, redeem us.

When hosannas
   turn to catcalls
   and we're tempted to deny you,
   give us faith that will not fade
   and the courage to stand by you.

Keep us faithful:
Keep us faithful.   PETER DAINTY

We were there to celebrate Passover

Reading: Matthew 26:17-20

On the first day of Unleavened Bread the disciples came to Jesus, saying, 'Where do you want us to make the preparations for you to eat the Passover?' He said, 'Go into the city to a certain man, and say to him, "The Teacher says, My time is near; I will keep the Passover at your house with my disciples."' So the disciples did as Jesus had directed them, and they prepared the Passover meal.

When it was evening, he took his place with the twelve; and while they were eating, he said, 'Truly I tell you, one of you will betray me.'

Meditation of Matthew

We were there to celebrate Passover,
    the twelve of us and Jesus, together in the upper room.
And I don't mind telling you
    our hearts were pounding,
    our pulses racing,
    our imaginations running riot.
I mean, the Passover!
You know the significance of that, surely?
A reminder of God delivering his people,
    setting them free from captivity,
    opening the way to a new and different life.
Well, what were we to expect?
Oh, it's easy now, looking back, to realise we were wrong,
    but at the time it seemed to all of us,
    all except Judas anyway,
    that this was it,
    the moment we'd been waiting for,
    the time when Jesus would pull the rabbit out of the hat,
    turn the tables on his enemies,
    show us he was in control after all.
 Only then, whilst we were eating together,
    enjoying ourselves more than we had in a long time,
    he stood,
    quietly,
    solemnly,
    and we could see from the look in his eyes,
    the set of his face,
    that he had other ideas.
 He took the bread,
    lifted it high,
    then broke it –
    enough for all of us –
    'This is my body, broken for you; do this in remembrance of me.'

And before we had time to argue,
    time even to take in what he was saying,
    he was holding the cup,
    passing it round –
    'Take this and drink. This cup is the new covenant sealed in my blood.'
We were staggered,
    horrified,
    and to tell the truth more than a little shocked.
All right, so he'd talked of death before,
    often,
    too often,
    but we'd never actually believed it.
We thought he was exaggerating, I suppose,
    painting the blackest picture to keep us on our toes.
But here he was, if we'd heard him right, offering his own epitaph,
    saying his final farewells,
    preparing us for the end.
And he was of course, in a sense;
    it was the end of a chapter,
    the last page of the book.
Yet it wasn't over,
    by no means the end of the story;
    that had only just begun,
    and we, astonishingly, were part of it –
    his body, here on earth,
    the sequel to what he had started!
Well, we've done as he said,
    week after week,
    year after year,
    breaking bread and sharing wine,
    reminding ourselves of who he is and who we are,
    of what he has done and what we have still to do;
    and we'll go on sharing his supper,
    gladly,
    humbly,
    confidently,
    until he comes.
                                                            NICK FAWCETT

Meditation of Philip, the Apostle

He couldn't mean me, surely? –
   that's what I kept telling myself –
   one of the others perhaps, but not me.
I would stay true, if nobody else did,
   dependable to the last,
   someone he could stake his life on if he needed to.
Yet could he?
Deep down, despite my protestations, I wondered,
   for, to tell the truth, I was scared out of my wits,
   dreading what the future might hold for us.
It was suddenly all too real,
   the prospect of suffering and death,
   those warnings Jesus had given
   no longer simply words we could push aside,
   but fact staring us in the face.
His enemies were gathering for the kill,
   greedily waiting their moment,
   and it was only a matter of time
   before they came for the rest of us.
We'd kept on smiling until then,
   putting a brave face on things as best we could,
   if not for his sake then our own.
But suddenly there could be no more running away,
   for in that stark sentence he spelt out the awful truth:
   'One of you will betray me.'
We protested, of course, vehement in our denials,
   yet one by one we looked away, unable to meet his gaze.
It *wasn't* me, I'm glad to say,
   but, of course, you'll know that by now, won't you?
It was Judas who finally couldn't take it,
   Judas whose name will go down in history
   as the one who betrayed Jesus
Yet somehow that doesn't help,
   for the truth is this:
   when the moment came we were all found wanting,
   all more concerned for our own safety than his.
Maybe we didn't betray him,
   but don't think we're feeling smug about it,
   still less like twisting the knife in Judas,
   for that moment – there in the upper room –
   made us all take a long hard look at ourselves,
   and we didn't much like what we saw.

NICK FAWCETT

Meditation of Peter

He was broken-hearted, if you ask me,
   and I can't say I blame him.
I think I'd have felt the same.
You see, he'd expected it from the others –
   the Scribes and Pharisees –
   he knew they had it in for him from the start.
And the crowds who'd followed him, welcomed him into Jerusalem –
   he wasn't taken in by them,
    not for a moment.
Even Judas,
   he saw the truth about him before anyone else had an inkling.
But the rest of us, I think he'd hoped for something better.
Not that he asked much.
He knew I'd deny him, despite all my protestations of loyalty,
   and he knew we'd all run for it when it was our skins on the line.
He'd accepted that, and still loved us, God knows why!
But there in the garden, that's when he needed us most,
   that's when he'd hoped for that little bit more.
Just to know we cared,
   that we were behind him,
   that we were there.
It would have meant so much.
And we failed him, even in that one simple thing.
I still don't know how it happened.
I tried,
   I really tried,
   but somehow I just couldn't keep my eyes open.
I can forgive myself the rest;
   it was my life at stake after all.
But to stay awake just one hour.
It wasn't much to ask, was it?
And I couldn't do even that.
He was broken-hearted,
   the stuffing knocked right out of him,
   and I know in large part it was all down to me.

NICK FAWCETT

Meditation of Peter

He was unsure of himself,
   for the first time in his life
   unsure of his ability to face the future,
   and it hurt him more than the pain he was finally to suffer.
You see, there'd never been any doubt until then,
   never even the slightest suggestion of hesitation.

Despite the hostility, the resentment, the abuse from so many,
   he'd set his face resolutely towards Jerusalem,
   knowing from the very beginning where it would all end.
He understood it all,
   the pain and humiliation he must suffer,
   conscious of it even way back
   in those heady days of his baptism,
   yet he'd carried on willingly,
   the prospect seeming to hold no fear for him,
   and we'd marvelled at the faith, the love,
   the courage of the man,
   the sheer commitment
   which gave him such awesome strength and inner purpose.
But suddenly, that evening, it was all so very different,
   a shadow blotting out the light which had shone so brightly.
I saw despair in his eyes rather than hope,
   fear rather than laughter,
   sorrow rather than joy,
   and, most terrible of all, that desperate look of uncertainty,
   so alien,
   so devastating,
   so crushing a burden.
It was all suddenly too real,
   no longer theory but fact –
   the agony and the isolation he was about to face –
   and, like any of us would in his place, he wanted to back away,
   find an easier course,
   a less dreadful option.
It struck me then, as never before,
   that he didn't know what lay beyond death
   any more than I did.
He'd always believed,
   always trusted,
   but he had no more certainty than you and me –
   only the assurance of faith,
   the conviction borne of trust,
   and there in the darkness,
   as the chill of night took hold,
   it all hung on a thread
   as he wrestled with the torment of doubt.
I know what I'd have done had I been him –
   quite simply, I wouldn't have stopped running
   until Jerusalem was just a memory!
But not Jesus.
He stayed quietly in the garden, as I knew he would,

and he offered not just his *faith* but his *doubt* to God –
  'not *my* will but *yours* be done'.
Well, he was sure of one thing after that –
  there was no way back,
  death now a cast-iron certainty;
  but it wasn't dying itself that was the problem for him,
  it was not knowing whether it would all be worth it,
  whether it could actually make a difference
  to this world we live in,
  and there was no way of answering that for certain
  this side of eternity.
He was unsure –
  of himself,
  of his faith,
  of his ability to face the future –
  but despite it all he risked everything,
  offering life itself,
  so that we might know the truth,
  and be free from death –
  free for all eternity!

NICK FAWCETT

Meditation of one of the Priests

Reading: Matthew 26:14-16

Then one of the twelve, who was called Judas Iscariot, went to the chief priests and said, 'What will you give me if I betray him to you?' They paid him thirty pieces of silver. And from that moment he began to look for an opportunity to betray him.

Reading: Matthew 27:3-5

When Judas, his betrayer, saw that Jesus was condemned, he repented and brought back the thirty pieces of silver to the chief priests and elders. He said, 'I have sinned by betraying innocent blood.' But they said, 'What is that to us? See to it yourself.' Throwing down the pieces of silver in the temple, he departed; and he went and hanged himself.

Meditation

Thirty pieces of silver, that's all it took –
  thirty measly pieces of silver to betray his closest friend.
Can you believe that?
We couldn't.
We'd expected a hundred at least, probably more,
  but we started low, just to play safe,
  expecting him to haggle,
  see how high we'd go.

You should have seen him though –
   hardly able to contain himself,
   eyes almost popping out of his head –
   he could hardly keep his hands off it, the greedy devil!
I honestly think he'd have settled for less if we'd pushed him.
But we were in no mood for playing hard to get –
   after three years of scheming,
three years of waiting,
   we'd finally got our man where we wanted him,
   for thirty pieces of silver!
Money – the depths people will sink to for it,
   selling their very souls;
   it's incredible, pathetic really.
As if anyone can really imagine it can buy them happiness!
Well, it didn't do Judas much good, that's for sure –
   just a few days later and there he was again,
   crawling over our doorstep, actually expecting sympathy.
'I've been a fool,' he told us.
   'Betrayed an innocent man.'
And he tried to give the money back.
Well, he was a bit late for that, wasn't he?
A little far on in the day to start having scruples;
   the damage was done, from his point of view anyway.
There was no going back –
   Jesus was done for,
   all over bar the shouting –
   we couldn't have undone his actions even if we'd wanted to,
   but we didn't, of course,
   and to be truthful we rather enjoyed watching him squirm.
Served the wretch right,
   that's how we saw it, even if he had done us a favour.
Anyway, we told him eventually to get lost;
   he'd made his bed, he could lie on it
Only he couldn't, not any more.
He couldn't live with himself,
   couldn't carry on with the knowledge of what he'd done.
He hanged himself apparently,
   and good riddance as far as we were concerned.
But there's an odd twist to it all,
   a little detail which even now I'm trying to make sense of,
   for that night in the garden when he betrayed Jesus –
   with a kiss of all things –
   do you know what Jesus said to him?
   'Friend, do what you are here to do.'
Friend!

God's truth, that's what he said.
Well, with friends like that who needs enemies, that's all I can say.
Yet Jesus, apparently,
   even though he knew what Judas was up to,
   even though he saw right through him,
   still had time for him.
It's a mystery to me,
   but then Jesus always was, wasn't he?
It may sound daft, but if Jesus has made it
   to that heavenly kingdom he was always on about,
   I actually think he'll have found room there even for Judas,
   despite everything!

Prayer

Lord Jesus Christ,
   it's easy to condemn Judas –
   the man who let you down,
   the man who, with so much going for him, threw it all away.
Yet in our hearts we know we have no right to judge.
Each day in so many ways we betray you,
   we betray ourselves, we betray our loved ones.
We say one thing but do another.
We talk of high ideals but we fail to reach them.
We mean well but we act foolishly.
Lord Jesus Christ,
   save us from judging others, lest we too be judged.

NICK FAWCETT

Meditation of Annas

Angry? You bet I was!
Wouldn't you have been?
It beggared belief the things this man had said and done –
   violating the sabbath,
   flouting the scripture,
   contradicting our teaching,
   presuming even to forgive sins –
   who did he think he was, the Son of God or something?
I was seething,
   barely able to restrain myself as he stood before me,
   so when one of my men lashed out
   and struck him across the face,
   let's put it this way, I made no attempt to intervene.

It wouldn't have been so bad had he been a priest or a rabbi –
   at least then he'd have had some claim to authority,
   some grounds perhaps to speak out.
But he wasn't any of those, was he? –
   just some self-styled teacher from Galilee
   without even the first idea
   about the finer points of the law.
Yet was he sorry when they dragged him in?
Was there any sign of remorse,
   even a hint of regret?
Not a bit of it!
Blatant defiance, more like,
   a total disregard for his spiritual betters.
I'll give him one thing, though –
   he made no attempt to duck the issue
   as some might have done,
   no cowering behind half-truths or lame excuses.
We'd been prepared for that,
   even hauled in some false witnesses just in case,
   but it was clear they wouldn't be needed,
   this man happy, apparently, to condemn himself
   out of his own mouth.
That's the one thing I can't understand –
   he made it easy for us,
   almost too easy,
   as though he wanted it all to happen,
   as though he welcomed the prospect of death.
It wasn't just the trial that set me thinking, but before that:
   why, for example, he came to Jerusalem in the first place –
he must have known the knives were out for him;
   and why he waited there in the garden
   after Judas slipped away into the darkness –
   did he really have no idea we'd set him up?
Perhaps he was just teasing us,
   believing God would deliver him at the last?
Or did he expect the mob to rise up in rebellion,
   to take us by storm and set him free?
Well, if he did, he showed no sign of it.
It's a mystery to me,
   I have to confess,
   and there are times when I catch myself thinking
   we were the ones set up that night,
   not *him* –
   that for all *our* scheming *he* was the one
   who finally called the tune.

I'm wrong of course,
   I must be,
   for where did it get him? –
   off to Caiaphas,
   off to Herod,
   off to Pilate,
   off finally to the cross and that ghastly, grisly end.
Not even Jesus could have wanted that, could he?
Surely not!   NICK FAWCETT

Don't be afraid to pray –
to pray is sometimes the only thing we can do.
Keep going . . . keep praying.
Pray through the shadow and the darkness,
pray through the Gethsemane experience.
God is there.
                        J. S. Steward   from *You're Never Alone*
                                                          ELIZABETH RUNDLE

Good Friday

Jesus offers his all to bring life to all

John 18:1-19:42

(also Isaiah 52:13-53:12; Psalm 22; Hebrews 10:16-25 or Hebrews 4:14-16, 5:7-9)

The last days

In the Garden   John 18:1-12

Jesus left the house with his friends and crossed the Kidron Brook to the other side of the valley. They came to a garden and went inside. They knew it well, for Jesus and his friends had often met there.

Judas knew this, and he led a detachment of Roman soldiers and a company of Jewish police straight to the spot. They were fully armed and carried lanterns and torches.

Jesus stepped out to meet them. 'Who do you want?' he asked.

'Jesus from Nazareth,' they answered.

'I'm the man you want, then,' said Jesus.

At these words, they stepped back and fell on the ground.

'Who do you want?' asked Jesus again.

'Jesus from Nazareth,' they repeated.

'I've told you – I'm the man you want,' he said. 'If it's me you're after, let these men go.'

Peter drew his sword and struck at a slave of the High Priest and cut off his right ear.

'Put your sword up,' said Jesus. 'Do you want to stop me facing what God the Father has set before me?'

The soldiers then arrested Jesus and handcuffed him.

Before Annas   John 18:13, 15-27

The soldiers took Jesus before Annas, the most powerful man in Jerusalem City. He was not the High Priest of the Jewish people. Caiaphas was the High Priest that year; Annas was his father-in-law.

Now Jesus had a friend whose name we do not know. He was not one of the 'Twelve', but belonged to one of the most important families in Jerusalem; the High Priest knew him well. He was the 'other friend'.

Peter and the 'other friend' followed Jesus along the road. When they got to the courtyard, the 'other friend' went straight in with Jesus; Peter was left standing outside at the door. The 'other friend' came back and had a word with the girl on duty at the door and then took him inside.

'You're one of this fellow's friends, too, aren't you?' the girl asked Peter.

'Not I,' said Peter.

It was a cold night, and the slaves and court officers had lit a charcoal fire. They were standing round it, trying to keep warm. Peter joined the crowd round the fire; he wanted to get warm too.

The High Priest asked Jesus about his friends and what he stood for.

'What I have had to say,' said Jesus, 'I have said openly for everybody to hear. I have talked in the Meeting Houses, and I have talked in the Temple to Jewish people from all over the world. I have not been plotting in back rooms. Why ask me questions now? Ask the ordinary people in the villages and in this city. They heard me. They know what it was I talked about.'

One of the court officials standing near him gave him a slap on the face. 'Is that the way to talk to the High Priest?' he said.

'If I did something wrong,' said Jesus to the officer, 'prove it. If I didn't, why hit me?'

Annas had Jesus handcuffed again and sent to Caiaphas.

Peter was still standing near the fire, getting warm.

'You are one of this fellow's friends too, aren't you?' said some of the men by the fire.

'Not on your life,' said Peter.

Now it happened that one of the court officers standing there was a relative of the man Peter had slashed with his sword.

'I saw you in the garden with him, didn't I?' he asked.

'No, you didn't,' said Peter.

At that moment, somewhere in the distance a cock crowed.

Before the Roman Governor   John 18:28-31, 33-40; 19:1-16a

It was now Friday, the day before the Great Feast.

Just before dawn Jesus was marched into the headquarters of Pilate, the Roman Governor.

The Jewish leaders stayed outside the building (it was 'unclean' to them because it belonged to foreigners, and, if they had gone inside, they would not have been allowed, by Jewish law, to take part in the Great Feast). So Pilate came outside.

'What's the charge against this man?' he asked.

'He's a criminal,' they said. 'Would we have brought him here if he wasn't?'

'Well, take him off and deal with him yourselves,' said Pilate. 'You've got your own laws and law courts.'

'But we can't pass the death sentence,' they replied.

Pilate went back into the building and had Jesus brought before him.

'So you're the Jewish King, are you?' he said.

'Are those your own words?' asked Jesus. 'Or are you just repeating what other people have told you?'

'Do I look like a Jew!' said Pilate. 'You've been brought here by your own leaders. What have you been up to?'

'I'm no nationalist,' said Jesus. 'My men would have been out on the streets fighting, if I were – they wouldn't have let me be arrested so easily. My "kingdom" has nothing to do with that sort of thing.'

'So you *are* a "king", then,' said Pilate.

'The word is yours,' said Jesus. 'I was born to defend the truth. Anybody who cares for the truth knows what I am talking about.'

'What is truth?' said Pilate.

And with that he went outside again.

'As far as this court is concerned,' he told the crowd, 'there is nothing this man can be charged with. I've been in the habit of setting one prisoner free for you at the Feast. What about letting "the Jewish King" go free this year?'

The crowd broke into a roar. 'Not this man, but Barabbas!'

(Barabbas was one of the terrorists in the Resistance Movement.)

So Pilate had Jesus flogged, and the soldiers – as was often their custom with prisoners – made sport of him. They made a crown out of some thorn twigs and crowned him with it, and dressed him in a soldier's purple cloak. Then they kept coming up to him, saluting him with 'Long live Your Majesty!' and slapping him on the face.

Pilate went out to the crowd again.

'Here he is,' he said. 'I'm going to bring him out to you to make it clear that there is nothing this court can charge him with.'

Jesus was brought outside, still wearing the mock crown and the purple cloak.

'There's the man!' said Pilate.

When the Jewish leaders and their officers caught sight of him, they started shouting. 'The cross! Let's have him on the gallows!'

'Take him and put him on a cross yourselves,' said Pilate. 'He's done nothing this court can deal with!'

'But we've a law of blasphemy,' they answered, 'and by that law he ought to be executed – he claims to be equal with God himself!'

That last sentence frightened Pilate. He went back again into the building.

'Where were you born?' he asked Jesus.

Jesus didn't speak.

'I'm the Governor, you know – why don't you say something?' said Pilate. 'Don't you know I can set you free or have you executed?'

'You would have no power over me at all,' said Jesus, 'if God had not given it to you. The man who handed me over to you is more guilty than you.'

From that moment Pilate made up his mind to set him free.

But the shouting of the crowd went on.

'If you let this man go, you're no friend of the Emperor! Anybody who calls himself a king is an enemy of the Emperor!'

Pilate heard what they were shouting.

He brought Jesus outside again, and took his seat as Governor and Judge at the place called 'The Pavement'. It was now just midday.

'Here's your "King"!' he said.

'Take him away! Hang him on a cross!' the crowd shouted.

'So it's your "King" I'm to hang on a cross?' he asked.

'The Emperor is the only King we've got!' they shouted back.

Pilate handed him over for execution.

At Skull Hill   John 19:16b-35, 38-42

The soldiers marched Jesus off, and, with his own cross on his shoulders, he went out of the building to Skull Hill, a place quite near the city. And there they hung him on the cross. Three men were hung on crosses that day – Jesus in the middle, the other two on either side of him.

Pilate had a notice written out in three languages, Jewish, Roman and Greek: JESUS OF NAZARETH, THE JEWISH KING. He had it fastened on the cross. Crowds of citizens read it.

'Don't put THE JEWISH KING,' the Jewish leaders protested to Pilate. 'Put – HE SAID HE WAS THE JEWISH KING.'

'It stays as I wrote it,' said Pilate.

When the four soldiers had carried out their orders, they picked up the clothes of Jesus and made four bundles, one for each of them. Then they picked up his tunic. This was one piece of cloth, woven from top to bottom, not made up of several pieces.

'We mustn't tear it up,' they said. 'Let's toss for it.'

That is what they did.

All this time, his mother, his aunt Mary, the wife of Clopas, and Mary from Magdala were standing near the cross itself. Jesus caught sight of his mother – and the friend he loved dearly standing by her side.

'Mother,' he said, 'take my friend as your son.'

'Take my mother as your mother,' he said to his friend.

And from that time, his friend took her into his own home.

'I am thirsty,' said Jesus.

A full jar of sour wine had been put nearby for the guard. The soldier soaked a sponge in it, stuck it on a javelin and put it up to his mouth. Jesus drank it.

'My work is done,' he said.

His head dropped, and he died.

The Jewish leaders did not want the bodies on the crosses to stay there over the Saturday, the Holy Day of the Jews, especially since this was a very important Saturday, the first day of the Great Feast. They asked Pilate to have the men's legs broken to make them die quickly, and then to have the bodies taken away.

This is what the soldiers began to do. They broke the legs of the two men hanging on either side of Jesus, one after the other. They went up to Jesus, but they found that he was already dead. They didn't break his legs, but one of the soldiers jabbed a lance into his side, and water and blood flowed out. (This is what happened; it is the evidence of an eyewitness who can be trusted.)

After all this, two men went to Pilate – Joseph from the village of Arimathea (he was a member of the Jewish Council; he had kept his friendship with Jesus a secret, for he was afraid of what the Council might do) and Nicodemus (who, as we have told, first met Jesus at night).

Joseph asked Pilate to let him take the body of Jesus down from the cross, and Pilate agreed. So his friends came and took his body away, and wrapped it in linen sheets with spices which Nicodemus had brought, more than seventy pounds weight of perfume mixture. (This is the Jewish method of burial.)

There was a large garden nearby. In it there was a new tomb – nobody had yet been buried there.

It was now getting on for six o'clock in the evening, the time when the Holy Day began. The tomb lay near at hand; so they put Jesus there.

ALAN DALE

Introductory material

How would you have acted had you been hanging on the cross in place of Jesus, listening to the sneers and shouts of your enemies as they watched you writhing there in agony? Would you have called curses down upon them from heaven? I think I might have done. Would you have cried out in anger, 'Why me? What have I done to deserve this?' Again, yes, I think I might. Or would you have been so preoccupied with your pain and misery that you had no thoughts for anyone but yourself. On reflection, that's probably most likely of all. The one thing I'm sure I wouldn't have done is say this: 'Father, forgive them, for they do not know what they are doing.' In the most appalling of suffering to think not simply of others, but of those who have brought such suffering upon you; in the throes of death to look them in the eye and seek God's forgiveness for your killers – amazing! That's why we're here today. That's the man we come to honour and the God we meet through him; the God who gives, and goes on giving; who loves, and goes on loving; who died, and goes on dying, even though he lives; until that day when each and every one of us has responded to his grace and been gathered into his kingdom. Come now, and worship him.

NICK FAWCETT

Prayers

Thanksgiving – A man apart

Lord Jesus Christ,
  we thank you again today for the wonder of your grace
    and the awesomeness of your sacrifice.
  Though you were human just as we are,
    experiencing the same feelings and sensations as we do,
    you were unlike anyone has been before or since,
    unparalleled in the extent of your love,
    matchless in your selflessness –
    truly, a man apart.
  For your willingness to give and go on giving,
    Lord, we thank you.

  You could have served yourself,
    secured wealth, influence, personal glory,
    anything you cared to name.
  You could have saved yourself,
    avoided the heartache of Gethsemane,
    the agony of the cross,
    no power able to hold you.
  But you didn't,
    resolved instead to stay true to your calling –
    truly, a man apart.
  For your willingness to give and go on giving,
    Lord, we thank you.

  You chose to suffer and die
    so that we might be set free
    from everything that holds us captive.
  You freely surrendered all
    so that we might inherit life
    and enter into the joy of your kingdom.
  You made yourself as nothing
    so that we might receive everything –
    truly, you are a man apart.
  For your willingness to give and go on giving,
    Lord, we thank you.

Lord Jesus Christ,
  there is no one like you,
    no one to whom you can be compared,
    your greatness beyond measure,
    your love beyond words.

In you we see human life as it has never been seen elsewhere,
yet we glimpse also what life could and should be for all.
Inspire us through your example,
renew us through your grace,
and refashion us through your Spirit,
so that we may reflect a little of your goodness
and live to your glory.
Come to us now and help us to be a little more like you –
truly, a man apart.
For your willingness to give and go on giving,
Lord, we thank you.
Amen.   NICK FAWCETT

Confession

Lord Jesus Christ,
today of all days we are reminded
just how much we owe you,
how great a price you were willing to pay
to give us the gift of life.
Forgive us for giving you so little in return,
for shying away from discipleship
when there is any suggestion it may be costly.
Lord, in your mercy,
hear our prayer.

We are reminded how you stayed true to your calling,
despite every attempt to deflect you from it.
Forgive us that we so often take the way of least resistance,
compromising our convictions for the sake of any easy life.
Lord, in your mercy,
hear our prayer.

We are reminded how you stayed true
to those who were to fail you,
more concerned for their own safety than your welfare.
Forgive us that we so readily put self-interest
before the interests of others,
our loyalty depending on how much is asked of us.
Lord, in your mercy,
hear our prayer.

We are reminded how you endured ridicule and violence
  without any attempt at retaliation,
  praying instead for those who persecuted you.
Forgive us that we lash out at the slightest provocation,
  that we are more often concerned with exacting revenge
  than offering forgiveness.
Lord, in your mercy,
  hear our prayer.

We are reminded of how you loved us so much that you died for us,
  willingly taking the Way of the Cross.
Forgive us that we love you so little,
  that we find it so hard to offer anything of ourselves.
Lord, in your mercy,
  hear our prayer.

Lord Jesus Christ,
  we thank you for this day and for all it calls to mind.
  Help us to hear its message
    and respond to its challenge.
  Lord, in your mercy,
    hear our prayer,
    for in your name we ask it.
  Amen.

NICK FAWCETT

Intercession

Jesus lays down his life for us. He yearns so much for us to be saved that he undergoes death, allowing the burden of the whole world's evil to rest on his shoulders. Not once does he stop loving or forgiving. His death is no failure, but a victory of cosmic proportions, through which we are saved.

As children of our heavenly Father,
and knowing the extent of his love for us,
let us pray to him now.

We pray for all whom you have called to serve you,
in different ministries and in every country;
may they work in your strength
and show your love and compassion.

Silence for prayer

Lord, how you must love us:
may we love you more and more.

We pray for all in positions of authority,
particularly when faced with moral dilemmas
and the temptation to act expediently;
may they see what is right
and be encouraged to stand firm.

Silence for prayer

Lord, how you must love us:
may we love you more and more.

We pray for the members of our family and all whom
we love and care for; may we always be ready to
forgive, respect and value them.

Silence for prayer

Lord, how you must love us:
may we love you more and more.

We pray for all who know the pain
of rejection, vulnerability or torture;
for all innocent sufferers
and prisoners of conscience;
may they know your love for them.

Silence for prayer

Lord, how you must love us:
may we love you more and more.

We pray for those who are nearing death
and those who have moved on into eternity;
may we one day be welcomed into your kingdon.

Silence for prayer

Lord, how you must love us:
may we love you more and more.

Lord, how can we ever thank you
for what you have done for us!
May our lives proclaim our thanks and praise.

Silence for prayer

Merciful Father,
**accept these prayers
for the sake of your Son,
our Saviour Jesus Christ, Amen.**

Susan Sayers

Act of witness – Beneath the cross of Jesus

Loving God,
   we gather around this cross in the name of Christ,
      thanking you again for its astonishing message,
      its power to speak and challenge in so many ways.

   We rejoice in the love it represents,
      the sacrifice so freely offered on our behalf,
      so that we might experience life in all its fullness.

   We celebrate the forgiveness it proclaims,
      an end to all that has gone before
      and a new beginning, the slate wiped clean.

   We praise you for the freedom it brings,
      liberation from everything that destroys love,
      devalues life and denies the future.

   May it be a sign of the faith we share,
      a simple witness to Christ reaching out into this community,
      and a challenge to all to consider his call
      and respond to his love.

Loving God,
   give us courage to take up our cross in turn,
      and to walk the way of Christ.
   May our lives speak of him,
      even as this cross speaks so clearly of you.
   In his name we pray.
   Amen.   NICK FAWCETT

Short prayers

Lord Jesus Christ,
   you gave your whole self for us.
Not just a little, not simply part, but everything,
   offering your life for the life of the world.
You took the way of the cross
   and endured the agony of death.
You experienced the pain of betrayal,
   the hurt of denial,
   the sorrow of being abandoned
   by your closest friends.

You suffered the awful isolation
　of separation from God
　　as you took our sins on your shoulders.
Forgive us that we find it so hard
　to offer anything in return.
Forgive us that we hold back,
　giving only grudgingly of ourselves.
Lord Jesus Christ,
　you went the whole way for our sakes –
　help us to come a little way in return.   NICK FAWCETT

Living God,
　in so many ways this is the blackest of days
　recalling the darkest of moments –
　a day on which hearts were broken
　and faith tested to the limit,
　a day of appalling suffering and agonising death,
　a day when all hell was let loose
　and love seemed overwhelmed.
Yet we can call this day 'Good Friday',
　for in all of that horror you were there.
In the despair, in the pain,
　in the humiliation, in the sorrow,
　you were supremely at work,
　demonstrating the immensity of your love.
Living God,
　as we recall those terrible yet wonderful events,
　give us new insight into what you did that day,
　for us and for all.   NICK FAWCETT

Reflective prayers

Inner

(Place a wooden cross in the centre of the room. Read the prayer facing the cross.)

Lord,
　I cannot begin to understand pain,
　thirst, hunger or humiliation.
It's totally beyond my comprehension.
It's totally beyond my imagination.
It's totally beyond me
　why you would go through so much
　for me.
You meant so much to everyone

who had followed your every move,
    listened to your every word
    and watched, amazed at your every action.
You had the chance to turn around,
    walk away
    and live to share your heart
    another day.
But you chose to face the cross,
    to put yourself
    in the hands
    of everyone
    who wanted you silenced,
    inactive,
    out of sight,
    extinct, totally dead.
They thought they'd won
    but we know better,
    or at least
    we should do.   PETE TOWNSEND

Outer

(Stand in front of the cross and stretch your arms out in front of you with the palms of your hands facing upwards.)

Lord,
    you suffered,
    knew rejection,
    endured insults,
    were falsely accused
    and paid the price.
All around,
    wherever the winds blow,
    there are people
    suffering,
    imprisoned,
    rejected by those who know them,
    falsely accused;
    and waiting
    for someone
    to speak their name,
    free them of the chains
    that shackle them
    to the walls of persecution.
Hear their cry, Lord,
    bring comfort,

dry their tears,
fill their hearts
with the warmth
of your love.
Teach us,
show us
how we,
each one of us,
can reach out
and be the voice
of the voiceless.
To stand for those
who cannot stand.
Be their light
wherever darkness falls.
Amen.   PETE TOWNSEND

Inner

(Have a bag/box of medium-sized stones available. Sit in a dimly lit area.)

Lord,
this life,
this journey through
a landscape
that's often littered with the debris
of fear,
rejection and hurt,
causes my feet
to stumble,
to trip
and bump
against every stone
that attempts
to batter my spirit,
causes my eyes to fill
with the tears of each
pain-soaked footfall.

(Take the stones and place them in a pile in front of you.)

Lord,
each of these stones
is a reminder,
a monument to hurt,
a visible marker
for others on this journey

to know that someone else
has trod the same path.
Lord,
even though
in the here and now
the pain
seems unbearable,
it's so good to know
that your Son
trod the path of pain
so that people like me
need never know
the absolute agony
of being separated
from your loving embrace.

PETE TOWNSEND

Outer

Lord,
even in the darkness of the night
and the incessant rainfall
which threatens to dampen
the embers of my heart,
let me always remember
that your heart
never grows cold,
never hardens,
never turns away
when those in need
turn to you
looking for shelter
in their dark moments.
Remind me
that just as you love,
so should I
be aware
of those
who suffer,
who hurt,
who cry out
from the desolation of their heart.
Wherever my journey takes me,
wherever my path crosses
that of another traveller,
let me be

as a signpost,
a guide
to a well in the desert
where the tired heart
can find rest
shelter
and drink
from the water of life.   PETE TOWNSEND

Inner

(Sit on a chair in the centre of the room to give the feeling of isolation.)

Lord,
    I'm really finding life
    kind of frustrating.
So many things
    demanding my attention,
    wanting my time,
    eating away at my sanity
    until
    I can't remember
    what it was I was supposed to be doing
    in the first place.
Sometimes
    I walk into a room
    and then spend the next ten minutes
    wondering what I'm doing there!
I look around me for a sign,
    a clue to my action,
    Why, when, how, what for?
And, Lord,
    if I'm honest
    that's exactly how I feel
    when I go to church.
It's not that I don't want to be there
    but it would be nice
    if I had a clue
    as to what I was supposed to be doing there!
It's a good job that my faith
    isn't in tradition, buildings or committees,
    or even in how many times
    someone remembers my name,
    but my faith is in the one
    who gave his all for me.   PETE TOWNSEND

Outer

(Stand up with the chair remaining behind you. Begin the prayer by facing north.)

Lord,
    let us never forget
    all those people
    who feel that they've come to the end.
Their strength has left them
    and it's just too much trouble
    to put one foot in front of the other.

(Turn to the West)

And, Lord,
    let us not forget
    all those people
    who feel the pressure
    of living up to other people's expectations,
    where the quality of your life
    is measured by the accumulation
    of material wealth.

(Turn to the south)

Lord,
    let us not forget
    all those people
    who feel the oppression
    of regimes
    that fear the expression
    of a human heart.

(Turn to the east)

And Lord,
    let us not forget
    all those people
    who suffer hatred,
    violence,
    and are forced to live
    as foreigners
    in their own land.
Lord,
    let us not forget.

PETE TOWNSEND

Lord Jesus Christ,
  you gave your whole self for us.
Not just a little, not simply part, but everything,
  offering your life for the life of the world.
You took the way of the cross
  and endured the agony of death.
You experienced the pain of betrayal,
  the hurt of denial,
  the sorrow of being abandoned
  by your closest friends.
You suffered the awful isolation
  of separation from God
  as you took our sins on your shoulders.
Forgive us that we find it so hard
  to offer anything in return.
Forgive us that we hold back,
  giving only grudgingly of ourselves.
Lord Jesus Christ,
  you went the whole way for our sakes –
  help us to come a little way in return.   NICK FAWCETT

Living God,
  in so many ways this is the blackest of days
  recalling the darkest of moments –
  a day on which hearts were broken
   and faith tested to the limit,
  a day of appalling suffering and agonising death,
  a day when all hell was let loose
  and love seemed overwhelmed.
Yet we can call this day 'Good Friday',
  for in all of that horror you were there.
In the despair, in the pain,
  in the humiliation, in the sorrow,
  you were supremely at work,
  demonstrating the immensity of your love.
Living God,
  as we recall those terrible yet wonderful events,
  give us new insight into what you did that day,
  for us and for all.   NICK FAWCETT

All-age-talk material

A heavy load

Aim

To bring home the truth that, whatever problems or troubles may weigh us down, Jesus, through his death on the cross, is able to carry those burdens and so set us free.

Preparation

Get hold of two large identical boxes. Pack one full to the top with the heaviest items you can get hold of – books, cartons of water, lead weights, for example. Pack the other with polystyrene foam.

Talk

Ask if anyone is feeling strong. Tell the congregation you hope someone is because you need help. You've been busy tidying up the church office and you have two boxes which you need carried to the back of the church ready to take home later. You are happy to take one, but who will help you with the other? Invite volunteers to come forward. Ask the first volunteer to pick up the heavy box, while you pick up the light one. Express astonishment at their inability to pick the box up or carry it. Invite other volunteers to have a go, until everyone who wants to has had a turn. Make a joke of the fact that you never realised you were so strong! Then ask if anyone can explain why you found lifting your box so easy while your volunteers found theirs so hard. Open the boxes and display what's inside.

Imagine if we had to carry a heavy load around with us all time! We couldn't do it, could we? Yet there is a sense in which we do just that all the time, allowing our lives to become full of problems and anxieties which burden us, or fears and doubts which hold us down, or past mistakes and present weaknesses which prevent us living life to the full. All too often we struggle along through life, getting by as best we can, yet feeling increasingly unable to cope.

If that is how you're feeling, then listen again to the wonderful words of Jesus from the Gospel of Matthew:

> Come to me, all you that are weary and are carrying heavy burdens, and I will give you rest. Take my yoke upon you, and learn from me; for I am gentle and humble in heart, and you will find rest for your souls. For my yoke is easy, and my burden is light.   (*Matthew 11:28-30*)

These are words of Jesus spoken not only to his disciples and followers long ago, but to each of us now. For through his life and his death Jesus has carried on his shoulders the burdens we bear. Whatever mistakes we may have made, whatever fears may haunt us, whatever problems may beset us, he has dealt with them on the cross. In the words of the prophet Isaiah:

Surely he has borne our infirmities and carried our diseases; yet we accounted him stricken, struck down by God, and afflicted. But he was wounded for our transgressions, crushed for our iniquities; upon him was the punishment that made us whole, and by his bruises we are healed.

(Isaiah 53:4-5)

For us all there are times when we feel weighed down by the troubles and difficulties of life, unable sometimes to take another step. But the truth we celebrate today and in the days ahead is that Jesus has taken our burdens upon himself, and is ready to release us from whatever load we bear, setting us free to live life to the full!

Finish with the hymn *Burdens are lifted at Calvary*.   Nick Fawcett

Reflective material
(sketches, meditations and poems)

Doing the right thing: something we would prefer to do (well, most of the time) but find it difficult to know *how* to do it and *if* we've achieved it.

Sometimes knowing that we've done the right thing is relatively simple. The box of chocolates, bunch of flowers, birthday present or jar of pickled gherkins usually gets a quick response with a thank-you or huge smile from the recipient (or a sickly grin in the case of the pickled gherkins). Knowing whether we should enrol on a particular course study or accept an offer of a job are not quite so easy.

In Jesus' case, knowing what to do wasn't the problem. Even knowing how things would turn out wasn't difficult to come to terms with. Convincing other people that he was doing the right thing *was* the problem.

Jesus accepted the crucifixion not from an acknowledgement of guilt but because he knew that's what his Father wanted him to do. However, even knowing the path to tread didn't make life, or death, any easier.

Throughout his life Jesus had decisions to make. Some decisions were easy, an automatic response to someone's need. Other decisions required thought and a lot of chatting to his Father. Although Jesus knew how to do the right thing, and why, he had to trust God the Father had everything under control.

You can read the Gospels and think Jesus was always going to do the right thing because God had told him what to do, how to do it and what would happen when he did. But even that didn't make the situation easy. Jesus cried, sweated and bled about the course of action that God had asked him to take. Jesus agonised over the details and whether there wasn't another way of doing what God wanted. In the end doing the right thing was all that mattered.

Our life choices may never be so demanding of us. But the decisions we make affect so many areas of our lives, and the lives of others, that doing the right thing is just as important.

Jesus had to place his trust in God. He had to have faith in God's actions. Even more importantly, he continually chatted with his father about whatever situation he faced. The same applies to us. We need to place our trust in God and have faith that he is looking after us every step of the way. And, just as Jesus did, we too need to constantly chat with God, even if it's to say: 'This is tougher than I expected!' or 'Haven't you got any better ideas?' Doing the right thing starts with God and ends with God. If we involve God at the beginning, even though we may stumble and fall over at times, we'll have someone with us . . . Whatever the outcome, doing the right thing means getting God involved.

PETE TOWNSEND

It is finished

After Jesus drank the wine, he said, 'Everything is done!' He bowed his head and died. John 19:30

The ragged trade

They think it's all over . . . well . . . it's only just begun. How easy it is to think that death means the end, the finish, the completion of all that went before. How wrong can you get?

Characters

Bill and Ben are two market stall traders. Neither of them likes to miss an opportunity to ply their trade whatever the circumstances. Both are dressed in denim jackets, cloth caps and bright T-shirts.

Scene

It's the end of a busy trading day. Bill and Ben still have a few items for sale and are not too willing to leave while there still might be the possibility of a sale. Both are standing behind a stall on which a few items remain. The weather has taken a turn for the worse and both Bill and Ben are feeling the chill.

Props

Denim jackets, brightly coloured T-shirts, two tables with a selection of items scattered on them. Recording of crowd noises and the occasional crack of thunder.

Bill   (*Pulls collar of jacket up and shivers*) So that's it then. It's finished.

Ben   Looks like it. (*Looks up at sky*)

Bill   It's a pity.

Ben   Yeah. Shame really.

Bill   (*Nods*) A real waste.

Ben	A crying shame.
Bill	An opportunity wasted.
Ben	Well, not that wasted, surely.
Bill	No, not totally.
Ben	It's not been all bad.
Bill	*(Shrugs)* No, that's true.
Ben	There were some good moments.
Bill	One or two. *(Frowns)* Could have been better, though.
Ben	Yeah. Just a bit.
Bill	Still, can't complain, can we.
Ben	We shouldn't really.
Bill	We've had a good run, haven't we.
Ben	Not too bad.
Bill	It's a pity, though.
Ben	*(Nods in agreement)* Yeah. Real pity.
Bill	Oh well, there's always another day.
Ben	*(Looks as Bill enquiringly)* Hey, we're not done yet, are we?
Bill	What do you mean?
Ben	We've still got all this stock left. *(Points to several items on the table)*
Bill	*(Shrugs and holds hands out)* The punters are all going home now.
Ben	Wait a minute. *(Looks around anxiously)* Isn't there anyone else to crucify?
Bill	Doubt it. It's getting a bit late. Anyway, *(Looks skywards)* it's gone all dark. Bet there's rain on the way. *(Pulls cap down over eyes)*
Ben	Don't give up so easily. Look, *(Points towards audience)* offer that bloke over there a free sample if he'll go and get himself arrested and crucified.
Bill	*(Lifts cap up)* Free sample won't do him much good then, will it?

Ben	It's all business. Never turn down an opportunity.
Bill	That's what I admire about you.
Ben	What's that then?
Bill	Your willingness to offer someone a deal that's always worth refusing.
Ben	*(Sniffs)* Never been known to miss a potential customer.
Bill	*(Nods knowingly)* Don't they know it!
Ben	*(Taps chest)* You can always rely on me. And that's more than can be said for some of these blokes *(Points into distance)* who go and get themselves crucified.
Bill	*(Sighs)* You're all heart.
Ben	Well, you can't go letting folk down by going and getting yourself put out of business. Don't make sense. *(Rearranges some of the items on the table)*
Bill	Perhaps it wasn't their fault. They might have been set up. You never know.
Ben	What are you talking about. Are you suggesting a conspiracy theory.
Bill	I've heard stranger things.
Ben	You've been indulging in the fermented camel's milk again, haven't you.
Bill	No, seriously, I've heard rumours that the local big noises don't like anybody making trouble on their patch. *(Looks around anxiously)*
Ben	That's OK. I don't stand for any nonsense on my patch either.
Bill	Yeah, but you don't go and crucify them, do you? *(Rearranges some of the items on the table)*
Ben	I make them feel damned uncomfortable if that's what you mean. *(Picks up an item, looks at it for a few seconds and then bangs it down onto the table)*
Bill	Hey! Don't do that. Made me jump, you did. Anyway, I mean, you wouldn't go to such extremes as to have them permanently silenced, would you?
Ben	From what I hear, that was one of the problems with a bloke that was hung up today. *(Sniffs and buttons jacket up)*

Bill   What's that?

Ben   Couldn't gag him. So they had to employ other, less subtle methods. *(Taps side of nose)* Know what I mean?

Bill   *(Snort of indignation)* Don't call crucifixion subtle.

Ben   Works though, don't it?

Bill   From what I hear, that bloke said it was only a temporary measure.

Ben   Leave it out. You can't very well be hung up with nails and then after a few minutes shout, 'OK, I'm sorry. I've had enough, you can let me own now.' The authorities would be a laughing stock.

Bill   No. What I mean is, that bloke said they couldn't kill him.

Ben   They had a damn good try.

Bill   He said he would die and then come back to life.

Ben   Best bit of marketing I've ever heard. Perhaps we should try that. *(Turns to audience and shouts)* 'Hey, come and get your sandals here. *(Waves an imaginary pair of sandals)* They'll never wear out, they've got an eternal sole!'

Bill   You're just a hard-headed, ignorant opportunist.

Ben   That's the nicest thing anyone's ever said about me.

      Both begin to tidy the items on the table as the lights go down.

The dark clouds, the thunder and chill in the air must have been enough to convince most of the onlookers that it really was finished. It was the end of all they had hoped and dreamed of. The crucifixion had put an end to every promise and vague expectation . . . or had it?

The mood that afternoon was one of extreme sadness and disappointment. Jesus had been mocked: 'He can save others but can't save himself' and a board put above his head declaring: 'King of the Jews'. Not only were the taunts and barbed comments aimed at Jesus, they were directed at anyone who believed that Jesus was God's Son, the Saviour. To underline the point, Jesus was seen by everyone to be humiliated, whipped and nailed up on a cross just the same as anyone who dared to challenge the civil and religious authorities. And now, from his own lips, Jesus admits, 'It is finished'.

You can imagine the number of heads that were lowered in despair and sadness. But it was only a matter of days since Jesus had reminded his disciples again of what lay ahead:

Jesus left with his disciples and started through Galilee. He did not want anyone to know about it, because he was teaching the disciples that the Son of Man would be handed over to people who would kill him. But three days later he would rise to life. The disciples did not understand what Jesus meant, and they were afraid to ask.   Mark 9:30-32

Even if they had remembered, would they have taken the comment about rising after three days as just another false hope?

For Jesus, the words 'It is finished' were a statement that he had accomplished what he set out to do. The journey from virgin birth to crucifixion had been completed. It was never meant to be a statement of 'So, that's that, then. It was nice while it lasted!' It was the sole purpose of Jesus' ministry to reconcile humanity with God. The relationship no longer depended on animal sacrifice and the priestly rituals. From that point on anyone could approach God and develop a relationship with the creator. For Jesus, not so much a full stop at the end of a life but a question mark. A sort of 'Now it's up to you. What are you going to do about your relationship with God?'   PETE TOWNSEND

Meditation of one of the mob

What got into us that day?
Can you make sense of it?
I look back now incredulous,
    unable to believe we could have been so false, so fickle,
    one day protesting our undying loyalty,
    and the next baying for his blood like a pack of wolves.
Yet that's what we did,
    our cries of 'Hosanna!' in just a few days turning to 'Crucify!',
    our shouts of welcome to jeers of rejection.
It was partly, I suppose, borne of disappointment,
    the truth slowly dawning on us
    that Jesus wasn't the sort of Messiah we expected,
    his kingdom of an altogether different nature
    from the one we looked for.
That was a blow, undoubtedly,
    for many of us, me included, really believed
    he was the one we waited for,
    the promised deliverer who would set us free
    from the yoke of Roman oppression.
Then, of course, there was fear,
    for we were well aware that the Pharisees were watching us,
    their beady eyes on the lookout
    for anyone less than enthusiastic in their cause –
    we all knew it wouldn't take much

for us to suffer the same fate as Jesus.
Yet deep down those are only excuses,
   incidental to the main cause.
The ugly fact is this:
   we followed the crowd,
   caught up in the hysteria of the moment,
   until we blindly followed the one next to us
   like a bunch of sheep.
It all happened so quickly, that's the chilling thing –
   one moment we were sane, rational human beings,
   and the next no longer people at all,
   simply part of a faceless crowd,
   a senseless, soulless mob,
   all reason forgotten,
   all sanity suspended.
I thought I was different –
   able to think for myself,
   make my own decisions,
   resist the pressure to compromise –
   but I learned the hard way that I wasn't;
   I caught a glimpse of the person I really am,
   and I'm still struggling to take it in.
Do you know what bothers me most, though?
It's how Jesus must have felt as he stood there,
   listening to our shouts,
   and the truth dawned on him
   that he was wasting his life on people like us –
   it must have all but finished him.
The only surprise is he didn't realise it sooner,
   for he saw everything else so clearly;
   but he couldn't have done, could he,
   or he'd have called a halt somewhere –
   it stands to reason.
Yes, I know he was special, no question about it,
   but no one in their right mind
   would have gone to their death for us
   had they seen us that day,
   had they witnessed what we were really like –
   not even Jesus would do that,
   surely?

NICK FAWCETT

Meditation of Nicodemus

His back was cut to ribbons,
   a criss-cross of bloodied weals,
   the skin hanging in tatters where the whip had torn away the flesh.
Yet still he said nothing –
   no cry for mercy,
   no howl of protest,
   no shout of abuse –
   nothing!
Apart from the grunts of pain,
   the involuntary gasps,
   he was silent.
And we were all amazed.
We'd seen hardened killers grovel under the lash,
   prize-fighters cry like babies,
   but not Jesus.
I have to admit it, I thought he'd crack, for all my admiration of the man;
   I never imagined he could take such punishment.
A few strokes, perhaps,
   a token resistance,
   but then they'd break him and he'd say what they wanted him to,
   admit he'd been wrong.
But it never came,
   never happened,
   never even looked like happening;
   and suddenly I recalled the words of the prophet Isaiah,
   that great vision of God's chosen servant
   all at once imbued with new meaning –
   'Like a lamb led to the slaughter
   and like a sheep silent before its shearers,
   so he did not open his mouth.
   He was wounded for our transgressions,
   crushed for our iniquition,
   upon him was the punishment that made us whole,
   and by his stripes we are healed.'
It was like a flash from heaven,
   a ray of sunshine in a dark and dismal wilderness,
   for I realised that there, in the face of such appalling suffering and evil,
   there in the wretchedness of sorrow and death,
   God was at work,
   bringing health,
   wholeness,
   love,
   life.
Did Jesus see it like that?

Was that the secret which gave him strength?
We'll never know.
But I'll tell you one thing:
   it changed my life, seeing him suffer like that.
It made me realise that I had to respond,
   had to follow him;
   there was no other way.
For I knew it should have been me standing there enduring that agony;
   it should have been you,
   Caiaphas,
   Pilate,
   anyone –
   anyone other than Jesus.
He poured himself out to death,
   cut off from the land of the living,
   and somehow, in a way I don't fully understand,
   but a way I shall never, never forget,
   he did it for us!

NICK FAWCETT

Meditation of a soldier beside the cross

He was in agony,
   believe me, I know.
I've seen it often enough, crucifixion.
All in a day's work for me.
And I've heard a few howl for mercy over the years.
There's few things to touch it so they tell me for sheer pain,
   slow, lingering, dreadful.
But he was different, that was the curious thing.
I could see he was suffering all right;
   it was there in his eyes,
   in the gritted teeth,
   in the writhing body,
   in the sweat pouring from him,
   and most of all in that last awful groan.
But he never complained,
   never screamed,
   never swore.
Funny that.
To be honest, I've never seen anyone quite like him.
That look he had, even in death,
   as though we were the ones suffering,
   as though we were the criminals deserving punishment,
   as though he felt sorry for us.
Ridiculous, of course.

But you know, I could swear as he drew his last breath
   there was a smile on his face,
   almost like he felt he'd achieved something.
An odd business,
   very odd.

NICK FAWCETT

Meditation of Mary, wife of Clopas

He was silent,
   quite still,
   his body limp and lifeless,
   like a rag doll,
   like a broken puppet.
And I thanked God that at last it was over,
   his ordeal finally ended.
But it wasn't,
   not quite.
He moved again,
   just the faintest twitch,
   the last flickering ember of life,
   but enough to prolong our hopes,
   enough to prolong his pain.
He was still breathing,
   still suffering.
We watched wretchedly, torn by conflicting desires –
   the longing to see him come down and prove his enemies wrong;
   the longing to see him find peace in the cold embrace of death.
But suddenly his eyes were open,
   wide,
   bright,
   triumphant;
   the lips were moving,
   eager,
   excited,
   exultant;
   and his voice rang out:
   'It is finished!'
An acknowledgement of defeat, some said afterwards,
   a last despairing cry of sorrow.
But it wasn't,
   not for those who heard it,
   not for those with ears to hear.
It was altogether different –
   like sunshine after storm,
   like rain after drought,

like laughter after tears –
  gloriously unexpected,
  wonderfully surprising.
He had stooped and conquered,
  staked all and won.
Defeat was victory,
  darkness was light,
  death was life.
I didn't see it then, mind you,
  I can't pretend that.
It was just a glimpse at the time,
  a glimmer barely understood.
But what I did see, with sudden staggering clarity,
  was that until that moment,
  until that last victorious shout,
  he had lived with the awful burden of holding the world's fate in his own
  and wondering whether he could see it through.
At last it was done –
  he had honoured his calling,
  fulfilled his mission,
  walked the way of the cross.
It was finished,
  and with a song in his heart and joy in his eyes
  he bowed his head and surrendered his spirit.   NICK FAWCETT

Meditation of Joseph of Arimathea

It was the least I could do,
  the very, very least.
And yes, I should have done more;
  I know that,
  no need to rub it in.
I ought to have spoken out before the Council,
  begged them to reconsider,
  publicly declared my faith.
I should have told Pilate of their perjury,
  pleaded with him to show mercy,
  explained what sort of kingdom Jesus was talking about.
But I didn't, did I?
I didn't say anything, just watched and listened;
  I didn't do anything, just kept my own counsel;
I skulked in the shadows,
  observed from the outside,
  bit my tongue,
  and let them crucify the Messiah.

Could it have been any different?
Would my intervention have changed anything?
I doubt it,
    not given the mood they were in –
    his fate was sealed long before
    and no one was going to rob them of their prize.
Yet though I keep on telling myself that,
    vainly attempting to excuse my silence,
    it doesn't help,
    for in my heart I know I failed him.
When the chance was there to declare my allegiance, I chickened out;
    when the moment came to make my stand, I was afraid.
My concern was all for me, and none for him.
Yes, I know it's understandable,
    that most likely you would have done the same,
    but that's not the point.
It's me we're talking about,
    me who will have to live with the knowledge of my failure
    until my dying day,
    and so that's why I've acted now,
    offering my tomb to provide for his burial.
It's not much, I realise that,
    a bit like shutting the stable door after the horse has bolted.
But it's all there is left,
    some small way in which I can make amends.
A token gesture?
You may be right.
A feeble attempt to salve my conscience?
Most probably.
But I hope it's more than that.
You see, I've had enough of hiding,
    enough of closet discipleship,
    enough of this faith that's afraid to call its name.
So I've thrown caution to the wind and nailed my colours to the mast.
It may cost me my position,
    it will certainly cost me my friends,
    it might even cost me my life;
    but if Jesus could willingly sacrifice all that for me
    who deserves so little,
    surely I can do something for him who deserves so much.　　NICK FAWCETT

When Jesus asked for a drink he was given a sponge soaked in cheap wine (with a distinct tang of vinegar) which was held up to him on the stem of a hyssop plant. The hyssop plant is small and bushy and similar to strong grass, and about 60 centimetres long at best. Therefore, Jesus would only have been head and shoulders above his mother, who would have been able to see every flicker of pain on his face.   PETE TOWNSEND

Order of service

Journey with Jesus – A meditation on the Way of the Cross

These readings and prayers are intended to help the children to follow the foot-steps of Christ's last journey to the cross, and to enter into the Passion story in a more personal way. They make the journey beside Jesus, stopping along the way to remember his suffering, but also to recall the faith and love he showed right up to the moment of his death.

In preparation for making this journey together, the children should be split into small groups and asked to prepare a visual representation or symbolic focus for each station and the resurrection (suggestions are given). These should be kept simple and numbered appropriately, so that the children can move from one to another using the relevant readings and prayers. Another group could design and make a simple banner which reads, 'Come, follow me', to be carried at the front of their procession. Depending on the space available, the symbol for each station can be placed around the crucifix or cross which forms the central focus.

The first station

Jesus is sentenced to death

Focus

Coil of rope, brambles twisted to make a thorny crown.

Reading

Early the next morning, Jesus was bound and taken to Pontius Pilate, the Roman governor. Pilate questioned Jesus carefully, 'Is it true that you are the King of the Jews?' he asked. 'It is you who say this,' Jesus replied. Despite the many accusations made by the chief priests, and the questions asked by Pilate, Jesus stood silent and made no attempt to answer any of them. Reluctantly, Pilate sentenced Jesus to be crucified and handed him over to the guards.

Reflection

The prisoner said little in his own defence.
His silent acceptance and calmness
angered his accusers.
Words would make no difference anyway:
they had already agreed his guilt.

Prayer

Lord, forgive me when I fail
to recognise your presence among us;
for the times when I shut my ears and mind,
and refuse to listen to what you have to say to me.

The second station

Jesus is crowned with thorns and receives his cross

Focus

Simple cross made from two sticks or branches tied together.

Reading

The Roman soldiers who took charge of Jesus made fun of him and mocked 'the King of the Jews'. They wrapped him in a robe of royal purple, and plaited thorns to be his 'crown'. When they had finished taunting him, they dressed Jesus in his own clothes, and gave him a cross to carry.

Reflection

Mocked and abused,
taunted and torn,
they laughed at your misery,
and crowned your gentle head
with cruel thorns.

Prayer

Lord,
bruised and bleeding,
you accepted your lonely cross
and carried the weight of the world's sin.
Forgive me when I complain
about my own cross.
Help me to carry it gladly
on my journey through life.

The third station

Jesus falls for the first time

Focus

If available, use a simple wooden manikin of the type used in art departments, to depict a falling figure; otherwise a simple picture or 'stick' drawing can be used or a figure made from modelling clay or plasticine.

Reading

Exhausted and weak after being beaten and abused, Jesus had walked only a short distance before he stumbled under the weight of the cross, and fell for the first time.

Reflection

The road is long and the journey hard.
The cross grows ever heavier
and there is no one to help.
You stumble and fall.

Prayer

Lord,
how many times have I faltered and fallen?
Tripped up by my lack of understanding,
and stumbling over pebbles of doubt.
Help me to get up and begin again.

The fourth station

Jesus meets his mother

Focus

Cut-out heart, pierced with a cut-out sword, toy sword, letter opener or similar.

Reading

Many people had gathered to watch the sad procession making its way to Golgotha, and among them stood Mary, the mother of Jesus, who wept with sorrow when she saw her beloved son's suffering.

Reflection

Step by painful step
she shares your suffering,
her heart pierced by a sword of sorrow and pain.
A glance is enough,
her loving look says everything,
and then she is gone.

Prayer

Walk with me, Mary.
Stay beside me on my journey,
and comfort and strengthen me
with your mother's love.

The fifth station

Simon helps Jesus

Focus

Imprint of hands in damp sand or plaster; poster of handprints made with various colours of paint.

Reading

When the soldiers saw Jesus struggling, they were afraid that he would not survive the journey to the place of execution. So they chose a man from the crowd to share their prisoner's burden. The man came from Cyrene and his name was Simon. He helped Jesus to carry his heavy cross.

Reflection

A stranger in the crowd
is chosen to help you.
His hands lighten your load,
his shoulder shares your heavy burden.

Prayer

Lord,
a stranger's help
made all the difference
to your struggle.
May I help others along the way
as they struggle
with the crosses they bear.

The sixth station

Veronica wipes the face of Jesus

Focus

A simple piece of white cloth with a face roughly sponged or painted in outline; or if someone doesn't mind getting messy, apply face paint and gently press a cloth against their face to create an image.

Reading

Among the crowd watching Jesus suffering was a holy woman named Veronica. Seeing his plight, she was filled with pity and compassion, and she stepped forward to gently wipe his bloodstained face with a towel. As she lifted the towel away, the image of Christ's face remained imprinted there.

Reflection

She saw your suffering
and was moved to help.
She did not stand aside,
or pass you by.
You touched each other
with love.

Prayer

Lord,
give me the courage
to step from the crowd of indifference,
and do something positive
to show my love for others.

The seventh station

Jesus falls for the second time

Focus

Use a similar picture or figure as the third station.

Reading

Jesus stumbled, and the weight of the cross made him fall for a second time.

Reflection

Each step grows more difficult.
The weight of your cross
seems ready to crush
as once more you fall.

Prayer

Lord, however crushed
I feel by the troubles
and worries of life,
help me to my feet,
knowing that all will be well
with you by my side.

The eighth station

The women of Jerusalem weep for Jesus

Focus

Cut out one or two large tear shapes from silver card or some plain card covered with silver foil. Give the children a selection of magazines, and help them to find and cut out pictures of people who are sad or crying. These can then be stuck on the tear shapes to make a collage.

Reading

Many of the women wept with sadness when they saw the pitiful state of Jesus as he struggled along the way to Golgotha. Seeing them crying, he said to them, 'Do not cry for me, women of Jerusalem, but save your tears for yourselves and your children.'

Reflection

The women wept for you,
but their tears made no difference
because no one would listen.

Prayer

Lord, you made time to listen,
even on your way to die.
Let me open my heart
to hear and understand
those who cry out
and are ignored.

The ninth station

Jesus falls a third time

Focus

As third and seventh stations.

Reading

The cross was heavy and Jesus was exhausted. Urged on by the soldiers' spears, he staggered on slowly and painfully, until finally he fell for a third time.

Reflection

Almost there now.
Not much further to go.

Face down in the dirt,
you must get up and carry on.
Your journey is almost complete.

Prayer

Lord, don't let me give up,
when I fall time and time again.
Disheartened and feeling sorry for myself,
help me to continue on my way.

The tenth station

Jesus is stripped of his clothes

Focus

A pile of clothes; a couple of large dice made from covered cardboard boxes, and marked with appropriate spots.

Reading

When they reached the place of execution, the soldiers stripped Jesus and threw dice to divide his clothes among them.

Reflection

Stripped of clothes
and stripped of dignity,
standing naked before the crowd,
you suffer the final act
of humiliation.

Prayer

Lord, strip me of everything
which keeps me from being close to you
and your love.

The eleventh station

Jesus is nailed to the cross

Focus

Arrange a selection of the largest nails you can find, together with a mallet or hammer, next to a scroll of paper on which is written, 'Jesus of Nazareth, King of the Jews'.

Reading

When they reached the place called 'the skull', they nailed Jesus to the cross and raised it up to stand between two thieves. Above him they placed a sign which read, 'Jesus of Nazareth, King of the Jews'.

Reflection

They pierced
your gentle hands and feet,
and nailed you to the wood.
Stretched out in love,
you hang above the world
you came to save.

Prayer

King of love,
forgive me when I wound
and hurt you
by turning away
from your outstretched arms.

The twelfth station

Jesus dies on the cross

Focus

A crucifix or cross with a piece of black cloth draped over it.

Reading

For three hours darkness fell over the land like a blanket, and the sun lost its brightness. Then Jesus called out, 'My God, my God, why have you abandoned me?' And a short time later he cried out again, 'Father, I place my spirit into your loving hands.' Then he bowed his head and died.

Reflection

You hang there lifeless.
Your task is finally complete.
Your journey has finished.

Prayer

Lord,
when everything seems lost,
and darkness surrounds us,
may we look at your cross
and be filled with hope.

The thirteenth station

Jesus is taken down from the cross

Focus

Lay a plasticine figure on a brick or piece of rock or stone, and drape a cloth over the 'body'.

Reading

Joseph of Arimathea, who was a disciple of Jesus, asked Pilate for permission to remove his body from the cross. Together with Nicodemus, he gently lifted Jesus down and placed him in the arms of Mary his loving mother.

Reflection

Once more you are held
in the loving arms
which first held you
in a stable long ago,
and wrapped you
in a lifetime of love.

Prayer

Lord,
like Mary your mother
may I welcome you
into my life
with open arms.

The fourteenth station

Jesus is laid in the tomb

Focus

With a little imagination there are many different ways to create a tomb scene depending on the time and resources available – for example, a 'living garden' in a tray or bowl, something constructed from papier-mâché, or a simple collection of suitably arranged stones.

Reading

Joseph and Nicodemus wrapped Jesus in a shroud, and, together with the women, they carried his body to the tomb where he was to be buried. They laid him inside and rolled a stone against the entrance.

Reflection

They left you covered
and alone
in the darkness of the tomb,
and the darkness of sorrow.

Prayer

Lord,
let your tomb
be a symbol of hope and joy
in moments of sadness and sorrow.

Resurrection

Jesus is alive!

Focus

A large candle or resurrection cross, covered with fresh or paper flowers, can be used to represent the joy of Easter.

Reading

Before sunrise on the Sunday morning, Mary of Magdala went to the tomb. As she reached the entrance, she saw that the stone had been rolled away and the tomb was empty. She ran to the disciples, saying, 'They have taken the Lord from the tomb and we don't know where they have put him!' Peter and another disciple, John, ran to the tomb and found it just as Mary had described, with the linen burial cloths lying on the ground. The cloth which had been wrapped around Jesus' head lay rolled up separately from the other pieces of cloth. Peter went into the tomb first, followed by John. Until this moment they had not understood the Scriptures, which had said, 'He must rise from the dead.' But now they saw, and they believed.

Reflection

The cloths which bound you
have been cast off with death.
A new day dawns,
a new life rises
to greet the world.

Prayer

Lord,
may the glory of your resurrection
and the promise of eternal life
fill my lifelong journey
with hope and joy.

KATIE THOMPSON

Easter

Easter Day

The triumph of God's love over evil, suffering and death

John 20:1-18 (or Luke 24:1-12)

(also Acts 10:34-43, or Isaiah 65:17-25; Psalm 118:1-2, 14-24;
1 Corinthians 15:19-26 or Acts 10:34-43)

A reading from the Gospel of John (20:1-9)

Very early on the Sunday morning Mary of Magdala went to the tomb where Jesus had been laid. Seeing that the stone had been rolled back from the entrance to the tomb, Mary ran to find Peter and John.

'They have taken the Lord,' she cried, 'and I don't know where they have put him!'

The apostles ran to the tomb, and John, arriving first, saw the cloths lying on the ground. When Peter reached the tomb, he went in and he too saw the cloths that had once been wrapped around the body of Jesus.

Standing together, John and Peter understood for the first time what the Scriptures had meant about Christ rising from the dead.

This is the Gospel of the Lord
Praise to you, Lord Jesus Christ   KATIE THOMPSON

Introductory material

We are here in the season which gives meaning to all seasons, for without Easter there would be no gospel, no message, no Church, no faith. We could talk still, it's true, of the birth of Jesus, his life, his ministry and his death, but without the empty tomb and the risen Christ all this would finally be a tale of tragedy rather than triumph – a mirror of this world's ultimate impermanence rather than a window into the eternal purpose of God. No wonder today we celebrate!
                                                        NICK FAWCETT

'He is not here. He has risen.' Words which were to change not only the lives of those who first went to the tomb to anoint the body of Jesus, but the very course of history. For here is the message which turns our human expectations upside down, bringing laughter out of tears and victory out of defeat. What looked to be a conclusive end turned out instead to be a new beginning, holding promise not just for one but for all; and across the centuries countless people have experienced the full wonder of that promise for themselves. Listen again, then, to the testimony of scripture to the events of that first Easter; reflect on what they meant and what they continue to mean; and open your heart again to what God is able to do in your life through Christ crucified and risen!   NICK FAWCETT

Prayers

Praise – Good from evil

Lord Jesus Christ,
  when you were taken before Herod and Pilate,
    when you suffered in agony on the cross,
    and when your body was sealed in a tomb,
    it looked as though evil had triumphed,
    as though love, goodness and truth had finally been defeated.
  But you rose again,
    love triumphant,
    goodness vindicated,
    truth victorious.
  Living Lord,
    to you be the praise and glory.

Your enemies had done their worst,
  mocking you,
  beating you,
  nailing you to a cross,
  and for three days it seemed that hatred, deceit and violence
  had won the battle.
But you rose again,
  renewing,
  restoring,
  redeeming.
Living Lord,
  to you be the praise and glory.

It looked as though hope was groundless,
  faith futile,
  the future empty,
  for your purpose appeared to be destroyed,
  broken beyond redemption.
But you rose again,
  reviving confidence,
  rekindling trust,
  recreating life itself.
Living Lord,
  to you be the praise and glory.

Your friends had failed you when you needed them most –
  betraying you,
  denying you,
  abandoning you,
  and they were consumed by guilt and shame.

But you rose again,
  forgiving,
  accepting,
  affirming.
Living Lord,
  to you be the praise and glory.

Lord Jesus Christ,
  it's hard sometimes not to question,
    not to be perplexed at life's injustices
    and ask if your kingdom can ever truly come.
  But you rose again,
    light in our darkness,
    faith in our confusion,
    heaven touching earth.
Living Lord,
  to you be the praise and glory.

For your name's sake.
Amen.   NICK FAWCETT

Confession and petition

Almighty God,
  today is the most special of days –
    a day of victory, celebration and praise!

  A day on which we remember your great triumph –
    the defeat of evil, suffering and death.

  A day on which we recall the transformation you have brought –
    joy after sorrow, hope after despair, faith after doubt.

  A day on which we give thanks for all you have given us –
    love, laughter, life!

Almighty God,
  forgive us that we lose sight of those truths.
  We are so quick to become disheartened.
  We so easily forget all you have done for us.
  Forgive us for the limits we set upon your love.
  Forgive the feebleness of our response.
  Forgive the smallness of our vision.

Speak to us through this joyful season,
   and fill us with greater trust and deeper faith.
So may we live not just this day but every day
   as your Easter people,
   through Jesus Christ our Lord.
Amen.   NICK FAWCETT

Petition – Confidence from confusion

Lord Jesus Christ,
   it is hard to believe in you sometimes –
      hard to believe in the message you preached,
      the victory of love you proclaimed,
      the way of sacrifice and self-denial you urged us to follow.
   There is so much in life which challenges our faith,
      speaking instead of the way of self,
      of greed and avarice,
      of evil, injustice and exploitation.
   Yet you rose again from the tomb,
      triumphant over the darkness.
   Your love could not be defeated:
      may that truth turn our doubt to faith.

   We look at the course of human history,
      and time after time it is the same –
      a catalogue of hatred, violence, evil and oppression;
      a world in which the strongest survive,
      the wicked prosper
      and the innocent are led like lambs to the slaughter.
   Yet you rose again from the tomb,
      triumphant over the darkness.
   Your love could not be defeated:
      may that truth turn our doubt to faith.

   We look at the world today,
      and still it is the same story –
      nations racked by division and war,
      an economic order in which the few indulge their every craving
      while the many are deprived of even their most basic needs;
      an international system in which money outweighs principle;
      a world of drugs, rape, vandalism, child abuse;
      all this and so much more which scars the face of society.
   Yet you rose again from the tomb,
      triumphant over the darkness.
   Your love could not be defeated:
      may that truth turn our doubt to faith.

Give us new heart today through the message of Easter.
Help us to remember
    that your death made no sense to your followers,
    that violence appeared to be triumphant,
    goodness crushed
    and evil victorious;
    everything they had lived for seemingly sealed in the tomb,
    and faith replaced by confusion.
Yet remind us, too, that you rose again,
    and at your coming the clouds were lifted,
    the darkness was dispelled
    and faith began to shoot again.
Your love could not be defeated:
    may that truth turn our doubt to faith.

Lord Jesus Christ,
    it's hard to believe in you sometimes,
        for there are no easy answers to the harsh realities of life,
        no glib explanations as to why suffering is allowed to continue,
        evil go unchecked and good be unrewarded.
But you have shown us through your resurrection
    that, whatever it may face,
    love will not finally be extinguished,
    and your purpose cannot be denied.
One day your will shall be done and your kingdom come.
Your love could not be defeated:
    may that truth turn our doubt to faith.

We ask it in your name.
Amen.   Nick Fawcett

Intercession

Jesus is risen from the dead! Having passed through death to life, Christ has won the victory over everything evil and destructive. Full of glory and power, he enables us to bring the hope and joy of resurrection into the world's problems and tragedies. With God, nothing is impossible.

In the joy of this Easter morning let us pray to the God
who loves us completely.

We pray that the joy and conviction of Christians
may be so radiant
that all who are lost, weary and searching
may be directed towards your lasting, inner peace.

Silence for prayer

Risen Lord:
live in us all.

We pray that from every world crisis
and tragedy some good may come;
every problem become an opportunity
for development and spiritual growth.

Silence for prayer

Risen Lord:
live in us all.

We pray for the newly born,
and for all families,
that the children may be nurtured,
and the elderly cherished
through your wide, accepting love.

Silence for prayer

Risen Lord:
live in us all.

We pray that those in mental,
physical or spiritual distress
may recognise in their suffering
a privilege of sharing Christ's passion,
until they also share
the joy of a new life in you.

Silence for prayer

Risen Lord:
live in us all.

We pray that all those who have died
may share your risen life for ever.

Silence for prayer

Risen Lord:
live in us all.

In silence we praise you, Father,
for your abundant blessings.

Silence for prayer

Merciful Father,
**accept these prayers
for the sake of your Son,
our Saviour Jesus Christ, Amen.**

SUSAN SAYERS

Intercessory reflection – Hope from despair

Lord Jesus Christ,
    in this world where hopes are so often dashed
      and dreams so often broken,
      we remember today the faith in the future
      you brought to so many,
      both through your coming
      and through your resurrection from the dead.
    Lord Jesus, where faith has died and dreams have faded,
      may hope flower again.

We remember how Mary and Joseph looked forward
    to the day of your birth,
    how shepherds and magi caught their breath in wonder
    as they knelt before you,
    how the hearts of Anna and Simeon leapt in anticipation,
    and how your disciples and the crowds that flocked to hear you
    gave thanks,
    convinced that you were the Messiah,
    the one God had promised,
    the long-awaited deliverer come to set them free.
Lord Jesus, where faith has died and dreams have faded,
    may hope flower again.

We remember how that vision of the future
    was shattered by events to follow –
    your pain, humiliation, suffering and death –
    hope ebbing away as the lifeblood seeped from your body –
    an end to their dreams,
    an end to everything.
Lord Jesus, where faith has died and dreams have faded,
    may hope flower again.

We remember how the news spread that the tomb was empty,
    the stone rolled away,
    your body gone,
    and how, despite it all,
    your followers could scarcely bring themselves to hope –
    afraid to take the risk of faith
    in case they should face the heartache of losing you once more.
Lord Jesus, where faith has died and dreams have faded,
    may hope flower again.

But we remember finally how you appeared,
   in all your risen glory –
   in the garden,
   in the upstairs room,
   on the Emmaus road,
   by the Sea of Galilee –
   and the dream was born again,
   the smouldering embers of faith rekindled.
Lord Jesus, where faith has died and dreams have faded,
   may hope flower again.

Lord Jesus Christ,
   a world is waiting, hurting, longing,
     searching for hope,
     crying out for meaning,
     hungry for some reason to believe in the future.
Come again in your living power,
   and bring new life to all.
Lord Jesus, where faith has died and dreams have faded,
   may hope flower again.

In your name we pray.
Amen.

NICK FAWCETT

Short prayers

Loving God,
   we catch a glimpse today
   into the mystery of this world,
   into the strange puzzle
   that there can be no life without death,
   no light without darkness,
   no joy without sorrow,
   no starting the new without ending the old.
May that truth give us strength
   when days are hard to bear.
Reassure us with the knowledge
   that in the bleakest moments you are there,
   and that it is often in such times
   that you are supremely at work.
Though we do not see or understand,
   teach us still to trust,
   confident that in Christ
   all things will be made new,
   to the glory of your name.
Amen.

NICK FAWCETT

Loving God,
   we praise you again for this season
   and the assurance it brings
   that nothing can ever finally overcome your love.
You confronted the forces of evil,
   allowing them to throw everything
   they could muster against you,
   and when they had done their worst
   you emerged victorious,
   no power able to hold you down.
Teach us always to hold on to that truth,
   and so to live each moment in the knowledge
   that, whatever we may face,
   your love will see us through.
In the name of the risen Christ we pray.
Amen.   NICK FAWCETT

Lord Jesus Christ,
   we praise you that we can worship you
   not simply as the crucified Christ
   but as our risen Lord and Saviour.
We praise you that death was not the end
   but a new beginning,
   not simply for you but for us!
We praise you then for this time of joy,
   of thanksgiving and celebration –
   a time that speaks of victory, renewal and hope.
Lord Jesus Christ,
   we praise you for the great message of Easter
   and the wonderful truth
   that countless generations across the years
   have found it to be true in their own experience.
Open now your word to us
   so that we may meet with you
   and receive your life for ourselves.   NICK FAWCETT

All-age-talk material

JESUS is alive for EVER!

CUT TO LENGTH TO FIT

Put it round your head like this:

Colour the crown.
Cut along the lines.
Join them up to make a long strip.

SUSAN SAYERS

Colour the dotted shapes.

Help the women get to the tomb.

WORDSEARCH
Find the following words in the grid:
MAGDALENE, JOANNA, MOTHER,
WOMEN, CROSS, SUNDAY, JESUS,
RESURRECTION, TOMB, STONE,
GOOD NEWS, SPICES, SOLDIER.

```
M A G D A L E N E O T S
O M B W O L D I E R T J
T V G O O D N E W S O E
H J D G A M O T H A M S
E E E S U R E T N E B S
R S P S I C F N O R M S
X U J E U S A C D E O E
C T N E V S O R A I S C
S U N D A Y G O L D P I
G O O E N O T S E L I P
R E S U R R E S N O R S
N O I T C E R R U S E R
```

MICHAEL FORSTER

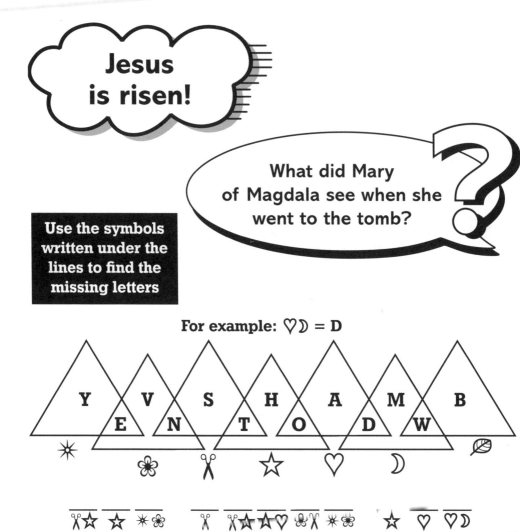

Jesus is risen!

What did Mary of Magdala see when she went to the tomb?

Use the symbols written under the lines to find the missing letters

For example: ♡☽ = D

John 20:1

KATIE THOMPSON

> Mary ran to
> tell two of the disciples that
> Jesus had gone

Follow the arrows to spell out their names

S	A	C	N	F	E
I	J	P	H	N	O
E	M	O	T	S	L
P	N	L	J	A	D
N	E	A	R	H	M
B	T	E	C	D	T

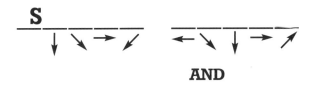

S _ _ _ _   _ _ _ _ _

AND

_ _ _ _

KATIE THOMPSON

They found the tomb empty! The linen cloths lay rolled up on the ground. Now they understood the Scriptures!

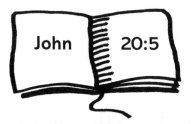

John 20:5

Using the code, see if YOU can understand what was written!

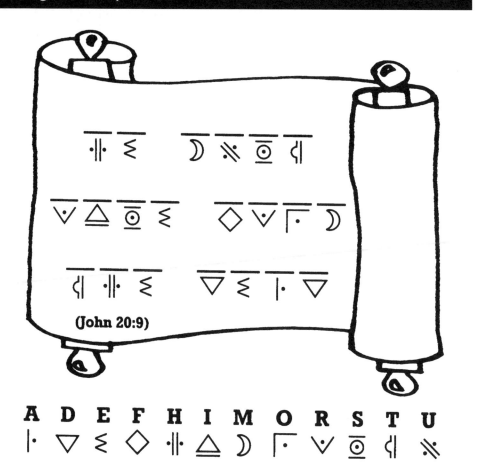

(John 20:9)

A	D	E	F	H	I	M	O	R	S	T	U

Katie Thompson

The disciples did not believe them, so Peter went to look for himself

Write the first letter of each object to see what he found

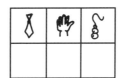

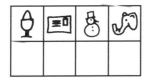

KATIE THOMPSON

At sunrise on the Sunday
morning, the women made their
way to the tomb where
Jesus was buried

**Help them to find their way through
Jerusalem's streets using these directions**

7A, 6B,
5C, 4C,
4D, 3D,
3E, 3F,
3G, 2G,
2F, 1F

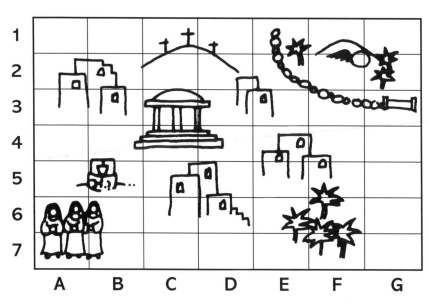

KATIE THOMPSON

They were puzzling over the empty tomb, when suddenly two men appeared beside them!

Write the next letter of the alphabet on the lines above to read what the men said to them.

A B C D E F G H I J K L M N O P Q R S T U V W X Y Z

'<u>H E</u> <u>I S</u>
<u>N O T</u> <u>H E R E</u>.
<u>H E</u> <u>H A S</u> <u>R I S E N</u>
<u>F R O M</u> <u>T H E</u>
<u>D E A D</u>!'

(G D) (H R)
(M N S) (G D Q D)
(G D) (G Z R) (Q H R D M)
(E Q N L) (S G D)
(C D Z C)

Luke 24:6

KATIE THOMPSON

The three women went off to tell the disciples their news

Use the code to find the women's names

T	M	A	O	F	R	E	Y	D	J	S	H	L	N	G
1	2	3	4	5	6	7	8	9	10	11	12	13	14	15

2 3 6 8   4 5

2 3 15 9 3 13 3

10 4 3 14 14 3

2 3 6 8   1 12 7   2 4 1 12 7 6

4 5   10 3 2 7 11

Luke 24:10

KATIE THOMPSON

Sense or nonsense?

Aim

To show that, while some may ridicule the idea of resurrection, to the eye of faith it is a truth which makes sense of everything.

Preparation

Display the following on a board:

$E = MC^2$

$2 = 2 = 5$

$4 \times 4 = 16$

$5 - 3 = 7$

Tfotf ps opotfotf

Twas brillig and the slithy toves

$101 + 110 = 11$

Ring a ring of roses

All dogs are animals, therefore all animals are dogs

A bird in the hand is worth two in the bush

'emeism de kerussomen Xriston 'estauromenon

He is not here; he has risen

Talk

Tell the congregation you need their help to sort out some sense from nonsense. Taking each of the displayed statements in turn, ask whether they make any sense or not. After giving time for answers, make the following comments about each:

$E = MC^2$
We may not be able to understand this, but it is central to Einstein's theory of relativity.

$2 = 2 = 5$
This is clearly nonsense.

$4 \times 4 = 16$
This makes perfect sense.

$5 - 3 = 7$
This is clearly nonsense.

Tfotf ps opotfotf
This looks like nonsense, but in fact is code for 'Sense or nonsense' (A=B, B=C, C=D, etc.).

Twas brillig and the slithy toves
These are the opening words of a nonsense poem by Lewis Carroll, but although the poem is nonsense it sounds like it makes sense!

$101 + 110 = 11$

This is nonsense using Arabic numbers, but perfect sense using binary numbers.

Ring a ring of roses

This dates back to the days of the Black Death.

All dogs are animals, therefore all animals are dogs

This sounds logical but, of course, is complete nonsense.

A bird in the hand is worth two in the bush

Taken literally this is nonsense, but the point this proverb is making makes good sense.

'emeism de kerussomen Xriston 'estauromenon

This may look like nonsense, but in fact is Greek for 'Yet we proclaim Christ crucified' (1 Corinthians 1:23).

He is not here; he has risen

There are many who will tell us this is nonsense, but as Christians we believe it is true.

Some of the statements are nonsense, some look like nonsense but in fact are good sense, some seem to make sense but are actually nonsense, and some make perfect sense as they stand. All of which goes to show that making sense of something is not always as easy as we might think. And if we still doubt that, let's look back to the reaction of the disciples of Jesus when the women ran back from the tomb to tell them that the tomb was empty and Jesus had risen:

> They did not believe the women, because their words seemed to them like nonsense. (Luke 24:11)

It wasn't that the disciples didn't want to believe; simply that for a moment it seemed too good to be true. Only when they saw Jesus for themselves were they finally fully convinced.

There are still, of course, many today who claim that the resurrection of Jesus is nonsense, that there is no way it could ever have happened.

We cannot prove them wrong, any more than they can prove themselves right, for the truth of the resurrection can only be discovered through personal experience. But when we open our lives to the reality of the risen Christ, then not only do we discover the truth about resurrection; we discover a faith that makes sense of life itself.   NICK FAWCETT

From the known to the unknown

Show the children something that's broken – perhaps a watch or an old radio that doesn't work any more. If you think it appropriate, you could also ask if any of them has ever broken something, either out of carelessness or perhaps because they were angry. We must all have done that at some time, so there's no need to be embarrassed about it, but it does show that the power to damage and destroy is nothing special – we can all do it, but hopefully we don't choose to most of the time. The power to mend, though – to heal, to give life – now that really sets someone apart. That's *real* power!   MICHAEL FORSTER

Select a variety of pictures taken from a wide range of magazines and/ or newspapers. Cut out a portion of the picture so that the image is incomplete (remember to keep a note of what the picture was originally). Stick/glue the images onto a flipchart and number each image.

Distribute pens and paper to the group and ask them to guess what the original picture was. The person with the most correct answers is the winner.

Images are open to our interpretation. It isn't always as easy as we think to identify even familiar images from a small portion or a strange angle.

Read Luke 24:1-12

It was extremely early on Sunday morning. It was still dark although the sun was just starting to signal its arrival for the day. Mary and several other women went to the tomb of Jesus to complete the last functions of the burial ceremony. The spices they took with them would have been a mixture of myrrh and aloes which acted as a sort of disinfectant and deodorant. It would have been a very sad occasion for the women. After three hectic yet incredible years, where Jesus had literally changed people's lives, the end had come. The final act of putting spices on the dead body was almost like closing a book; it was finished.

Jesus had used these very same words a couple of days earlier as he had hung on the cross: 'It is finished.' But his idea of 'finished' was very different from that of the women who came to his tomb. What Jesus had struggled for and eventually died for was finished. Stage One was complete and now Stage Two was about to begin.

When the women arrived at the tomb, the heavy circular stone had been moved, the tomb was open. Inside the tomb, the body had vanished. Various questions must have gone through the women's minds. What could have happened? Who could have taken the body? The women's thoughts were occupied with the practical side of things: who, what, where? They'd seen Jesus die – that was it, over and done.

In the gloom two men appeared. Their clothes shone in the darkness. The sight must have been frightening. The women were already concerned about the loss of the body and now here was something else to think about. The response from the two men was incredible. Why were the women looking where dead people were buried? Well, what else are you supposed to find in a graveyard? Then the amazing statement: 'Jesus isn't here, he's alive!'

The women ran back to the disciples and told them what they had and *hadn't* seen. The Greek word, which the disciples used to describe the women's report is one more often used by ancient Greek doctors to define someone who is 'babbling', someone who has a fever or is insane. The women's mixture of amazement and excitement didn't seem to make any impression on the disciples who must have been more interested in what was for breakfast.

Only Peter, who had denied Jesus three times, had the courage to check the story out. He also returned confused and wondering what had happened. Now it wasn't so much who had done it, but why?

Ask the group what words they think would describe the thoughts and feelings of the women when they went to the tomb of Jesus. Write them up on the flipchart. Then ask them for words to describe the thoughts and feelings of the disciples after the women had come back with their report.

- Do any of these words describe our thoughts or the way we feel about God, Jesus, the Holy Spirit?
- Is there a problem with us having these kinds of thoughts?
- If even the people who had known Jesus well could feel that way, then isn't it only reasonable for us to have the same thoughts and feelings whenever we try to understand what God wants with us?   PETE TOWNSEND

Reflective material
(sketches, meditations and poems)

Meditation of Mary Magdalene

They're not going to listen, I can tell you that now.
They've always been suspicious of me, right from the start,
    wondering what Jesus was thinking of,
    getting mixed up with someone like me.
I know what they'll say, you mark my words –
    'Making it all up.'
    'Wanting to be the centre of attention as usual.'
    'A lovesick fool.'
Not that I can blame them;
    it didn't do his cause any good, after all, when I came along.
A few tax collectors those Pharisees could stomach,
    but me, I really put the cat among the pigeons.
I know how the tongues wagged,
    how easy it became to criticise.
Maybe I should have stayed away,
    kept my distance,
    but I loved him.

No, not in the sense they meant with their sly, dark innuendo,
   but deeper,
   with everything I am,
   everything I've got,
   in a way that I've never loved before.
Yet not even the disciples really trusted me, I know that.
They found it hard to accept,
   hard to forgive what I'd been.
And I can understand that –
   let's face it, I'm finding it hard to forgive them for running away,
   failing him when he needed them most.
But what I hold on to is those words from the cross:
   'Father, forgive them, for they do not know what they do.'
He understood we all fail him,
   that we're all unworthy,
   none of us perfect,
   yet he forgave us and loved us despite that.
I thought I'd lost him,
   the only one who ever truly accepted me,
   and I was reconciled to struggling on alone,
   no one to understand,
   no one to offer their support.
But I was wrong, for he came to me.
There in the garden, overwhelmed by my grief,
   he came to me, and hope was born again.
Not that I could believe it at first.
The voice was familiar,
   the face,
   the eyes,
   but I told myself it couldn't be,
   that it had to be the gardener,
   anyone but Jesus.
And they'll do the same, I'm sure of it,
   tell me I got it wrong,
   that I'm overwrought,
   ready to believe anything.
They won't listen, I can tell you that now,
   but then I'm used to that, aren't I?
And it doesn't matter any more,
   for he's accepted me
   as he's accepted them,
   as he accepts everyone who's ready to respond to his love
   and receive his forgiveness.

NICK FAWCETT

Meditation of Peter

It seemed too good to be true,
   too wonderful even to contemplate he might be alive again –
   so we shook our heads,
   raised our eyebrows,
   and laughed between our tears.
We wanted to believe it, of course we did,
   more than anything else in the world,
   but how could we after all we'd seen,
   everything we'd been through?
Oh, it's all right for *you* –
   anyone can be wise after the event –
   but put yourself in our shoes;
   imagine what it must have been like
   having seen Jesus die as we did,
   and then ask yourself honestly:
   would you have felt any different?
Our faith was in tatters,
   life seeming an empty void,
   for how could God have let it happen,
   how could he have allowed a man like that
   to endure such a terrible end?
Yet he had,
   and we just couldn't get that knowledge out of our minds.
It had been different when Jesus was with us –
   we'd looked forward then,
   confident,
   full of hope,
   no promise too wonderful,
   no vision beyond fulfilment;
   for in those few short years of his ministry
   he'd shown us another way –
   the way of love, goodness, mercy –
   and we'd actually believed
   such things could finally triumph over evil,
   no matter how impossible it seemed.
Not any more, though.
It was back to the cold harsh world of reality
   where hopes are dashed and dreams lie broken,
   where goodness is trampled underfoot
   and love tossed back in your face,
   and this time we were resolved
   to keep our feet firmly on the ground,
   the thought of another disappointment, another let-down,
   too much to bear.

And yet, despite it all, I had to be sure,
    that flicker of hope their words had kindled
    either fanned into life or laid to rest once and for all;
    so I ran to the tomb, scarcely knowing what I did,
    and found the stone rolled away just as they had said,
    the grave clothes cast aside,
    the tomb, empty!
Can it really be,
    our Lord risen, alive?
I want to believe it so much,
    more than you'll ever know,
    but dare I take the risk of faith again?
What do you think –
    is it too good to be true?   NICK FAWCETT

Meditation of Bartholomew

What's done cannot be undone, isn't that what they say?
As much as we might wish otherwise,
    it's impossible to turn the clock back.
And that's exactly what we'd thought just a few days before,
    as we stood in desolation
    and watched the Master suffer on that cross,
    as we watched him breathe his last,
    as we saw him cut down, limp and lifeless,
    and carried to the tomb.
It was over,
    finished,
    those three wonderful years we'd spent with him at an end,
    never to be repeated.
What possible reason was there to think otherwise?
So when the women burst in on us,
    babbling about the tomb being empty,
    the stone rolled away,
    well, I hate to say it, but we didn't pay much attention.
It just couldn't be, could it?
At least that's what the theory said;
    the facts told a different story –
    and what a story it was!
For the next thing we knew he was there amongst us,
    the one they thought they'd destroyed, back from the grave,
    the one we all believed dead and buried, alive!
And in that moment the world itself was turned upside down,
    for suddenly we knew beyond doubt
    that what's done *can* be undone,
    the proof right there, before our very eyes.

Defeat had become victory,
   despair, hope,
   sorrow, joy,
   darkness, light,
   tears, laughter!
The forces of evil had conspired to do their worst,
   only for the havoc they'd wreaked
   to be wiped away in a moment,
   rolled back, as surely as the stone from the tomb,
   by the power of love!
Do you realise what that means?
That no situation is too hopeless,
   no person too dreadful,
   to be beyond redemption.
That no matter who we are or what we do,
   however much we fail,
   however far we stray,
   still he can turn us round and transform our lives.
That there is nothing in heaven or earth,
   in life or in death,
   that can finally separate us
   from the love of God revealed in Christ!
He'd been to the cross,
   he'd carried our sins,
   he'd wrestled with the powers of darkness,
   and he triumphed over it all.
Life was beginning again,
   for you,
   for me,
   for everyone willing to receive it.
That, and that alone, cannot be undone!

NICK FAWCETT

Additional Easter Material

(covering second and third weeks of Easter)

John 20:19-31; John 21:1-19

(also Luke 24:13-35; Revelation 5:11-14)

A reading from the Gospel of John (20:19-31)

On the Sunday after Jesus had died his disciples sat huddled together in a locked room, hidden away for fear of being arrested.

Suddenly Jesus appeared in the room with them. 'Peace be with you,' he said and he showed them the wounds in his hands and his side. The disciples were overjoyed to see their master again.

'As my Father sent me, so I am sending you,' said Jesus. Then, breathing on them, he said, 'Receive the Holy Spirit, and know that whoever you forgive I will forgive also!'

The disciple called Thomas was not with the others when Jesus had appeared, and because he had not seen him with his own eyes, he did not believe that Jesus was alive.

A week later Jesus appeared to them again and greeted them with the words, 'Peace be with you.' He showed his wounds to Thomas and said, 'Doubt no longer, Thomas.'

At once Thomas fell to his knees and cried, 'My Lord and my God.'

Jesus said to him, 'You believe because you have seen me with your own eyes. Blessed are those who have not seen and yet believe.'

Jesus performed many other miracles which his disciples witnessed, but they are not written down in this book. The ones recorded here have been written so you may believe that Jesus is the Son of God, and through this belief you may have everlasting life.

This is the Gospel of the Lord
Praise to you, Lord Jesus Christ   KATIE THOMPSON

A reading from the Gospel of John (20:24-29)

I've never met anyone who believes this story. Try it out. Ask people whether they would prefer actually to see and touch the risen Lord, or 'only' to believe. They'll all choose the first. For them, seeing is believing. What on earth could John mean by saying it is the believers who are more fortunate? He means that only those who believe can really see. Thomas' seeing and touching obviously feels more real. But that is only because it is a dramatic story, not a video recording. In actuality, no one can be in contact with the risen Christ until he believes that Jesus is alive. In the real world, believing that Christ is risen cannot mean physically touching him, whether we are talking of the first century or the twenty-first. What a materialistic view of our world to think otherwise!

It was on the Sunday after Jesus died
that his disciples first understood
that his death was not the end of him:
they actually experienced him as still being present with them.

One of the disciples, Thomas Twin,
had missed this experience because he was away.
So when the others told him they had actually seen Jesus,
he refused to believe them.
'I must see the nail-marks in his hands for myself,
and feel them for myself,' he said,
'and put my own hand into his wounded side.'

The following Sunday, the disciples
were again gathered together behind locked doors,
and this time Thomas was with them.
Suddenly Jesus was there in their midst.
He greeted them and said,
'May God's peace be with you.'
Then he turned to Thomas.
'Give me your finger,' he said,
'and feel my pierced hand.
Give me your hand and touch my wounded side.
Stop being such a sceptic,
and become a real believer like the rest.'

Thomas fell on his knees,
a verse of the psalms on his lips.
'My Lord and my God,' he murmured.
Jesus smiled as he said,
'You're saying that seeing is believing.
I'm saying that there's no seeing me without believing!'   H. J. RICHARDS

A reading from the Gospel of John (21:1-19)

Jesus appeared again to his disciples by the sea of Tiberius. Simon Peter and some of the disciples had been fishing all night but had caught nothing. As daylight dawned Jesus stood on the shore, although they did not recognise him, and he asked them, 'Have you caught anything?' As they shook their heads in reply, he said to them, 'Try once more over there, and you will catch something!'

They threw their nets back into the water and caught so many fish that their nets were ready to burst. As soon as Simon Peter recognised Jesus, he jumped into the water and swam to meet him.

On the beach Jesus had made a fire and was cooking breakfast for his friends, and they shared a meal together of bread and fresh fish.

When they had finished eating, Jesus turned to Peter and asked, 'Do you love me more than anyone?'

'Yes, Lord, you know that I love you,' Peter replied.

'Then feed my lambs,' Jesus said.

Again Jesus put the same question to Peter, and again Peter gave the same reply: 'Lord, you know I love you.'

Jesus said to him, 'Take care of my sheep.'

When Jesus asked Peter the same question for a third time, Peter felt sad and hurt, and he said to Jesus, 'Lord, you know everything, so you must know how much I love you!'

Again Jesus said to Peter, 'Take care of my sheep.' He told Peter how he would give glory to God, and then he said to him, 'Come, follow me.'

This is the Gospel of the Lord
Praise to you, Lord Jesus Christ   KATIE THOMPSON

Prayers

Praise – The victory of love

Loving God,
    we praise you once more for all you have done in Christ,
        for your victory through him over sin and evil,
        darkness and death.
    We praise you for your love that cannot be kept down,
        whatever it may face.
    May the knowledge of that love inspire us
        to keep on following you
        through good and bad.

When life seems hard,
    when good seems frustrated,
    when we feel ourselves in danger
    of being overwhelmed by trials and temptations,
    assure us once more of your love
    that will not be defeated.

When our work seems to bear no fruit,
    when our efforts go unrewarded,
    when our hopes appear unfulfilled,
    teach us to trust in your purpose
    that presses on towards fulfilment.

When the innocent suffer,
  when evil prospers,
  when hatred seems to hold sway,
  help us to keep on believing
  that good will finally win through.

Grant us a deep unshakeable confidence
  that whatever life brings,
  whatever we face,
  however things seem,
  your will shall be done and your kingdom come,
  through Jesus Christ our Lord.
  Amen.   NICK FAWCETT

Confession – God of the unexpected

Mighty God,
  we praise you for the great surprise of Easter –
    your transformation of what had seemed the end
    into a new beginning;
    your turning of what had seemed the triumph of evil
    into the victory of love.
  God of the unexpected,
    hear our prayer.

We praise you for the way you changed the lives
    of Jesus' followers –
    turning sorrow into celebration,
    doubt to faith,
    questions to answers,
    confusion to confidence,
    darkness to light.
  God of the unexpected,
    hear our prayer.

Forgive us that we too,
    like the Apostles arriving at the tomb,
    are sometimes deceived by appearances.
  We make judgements based on our own limited assumptions,
    and we lose faith
    when life doesn't measure up to our expectations.
  We imagine we have all the answers,
    and we are frightened when we find we have not.
  We reject truths that do not fit in with our view of the world,
    and then are puzzled
    when we cannot make sense of things.
  God of the unexpected,
    hear our prayer.

Forgive us for doubting your love,
    for losing sight of your purpose,
    for questioning your power.
Forgive us for ignoring your promises,
    for diminishing your greatness,
    for forgetting that your ways are not our ways
    nor your thoughts our thoughts.
God of the unexpected,
    hear our prayer.

We pray for all those unable to make sense
    of the situations they find themselves in,
    their hopes shattered by their experiences of life –
    those who are anxious, fearful, disillusioned, depressed,
    faced perhaps by inexplicable suffering, sorrow or evil,
    or having lost their homes, their employment,
    their livelihoods, their loved ones;
    afflicted by disease, disability, disaster,
    or exploited, oppressed,
    deprived of their basic human dignity.
God of the unexpected,
    hear our prayer.

May the surprise of Easter burst afresh
    into their lives and our own,
    revealing new possibilities to life
    and a new dimension to your love,
    giving new meaning to each day and every moment,
    bringing new strength and opportunities,
    offering new hope for the future
    and renewed purpose in the present.
May this day we celebrate teach us to expect the unexpected!
God of the unexpected,
    hear our prayer,
    in the name of the risen and victorious Christ.
    Amen.   Nick Fawcett

Confession – Commitment from denial

Lord Jesus Christ,
    we marvel today at the extent of your love
        and the wonder of your grace.
    You were betrayed, denied and abandoned,
        yet still, willingly, you went to your death,
        offering your life for the life of the world.

And, after you rose again,
    you appeared first to those who had forsaken you,
    reaching out your hands in acceptance,
    speaking your word of peace.
Time and again we fail you.
Lord, have mercy.
Time and again you welcome us back.
Teach us to walk in faith.

We know that our faith is no better than that of those first disciples,
    our courage no stronger,
    our commitment no more able to withstand adversity.
All too often we betray you through the way we live,
    we deny you through the things we say and do,
    we abandon you,
    preferring the easy and undemanding road
    rather than the way of the cross.
Time and again we fail you.
Lord, have mercy.
Time and again you welcome us back.
Teach us to walk in faith.

Thank you for being ready to forgive and forget,
    to offer us the opportunity to make amends.
You understand our weakness
    and, through your grace,
    you do not simply invite us to start again,
    you give us help and strength to follow you more closely.
When we fall, you pick us up,
    when we lose our way, you show us the way forward.
Always you are there to restore and renew.
Time and again we fail you.
Lord, have mercy.
Time and again you welcome us back.
Teach us to walk in faith.

Lord Jesus Christ,
    we are not worthy to bear your name,
        for we fail you so often in so many ways.
    But we come in all our sinfulness,
        confessing our failure,
        acknowledging our faults
        and throwing ourselves once more upon your great mercy.
    Above all, we come committing ourselves afresh to your service,
        resolved to live more faithfully as your people,
        to stay true to you as you stay true to us.

Time and again we fail you.
Lord, have mercy.
Time and again you welcome us back.
Teach us to walk in faith.

We ask it for your name's sake.
Amen.   NICK FAWCETT

Thanksgiving – Faith from doubt

Lord Jesus Christ,
   we thank you again today for the great miracle of Easter
     and for everything it reveals about your awesome love.

We remember how women came to the tomb,
   intending to anoint your body,
   wondering who would roll the stone away;
   only to find the tomb empty,
   your body gone,
   good news there to greet them!
It is still good news for today!
Lord, we thank you.

We remember how the disciples refused to believe,
   dismissing the women's words as nonsense,
   an idle tale,
   a foolish fantasy;
   only suddenly you were there,
   standing among them,
   speaking your word:
   'Do not be afraid.'
It is still good news for today!
Lord, we thank you.

We remember how Mary stood weeping in the garden,
   confused,
   shaken,
   beside herself with grief,
   even mistaking you for a gardener;
   only then you spoke:
   'Mary',
   and tears gave way to laughter.
It is still good news for today!
Lord, we thank you.

We remember how two weary followers
  were walking on the Emmaus Road,
  dismayed,
  disappointed,
  disillusioned,
  their hope that you might be the Messiah in tatters,
  their dreams crushed;
  only, all at once, you were with them,
  and, as you broke bread,
  their eyes were opened so that they realised it was you,
  Christ crucified but risen.
It is still good news for today!
Lord, we thank you.

We remember how Thomas doubted, despite everything,
  adamant he could not accept your resurrection
  until he'd seen you for himself,
  until he'd put his hands in your wounds
  and met you face to face;
  only, once again, you were there,
  speaking the words he longed to hear:
  'Put your finger here and see my hands.
  Reach out and touch' –
  and after doubt there was faith.
It is still good news for today!
Lord, we thank you.

Lord Jesus Christ,
  we remember today how,
    though all questioned,
    all struggled to accept the glorious truth,
    still you came,
    restoring hope to hearts dulled by despair,
    joy to lives bowed down by sorrow.
It is still good news for today!
Lord, we thank you.
Amen.   NICK FAWCETT

Intercession – Sharing the news

Lord Jesus Christ,
  we thank you for the message of Easter –
    for the assurance it brings of your triumph over death,
    the proof it offers
    that love will always have the last word.
  Yet alongside that message there is another
    that perhaps we do not hear so often –

a challenge which sometimes we can ignore,
a call to action as well as to celebration.
You have given us good news;
teach us to share it.

Lord Jesus Christ,
you appeared to your followers,
demonstrating you had risen,
and then you sent them out
to proclaim your resurrection to all.
You met with them,
and then called them to lead others to you.
You gave them joy,
and then told them to share it.
Easter was not for the few but for all,
not just for them but the whole world!
You have given us good news;
teach us to share it.

Lord Jesus Christ,
forgive us that so often we forget that.
Having experienced your risen presence,
we keep it to ourselves.
Having met with you,
we fail to introduce others to you in turn.
Having received so much,
we have shared so little.
You have given us good news;
teach us to share it.

Lord Jesus Christ,
we thank you for those who have fulfilled your call –
those who first made the Gospel known to us,
those who proclaim it to others,
those who sow, nurture, and bring to fruition
the seeds of faith.
We pray for all you have specially gifted
to proclaim the Good News –
preachers and evangelists,
ministers and missionaries,
teachers and writers.
May many meet with you through their labours
and come to know you
as their living Lord and Saviour.
You have given us good news;
teach us to share it.

Lord Jesus Christ,
    you call each one of us to be your witnesses –
        to tell others what we have experienced of your love,
        to make known what you have done for us,
        to testify to the way you have changed our lives.
    Help us to do that faithfully,
        to play our part in your kingdom and purpose.
    And so through us may others come to meet you
        and know you for themselves.
    You have given us good news;
        teach us to share it,
        to your glory.
        Amen.   NICK FAWCETT

Short prayers

Loving God,
we thank and praise you for your love,
stronger than fear and even than death itself.
We thank you for being with your people
even when we don't recognise you.
Forgive us for the times
when our own actions and attitudes obscure your presence,
and help us to live so that others may recognise you.
Through Jesus Christ our Lord.
Amen.   MICHAEL FORSTER

Lord, I don't understand philosophy,
    I can't get my head around psychology,
    and theology leaves me cold.
I'm not trying to make trouble,
    or cause anyone a problem.
I just want to be honest,
    well, as honest as I can be.
Don't get me wrong,
    I'm not saying I know it all,
    I'm glad I don't,
    know it all, I mean.
I want my faith to be real,
    not based on some second-hand account,
    or a set of rules which make me choke.

If I'm going to believe in you,
    properly, not some Sunday saint,
    or weekend wonder,
    but real, like a proper relationship
    between two hearts,
    then help me see the truth
    of who you are,
    and what you mean to me. Amen

PETE TOWNSEND

Lord Jesus Christ,
    you appeared to different people
    at different places, at different times –
    to Mary in the garden,
    to Cleopas and his companion
    on the Emmaus road,
    to the disciples in the upper room,
    to your followers in Galilee.
Each had their own unique meeting with you,
    and it was only when you met with them,
    face to face,
    that the truth dawned;
    only then that they dared to believe
    you were alive.
Lord Jesus Christ,
    we cannot see you quite as they did,
    but we too can meet with you
    and experience the reality of your living presence.
Meet with us now, as we worship you,
    as we gather in your name.

NICK FAWCETT

All-age-talk material

Use the Gospel and tell the story of the disciples fishing and seeing Jesus on the beach.

Divide the group into two. One group prepares the acting out (give lots of help and encourage the shy ones to participate).

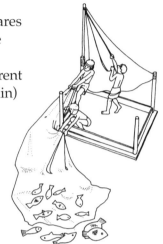

The other group cuts out lots of fish, all different colours, shapes and sizes. Have a net (old curtain) and an upturned table as a boat. Then the actors perform to the fish makers.

If this were prepared beforehand, the children could present their performance during the Gospel. Otherwise, let them take a fish home with them to remind them of what happened. Suggest they tell their families, or draw a picture of it to bring back next week.

SUSAN SAYERS

JESUS IS ALIVE — AND COOKING BREAKFAST!

In the SEA of TIBERIAS, PETER and his FRIENDS went fishing, but they CAUGHT NOTHING. Then they saw JESUS standing on the BEACH. He had lit a FIRE. He told them to FISH on the right SIDE of the BOAT. They caught lots of fish and ATE some for breakfast with Jesus.

"It is the Lord!"

Colour the picture

John 21:1-14

SUSAN SAYERS

Remind the children of how Peter had denied Jesus three times when he was frightened of what might happen to him if he told the truth. Discuss times when we feel scared of doing the right thing (like owning up, for instance) and how we don't feel really comfortable with someone we have hurt until we've said sorry and they have forgiven us.

Now tell or read how Jesus puts things right again for Peter, and even trusts him again. Jesus does the same with us – he will always give us another chance.

Help each child make a zigzag picture to show how turning away from God makes him and us miserable. Turning back to him makes him and us happy. Each picture is coloured, cut in strips and pasted on to thin card in the order: 1A 2B 3C 4D etc. Fold the finished card like a fan, and the two pictures will emerge when viewed from one side or the other. SUSAN SAYERS

  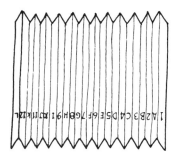

SUSAN SAYERS

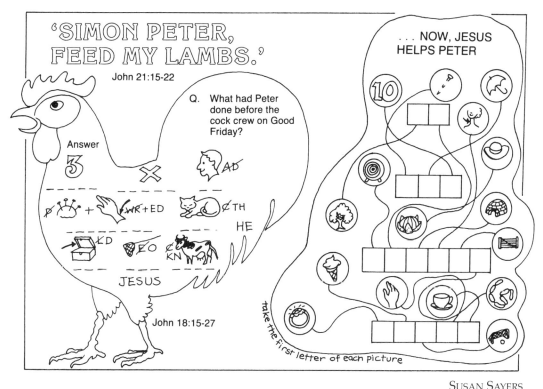

SUSAN SAYERS

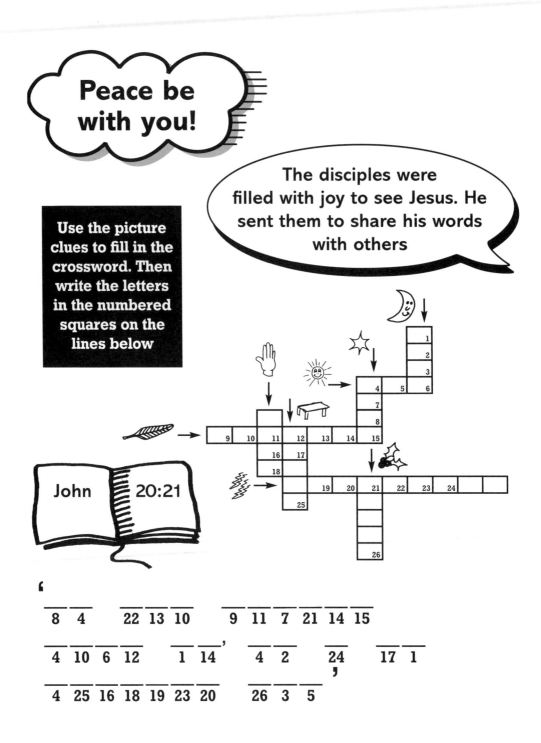

Peace be with you!

The disciples were filled with joy to see Jesus. He sent them to share his words with others

Use the picture clues to fill in the crossword. Then write the letters in the numbered squares on the lines below

John 20:21

'
___ ___　___ ___ ___　___ ___ ___ ___ ___ ___
8　4　　22　13　10　　9　11　7　21　14　15

___ ___ ___ ___　___ ___,　___ ___　___　___ ___
4　10　6　12　　1　14　　4　2　　24　　17　1

___ ___ ___ ___ ___ ___ ___　___ ___ ___
4　25　16　18　19　23　20　　26　3　5

KATIE THOMPSON

Then Jesus gave them a very special gift to help them with their work

Write the letter that is missing from the second word to spell out what it was!

In **HEART** but not **HEAR**

In **HAND** but not **BAND**

In **LIME** but not **LIMB**

In **HOUSE** but not **MOUSE**

In **OTHER** but not **EITHER**

In **LIGHT** but not **MIGHT**

In **YELLOW** but not **MELLOW**

In **WEST** but not **WET**

In **PAN** but not **CAN**

In **MAIN** but not **MAN**

In **WRITE** but not **WHITE**

In **VAIN** but not **VAN**

In **TABLE** but not **ABLE**

KATIE THOMPSON

One of the disciples was missing when Jesus appeared. He did not believe that Jesus was alive

John 20:24

Unscramble the letters to find his name

MHSAOT _____

Use the code to find what Jesus said to him

Jesus showed him his wounds and then he believed!

See John 20:29

1 A	14 N
2 B	15 O
3 C	16 P
4 D	17 Q
5 E	18 R
6 F	19 S
7 G	20 T
8 H	21 U
9 I	22 V
10 J	23 W
11 K	24 X
12 L	25 Y
13 M	26 Z

'
___ ___ ___ ___ ___   ___ ___ ___
8   1   16 16 25   1   18 5

___ ___ ___ ___ ___   ___ ___ ___
20 8   15 19 5   23 8   15

___ ___ ___ ___   ___ ___ ___
8   1   22 5   14 15 20

___ ___ ___ ___   ___ ___ ___
19 5   5   14   1   14 4

,
___ ___ ___   ___ ___ ___ ___ ___ ___ ___
25 5   20   2   5   12 9   5   22 5

KATIE THOMPSON

Jesus on the shore

John 21:1-19

> Peter and his friends had been fishing all night but had caught nothing. Then someone they did not recognise told them to try again

Solve each problem to find out how many fish they caught!

1. $5 \times 5 + 2 =$ _____

2. $14 + 22 - 3 =$ _____

3. $9 \div 3 \times 7 =$ _____

4. $17 - 2 \times 2 =$ _____

5. $3 + 3 \times 7 =$ _____

Answer = _____ **Fish!**

KATIE THOMPSON

Then Jesus
told Peter what he wanted
him to do

Add or subtract words and letters to find the missing words

feather ather
ed

Ke
m
key

lamp
b + s

e
t cake

car -Ø + e

shower ower
f feet feet
p

' _ _ _ _ _ _   _ _ _ _ _ _   of my   _ _ _ _ _ _ _ '

BY F hand

m + e eye
e

sheep

' _ _ _ _ _   _ _ _ _ _ _ '

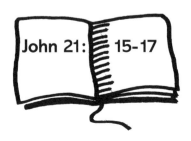

John 21: 15-17

KATIE THOMPSON

The disciples recognised Jesus and they came ashore to have breakfast with him. Jesus asked Peter the same question three times, and Peter gave the same answer each time

Use the code to find out what they said to each other

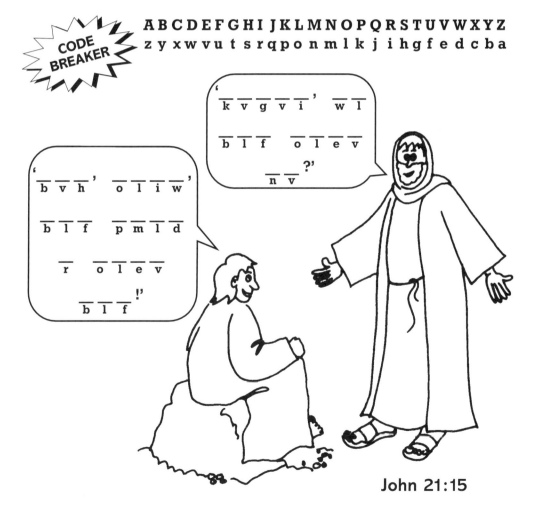

CODE BREAKER

ABCDEFGHIJKLMNOPQRSTUVWXYZ
zyxwvutsrqponmlkjihgfedcba

'<u>k</u> <u>v</u> <u>g</u> <u>v</u> <u>i</u>' <u>w</u> <u>l</u>
<u>b</u> <u>l</u> <u>f</u> <u>o</u> <u>l</u> <u>e</u> <u>v</u>
<u>n</u> <u>v</u>?'

'<u>b</u> <u>v</u> <u>h</u>' <u>o</u> <u>l</u> <u>i</u> <u>w</u>'
<u>b</u> <u>l</u> <u>f</u> <u>p</u> <u>m</u> <u>l</u> <u>d</u>
<u>r</u> <u>o</u> <u>l</u> <u>e</u> <u>v</u>
<u>b</u> <u>l</u> <u>f</u>!'

John 21:15

KATIE THOMPSON

Made known in the breaking of the bread. (Luke 24:35)

Help Cleopas and Judith back to Jerusalem.

WORDSEARCH

Find the following words in the grid:
ROAD TO EMMAUS, RISEN,
JESUS, CLEOPAS, STRANGER,
MESSIAH, PROPHETS,
BREAD, BROKEN,
BIBLE, HOPE.

Can you find 4 loaves of bread hidden in this picture?

```
E M M A R E G N A R T S
M P R O C H E T S R O A
M E R S H L E O P A S N
A B R O K E E N O A D G
U S P I P B R O K E N E
B E O K F H M F P S I R
R O A D T O E M M A U S
I S E N D B S T R A S U
S T R A I N S U S E N S
E B E B R E I X I B L E
N R L E A D A N G E R J
B E M M A U H R O K E N
```

MICHAEL FORSTER

Get the children to pass round some biscuits on paper plates with the words 'Jesus is here' written in non-toxic ink on them. Ask the congregation to let you know when they get the point of it.

Have the story read in either dramatised or narrative form and then point out to the congregation that Jesus was recognised in the act of sharing.

You can then elaborate further: the two disciples were having a dreadfully troubled time, and thought Jesus wasn't with them any more. Even when he was there, they couldn't recognise him, but *in the act of sharing* his presence was made clear. Maybe there are people today in their position – so troubled that all they can think of is getting away from whatever it is, and unable to see that Christ is walking with them. So who is going to share their journey, their story? And most importantly, who, by sharing friendship, is going to help them recognise that Christ is still with them?   MICHAEL FORSTER

Feelings of confusion and fear often make a situation appear hopeless.

Read John 20:19-31

It had been a horrendous few days for the disciples. Everything they had believed in and hoped for appeared to have gone for ever. All sorts of rumours were doing the rounds about what had happened to Jesus and what would happen to the disciples if the Jewish leaders got hold of them!

Confusion was the flavour of the day as the disciples gathered together in a room. Fear of being caught by the authorities drove them to lock the door. So many different thoughts must have been going through their minds. Why had the people suddenly turned against them? What more did Jesus have to do to prove who he was? What would happen to the disciples now? Where could they go? Was it possible for them to return to their former jobs and carry on as if nothing had happened? Questions, questions, fear and confusion, but no answers.

The feelings of dejection and hopelessness must have coloured their thoughts. Each of the disciples had experienced so much and seen so many amazing things happen that they must have been wishing for a miracle.

They hardly had time to blink before Jesus appeared in the middle of the room. The disciples probably thought that they'd all gone completely bonkers. This couldn't be happening, could it?

Jesus approached them with an everyday greeting: 'Peace be to you.' This carried a more significant meaning than simply 'I hope you don't get into trouble'! – although keeping out of trouble must have been just what the disciples wanted. The greeting means: 'May God give you every good thing.'

The disciples may have been a bit sceptical at first. You can imagine their first reaction to be: 'Yeah, we could do with a few good things, like how to get the authorities of our backs', but their scepticism was short-lived after Jesus had showed them his hands and side. The disciples may still have felt a little confused but at least they didn't feel as if they were on their own any more.

Although Jesus had explained to the disciples what was going to happen, when things began to get tough the disciples couldn't help feeling confused and frightened. Jesus had promised that he wouldn't just leave them to get on with life on their own.

It's never easy to feel confident when situations get a bit sticky. All too often we can feel as if we're up to our necks in it and completely on our own. But Jesus has given his word that he will never leave us to try and sort things out by ourselves. It may take some believing, but it's true.

Give each member of the group a pen and piece of paper. Ask them to think of situations or circumstances which have made them feel confused and/or afraid, or still do. You might like to start by sharing something that makes you feel uncomfortable.

Lord,
    at times –
    well, if I'm honest, quite a lot of the time –
    I feel as if my head
    is in a blender.
My thoughts whizz around,
    until everything
    is in a complete mess.
It makes my stomach churn,
    and my legs feel odd.
If I could close my eyes,
    stick my fingers in my ears
    and scream,
    then I would, if it made
    any difference
    to the way I feel.
You may have noticed
    that when I tried that last time
    people gave me funny looks
    and wondered
    if I was quite right in the head.
I couldn't admit to them
    that my head felt full of spaghetti
    and if I had told them
    it wouldn't have made any difference.
But telling you how I feel
    seems to make all the difference.
Thank goodness for that.   PETE TOWNSEND

Reflective material
(sketches, meditations and poems)

A stranger on the road

Based on Luke 24:13-35

Narrator	Cleopas and Joanna lived in a village called Emmaus, about seven miles from Jerusalem. They had gone to Jerusalem for a big festival, and to see Jesus. But Jesus had been captured by some bad people, and had been killed.
Joanna	Let's go home! I don't like it here any more.
Cleopas	Neither do I; the place is full of terrible memories.
Narrator	So they set out to walk the seven miles home. It was beginning to get dark when a stranger caught up with them, and heard what Joanna was saying.
Joanna	I can't understand how it happened. Jesus had so many friends, you'd have thought they'd have stopped it.
Stranger	Stopped what? What's happened?
Cleopas	You must have been walking around with your eyes closed! Jesus was killed – just because some powerful people were jealous of him.
Stranger	Oh, that! if you'd been reading your Bible, you'd have expected it. People like Jesus always get on the wrong side of powerful people.
Joanna	We did hear a rumour that God had brought him back to life.
Cleopas	Yes, but that was just some silly women – we men knew it wasn't true!
Narrator	Cleopas and Joanna did not know that this stranger was Jesus himself! The 'silly women' had been right! He walked with them talking of how the Bible said that God's special helper was going to get himself into trouble. By the time they got home, they were feeling better.
Cleopas	It's a dreadful shame that Jesus was killed, but perhaps God's at work in all this somewhere.
Stranger	Oh, yes, I think he is. God doesn't like bad things happening, but sometimes he can do amazing things with them when they do!
Joanna	Well, this is our house. Boy, am I glad to be home! Here we can feel safe. Nothing exciting happens here.

Stranger	Really? I wouldn't bank on that, if I were you. Goodnight.
Cleopas	Just a minute. It's late. Please come and stay with us.
Stranger	Thank you.
Narrator	The stranger followed them in to the house. They soon had a warm fire going, and put some bread on the table. Then the stranger did a very odd thing. Instead of being waited on like a guest, *he served them!*

- He *picked up* the bread
- He *broke it* into pieces
- He *handed it round*

Joanna	Good heavens! It's Jesus!
Cleopas	So it is!
Narrator	They both went to hug Jesus. But he'd gone!
Cleopas	Come on! We've got to get back.
Narrator	They scurried back to Jerusalem to tell their story. Philip said they already knew Jesus was alive because Simon had told them so. Everyone was wonderfully happy, and kept on telling the stories to each other.
Cleopas	Just think: a few hours ago, Jerusalem was a terrible place, and now it's the best!
Joanna	Yes. That often seems to happen when Jesus is around.

MICHAEL FORSTER

Meditation of Cleopas

So that's who it was!
I see it now, staring me in the face.
But how could we have not realised it before?
That's what I don't understand.
You see, we'd been to Jerusalem,
    watched with our own eyes what they did to him,
    even stood at the foot of the cross,
    yet we didn't recognise him when he walked beside us.
Why?
Was it sorrow that blinded us,
    our hearts too full of grief to glimpse the truth?
It's possible, for we were devastated, there's no denying that;
    we'd thought he was the one we longed for,
    coming to redeem our people,
    and it had been a terrible blow after arriving full of hope,

anticipating his kingdom,
  to see him nailed to that cross,
  bruised and broken,
  the life seeping from his bleeding body.
We'd been so certain,
  so sure he was the Messiah,
  but we'd seen his death
  and were making our way back home,
  our dreams in tatters,
  our lives in ruins.
That could have clouded our eyes, unquestionably,
  for we had little time for anything or anyone.
He was the last person we expected to meet, I can tell you that.
Oh, I know he'd talked of rising again,
  returning from the grave –
  we were talking of it even as we walked –
  but we'd taken it all with a pinch of salt,
  and in our hearts we'd given him up,
  reluctantly making our way back to reality.
We never imagined for a moment we might see him;
  the thought simply never entered our heads.
So yes, perhaps that explains it,
  why for all that time the penny failed to drop.
Yet it was more than that,
  for it wasn't finally the face we recognised at all.
It went far deeper –
  the way he spoke,
  the way he acted,
  the way our hearts burned within us as we walked.
And above all the meal that we shared.
He took the bread,
  and broke it,
  and suddenly we realised, with a certainty nothing could shake,
  that this was Jesus,
  risen,
  alive,
  victorious.
Yet even as we saw it he disappeared,
  vanishing before our eyes,
  and we've never seen him since.
It's funny that, isn't it,
  how we saw him most clearly when we couldn't see him at all,
  how our eyes were opened when we weren't even looking –
  and how we know he's with us now, even though he's departed from us!

NICK FAWCETT

Failures, fish and forgiveness (John 21:15-22)

Scene

Two people are standing watching Peter on the beach.

James	Look at him.
Salome	I know.

Peter is wandering up and down the beach.

James	What do you think's got into him?
Salome	You don't think he's going to try walking on water again?
James	No!
Salome	Perhaps it's the conversation he's had.
James	No!

Pauses.

James	Oh yeah.

Salome looks and nods.

Salome	Something's going through his mind.
James	It's OK. Look, John will sort him out.
John	Peter, why are you counting the fish?
Peter	I'm hyperactive. I always have been.
John	But you've counted them three times already.
Peter	I told you, I'm hyperactive. I need to do something.
John	Well, how many fish did we catch?
Peter	I don't know, I keep forgetting.
John	It doesn't matter.
Peter	Yes it does. I'll count them again.
John	Please don't. You don't have to.
Peter	But I want to.
John	It's not important.

Peter	I want to count!
John	We don't need an exact figure.
Peter	I love counting!
John	We . . . can't wait to find out how many.
Peter	Good.

Peter digs into the net and begins counting. After a while he stops.

John	Do you want a hand?
Peter	What?
John	You've stopped counting.
Peter	I know.
John	I wondered if you'd run out of fingers and thumbs.
Peter	Very funny.
John	Thank you.
Peter	I can't count now. I can't concentrate.
John	I'm not surprised.

Peter looks at John.

Peter	Can you believe it?
John	What? That you've stopped counting, you're standing still, and not doing anything?
Peter	No, not that.
John	Only kidding.
Peter	Very funny.
John	Thank you.
Peter	You know what I'm talking about, don't you?
John	I think so.
Peter	This time I really thought I'd blown it.
John	We all did.

Peter	I know we all ran, John, but I was the only one who denied knowing him.
John	Peter . . .
Peter	You don't have to say anything, John.
John	I don't know what to say.
Peter	Neither did I. At first when I saw him again, I couldn't believe it, I hardly dared hope.
John	We all felt the same.
Peter	But you didn't have my shame.
John	I'm sorry.
Peter	So was I. More than I could express. Even me, Peter. I was speechless.

There is a pause.

John	But Jesus spoke to you.
Peter	Yes, he did.
John	And . . . I don't mean to pry, Peter . . .
Peter	No, it's OK. I want to share. Do you know what he asked me?
John	No.
Peter	'Do you love me?' That's what he said. Can you imagine how I felt? What I thought? Of course I love him. More than life. I had wept bitter tears after my denial, I had cried myself to sleep over his death. I had mourned and gone without food because of my sadness. Of course I love him.
John	Did you tell him?
Peter	I think he knew. I'm sure he knew, but I told him. Yes, I told him.
John	What did he say?
Peter	He said, 'Feed my sheep.' Then he asked me again if I loved him.
John	Again?
Peter	He asked me three times.

John	Three?
Peter	I think I know why . . . And three times he told me to feed his sheep, take care of his lambs. John . . . he's forgiven me, he loves me, he has a job for me, for me!
John	Peter, I'm so happy. I'm so pleased for you. It's great. It's more than great, it's brilliant. What can I say?
Peter	That you'd like to count the fish for me?
John	What?
Peter	I'm too excited to count. You don't mind, do you, mate?
John	One, two, three . . .

TONY BOWER

But it won't last *or* Famous last words

Official	They were two of his disciples.
Soldier	Yes, Sir.
Official	Talking about the man they had been following.
Soldier	Yes, Sir.
Official	That's quite natural, quite normal behaviour – remembering their leader.
Soldier	In the present tense, Sir?
Official	Present?
Soldier	After his crucifixion.
Official	When he had been killed.
Soldier	Yes, Sir.
Official	This doesn't make sense.
Soldier	No, Sir.
Official	Dead men don't walk.
Soldier	No, Sir.
Official	Dead men don't talk.

Soldier	No, Sir.
Official	Dead men don't cook.
Soldier	No, Sir.
Official	Dead men don't eat fish.
Soldier	No, Sir, but people who are alive do.
Official	Alive?
Soldier	That's what the disciples say.
Official	Deluded, demented disciples is what I say.
Soldier	And all the thousands of people who've recently become converts. I have another rather thick file I could show you. Eye-witness accounts, testimonies, people who've been imprisoned but still say Jesus is alive. I could bring you the file . . .
Official	Burn it.
Soldier	Burn it, Sir?
Official	We don't need to tell Rome about this.
Soldier	No, Sir.
Official	It's not as if these rumours will ever reach Rome, is it?
Soldier	No, Sir.
Official	All this fuss will die down in a few weeks.
Soldier	Yes, Sir.
Official	A couple of months at the most.
Soldier	Yes, Sir.
Official	This time next year it will all be forgotten.
Soldier	Yes, Sir. And a thousand years from now no one will even remember his name.
Official	Whose name?
Soldier	Very good, Sir. Very funny.
Official	No, I'm convinced that this will all blow over.

Official stands up, walks away from his desk, pauses before the next line which is delivered in an emphatic tone.

Official   Dead men don't change the world.

Soldier   No, Sir. Dead men don't change the world.

Soldier says this with a question in his voice. Both look at each other. There are questions in their minds. They look away, to the audience, their faces showing that Jesus may well be . . . alive.

Freeze.   TONY BOWER

Jesus appears to his disciples at Emmaus

Thinking about it

What's the point?

Sometimes people who are finding life tough aren't able to see that Christ is with them. Often it's a simple act of sharing that makes him 'visible'.

Doing it

Prayer

Thank you, Lord Jesus,
for the time that we share here today.
Help us to see that you are sharing in it with us, too.
Amen.

From the known to the unknown

Have the children ever wanted to run away from home? (Virtually all children have threatened to do so at least once!) Perhaps something very upsetting had happened and they needed a bit of space? Here's a story about two people who were so sad when Jesus died that all they could think about was getting away. But Jesus went with them, even though they didn't recognise him!

Tell the story: Luke 24:13-35

(See page 407 for a dramatised version of this story.)

Walking from despair to hope

Cleopas and Judith were friends of Jesus – and they were terribly upset.

'I know Jesus offended a lot of people,' Judith said, 'but they had no reason to have him killed – and in a horrible way like that, as well.'

'He was too honest, that was his trouble,' Cleopas observed. 'Anyway, I don't like Jerusalem any more – let's go home to Emmaus.'

'Good idea,' Judith agreed. 'Let's get away from all these horrible memories.'

So they set out to walk to Emmaus, about seven miles away, and as they walked they tried to make sense of what had happened.

'He was such a good man,' Cleopas said. 'It just doesn't add up.'

'I thought he was the special man God had promised,' Judith added, 'but if he was, why did God let him be killed?'

'Don't look now,' Cleopas whispered, 'but we're not alone.'

He was right – a mysterious figure was catching up with them. 'What are you talking about?' he asked.

Cleopas and Judith stopped and stared. 'You mean, you don't know?'

Judith gasped. 'Are you the only person who's been in Jerusalem this weekend who doesn't know what's happened?'

'Why?' asked the stranger. 'What *has* happened?'

'Oh, nothing much,' sniffed Judith, tearfully. 'They've just gone and killed Jesus, that's all, and after all the wonderful things he did, as well.'

'Yes,' Cleopas added, 'and we were thinking he was the great promised Messiah.'

'That was on Friday,' Judith said, 'and now there are all kinds of rumours going round. Some of our friends went to his grave this morning and came back saying that he'd risen – said they'd seen some angels who'd told them so.'

'Women, you know,' said Cleopas. 'No one else saw anything.'

The stranger spoke kindly, but sounded disappointed. 'When are you going to learn to listen to the prophets?' he said. 'Wasn't all this foretold, that the Messiah would be treated badly, but then God would glorify him?' And before they could stop him he was giving them an off-the-cuff Bible study. They hardly noticed the miles they walked as they listened to him, and before they knew it they were at Emmaus. The stranger was still in full flood, but when they got to their door he stopped. 'Well, I'll say goodnight,' he said.

'Oh, you can't!' exclaimed Judith. 'Look, it's getting dark – why don't you come and stay with us?'

'That's kind of you,' said the stranger, and they went into the house.

'Not much for supper, I'm afraid,' Cleopas apologised. 'We weren't expecting to be home tonight, so the neighbours won't have got anything in for us. We can manage a bit of bread and wine, though.'

'That sounds terrific,' answered the stranger. 'You'd be amazed what you can do with a bit of bread and wine.'

Soon they had a roaring fire going to keep them warm, and the room was beginning to look almost cheerful in spite of everything. They sat down to eat, and Cleopas reached out to take the bread and hand it round, but the stranger got there first. He took the bread, and he said grace, and then, gripping the loaf between his hands he broke it. 'Here you are,' he said. 'Take and eat this.'

Suddenly, a shiver went down Cleopas' spine. It was as though they were back in that room where they'd shared their last supper with Jesus before he'd been killed. Something about the way he said grace . . . and broke the bread . . . and offered it to them. Cleopas looked at Judith, and knew she'd felt it, too. The same tingle, the same flash of recognition. Their eyes met, and lit up with joy. 'It's him!' they chorused, and together they reached out to take Jesus' hands. Laughing and crying at the same time, with joy, they grasped hold of . . . nothing. He wasn't there any more.

'Of course!' laughed Judith. 'He's alive, and he's free, and he's not to be clutched at or held or pinned down by anybody, ever again.'

They didn't say any more, but got up and dashed back to Jerusalem – all seven miles of it. 'This is the place to be!' said Cleopas. 'This is where God's bringing new hope out of all that pain.' And he was right.   MICHAEL FORSTER

Walking from despair to hope

Based on Luke 24:13-35

Narrator	Cleopas and Judith were friends of Jesus – and they were terribly upset.
Judith	I know Jesus offended a lot of people, but they had no reason to have him killed – and in a horrible way like that, as well.
Cleopas	He was too honest, that was his trouble. Anyway, I don't like Jerusalem any more – let's go home to Emmaus.
Judith	Good idea. Let's get away from all these horrible memories.
Narrator	So they set out to walk to Emmaus, about seven miles away, and as they walked they tried to make sense of what had happened.
Cleopas	He was such a good man. It just doesn't add up.
Judith	I thought he was the special man God had promised, but if he was, why did God let him be killed?
Cleopas	Don't look now, but we're not alone.
Narrator	He was right – a mysterious figure was catching up with them.
Jesus	What are you talking about?
Judith	You mean you don't know? Are you the only person who's been in Jerusalem this weekend and doesn't know what's happened?
Jesus	Why? What *has* happened?

Judith	Oh, nothing much – they've just gone and killed Jesus, that's all, and after all the wonderful things he did, as well.
Cleopas	Yes, and we were thinking he was the great promised Messiah.
Judith	That was Friday, and now all kinds of rumours are going round. Some of our friends went to his grave this morning and came back saying that he'd risen – some angels had told them so.
Cleopas	Women, you know. No one else saw anything.
Narrator	The stranger spoke kindly, but sounded disappointed.
Jesus	When are you going to listen to the prophets? Wasn't it foretold that the Messiah would suffer, but then God would glorify him?
Narrator	Before they could stop him the stranger was giving them an off-the-cuff Bible study. They hardly noticed the miles as they listened to him, and soon they were at Emmaus. The stranger was still in full flood, but when they got to their door he stopped.
Jesus	Well, I'll say goodnight.
Judith	Look, it's getting dark – why don't you come and stay with us?
Cleopas	Not much for supper, I'm afraid – we weren't expecting to be home tonight. We can manage a bit of bread and wine, though.
Jesus	That sounds terrific. You'd be amazed what you can do with a bit of bread and wine.
Narrator	They sat down to eat, and Cleopas reached out to take the bread and hand it round, but the stranger got there first. He took the bread, and he said grace, and then, gripping the loaf between his hands, he broke it.
Jesus	Here you are – take and eat this.
Narrator	Suddenly, a shiver went down Cleopas' spine. It was as though they were back in that room where they'd shared their last supper with Jesus before he'd been killed. Something about the way he said grace . . . and broke the bread . . . and offered it to them. Cleopas looked at Judith, and knew she'd felt it too. The same tingle, the same flash of recognition. Their eyes met, and lit up with joy.
Judith and Cleopas	It's him!
Narrator	Together they reached out to take Jesus' hands. Laughing and crying at the same time, with joy, they grasped hold of . . . nothing. He wasn't there any more.

Judith	Of course! He's alive, and he's free, and he's not to be clutched or held or pinned down by anybody, ever again.
Narrator	They didn't say any more, but got up and dashed back to Jerusalem – all seven miles of it.
Cleopas	This is the place to be! This is where God's bringing new hope out of all that pain.
Narrator	And he was right. MICHAEL FORSTER

Meditation of Peter

Three times he asked me,
    three times the same simple yet searching question:
    'Do you love me, Peter?'
And I was getting fed up with it,
    not to say a little hurt.
After all, he should have known by then, surely?
I'd followed him for three years,
    and I thought we'd become close –
    he gave that impression, anyway.
The 'Rock', he'd called me,
    the one on whom he'd build his Church –
    an expression of trust, if ever there was one –
    so how could he doubt me now,
    let alone question my love?
But then, of course, I remembered that bold, brash promise of mine:
    'Though all become deserters because of you,
    I will never desert you' –
    and suddenly I understood.
He'd known I would fail, even as I said it,
    not only abandon but deny him,
    and he knew too how sick I'd felt,
    how wretched and ashamed
    when the knowledge of my failure finally sunk home.
But there was no anger from him,
    no recriminations,
    no rebuke.
His concern was for me, not himself,
    his sole desire to wipe the slate clean and start again,
    and this was my chance to deal with the guilt,
    to exorcise the demon once and for all.
Three times I'd denied him,
    three times he put the question,
    and at last I could put the record straight,

declare to him what I should have declared to others:
  'Yes, Lord; you know that I love you.'
We couldn't change the past, we both knew that,
  but with his help we could put it behind us and change the future,
  and that's what he offered me that day;
  a new beginning,
  a fresh chapter,
  life dawning for me as surely as it had dawned again for him.
I was restored,
  cleansed,
  forgiven,
  the ghost finally laid to rest,
  and I owed it all to him,
  the man whom I abandoned so freely,
  yet who refused to abandon me!   NICK FAWCETT

Meditation of Thomas

Would you believe it!
They're all at it now, the whole daft lot of them!
I never thought I'd see the day.
Not Peter, anyway – I thought he had more sense.
And James and John, hot-headed at times perhaps,
  but they had their heads screwed on, or so I thought.
OK, maybe the others were a little suspect.
Simon for one.
To be honest, I felt like he'd believe anything sometimes.
And the rest, they had their moments too, to put it kindly.
But this? Jesus alive and kicking, dropping in on them for a quiet chat . . .
  who are they trying to kid?
It really is beyond me.
I mean, they were the first to mock when the women came back
  trembling and laughing like a bunch of mixed-up children.
We all agreed it was nothing more than hysteria, poor things.
So what's changed? What's got into them?
If you ask me it's this cursed waiting:
  waiting for the sound of footsteps,
  waiting for the knock on the door,
  waiting for the moment when we know it's all up for us
  just as it was for him.
That's enough to make anyone go off their trolley.
But even so you won't catch me rabbiting on about Jesus being alive –
  I'll want more than a few fanciful visions before I start doing that.

Let me touch him perhaps,
   see the scars, put my hand in that spear-wound,
   feel where they smashed those nails home,
   and then, who knows, it might be different.
But be honest, what chance is there of that?
Do you believe it could happen?
I don't.

Prayer

Lord Jesus Christ,
   it is hard sometimes to believe.
In the face of frustrated hopes and broken dreams,
   of sorrow, suffering and death,
   we too, like Thomas, can find ourselves doubting,
   wanting irrefutable proof before we dare accept what we are told.
You appeared to Thomas and gave him the assurance he wanted,
   but you also told him that those who have not seen but still believe
   are most blessed of all.
Help us then, even when faith is hard,
   even when it's a struggle to hold on,
   to put our trust in you, knowing you will not fail us.　　NICK FAWCETT

Meditation of Paul – Acts 8:1-3, 9:1, 2

So they claim he's alive, do they?
Back from the dead and offering new life to his followers?
Well, we'll see about that!
A few floggings,
   a few stonings,
   and we'll soon hear a different story.
What are they trying to prove, these people?
Do they really imagine we're going to swallow their nonsense?
He's dead, Jesus,
   nailed to the cross like a common criminal,
   and good riddance;
   so perish all blasphemers, that's what I say.
How can they still claim he's the Messiah?
I just don't understand it.
If he was, he'd hardly be dead now, would he?
And he definitely wouldn't have died in the way he did,
   humiliated,
   ridiculed,
   cursed,
   despised.

No, don't try telling me he's the Christ,
    I know better than that.
Product of the best Pharisaic education, that's me!
Acknowledged expert in the Law,
    got it all at my fingertips down to the last detail.
And I can assure you that this Jesus just does not fit the bill.
A jumped-up fanatic from Galilee,
    a misguided martyr from the sticks,
    a good-for-nothing layabout looking to cause trouble.
I must say I thought we'd seen the last of him,
    we all did;
    but even in death he continues to spread his poison,
    duping his followers with his empty promises.
You have to admire their courage though, I'll give you that;
    after watching him die I expected they'd soon climb down,
    keep as far out of sight as possible.
And they did for a time –
    no sight or sound for many a week –
    until suddenly there they were,
    for no reason I can think of,
    not a care in the world apparently,
    heedless of the risk,
    carrying on where he'd left off.
Well, if that's what they want, that's what they're going to get –
    they can carry on all right,
    follow in his footsteps all the way to the cross;
    I'll be more than happy to oblige.
I don't know what changed them,
    and I don't care.
No, really, it's of no interest to me.
My duty is to destroy this cancer,
    wipe out this heresy
    before it does the same to us.
Bring them back begging for mercy,
    string up their ringleaders,
    and then we'll see whether they still claim he's alive –
    then we'll see what life he has to offer!   NICK FAWCETT

Meditation of Paul – Acts 9:1-9

I was wrong,
    so terribly, totally wrong,
    and now I'm sick with shame.
To think that I, Paul, persecuted the Messiah;
    the one for whom we had waited so long,
    the one who we all longed to see.

I failed to recognise him,
   blinded by my own pride and bigotry.
I'd watched as his followers were killed,
   rejoicing in their deaths,
    glad to be associated with their destruction.
And then, when the opportunity finally came,
   I leapt at the chance to destroy them myself.
It was my mission,
   my great calling,
   and I pursued it gleefully,
   brutally,
   with unquenchable zeal.
They quaked at the sound of my voice, those Christians,
   and I gave glory to God.
They trembled as I approached,
   and I offered him my gratitude.
I have broken bodies,
   tormented minds,
   crushed spirits,
   all in the name of faith.
But then I saw it,
   there in the brightness,
   the face of Jesus,
   tears in his eyes.
I heard it,
   there in the silence,
   the voice of Jesus,
   'Why, Saul, why?'
And I knew then the awful, wonderful truth.
It was just as they had said –
   he was the Messiah,
   risen from the dead.
I know that now, but I wish I didn't,
   for I have become the one suffering,
   racked by guilt and sorrow.
Why did he spare me to endure this agony?
Why not finish me off there and then?
Or is this my punishment,
   his judgement on my foul, despicable crimes?
There's no way he can ever forgive me, I'm certain of that;
   not after all I've done.
And even if he did there's no way I could ever be accepted by his followers;
   they'd never believe someone like me could change that much.
So here I am,
   Paul, persecutor of Christ,

grovelling in misery before him;
  Paul, exterminator of the Church,
  wishing I could be exterminated.
I was wrong, so terribly wrong.
But it's too late for excuses,
  too late for tears,
  too late to make amends,
  too late for anything.   NICK FAWCETT

Read Acts 9:1-20

Saul, later known as Paul, had recently acted as a sort of coat-rack for a group of Jews (members of the Sanhedrin, a Jewish court or council) who handed Saul their outer clothes while they stoned a bloke named Stephen to death (see Acts 7:54-60). Saul thought that anyone who believed in Jesus was an absolute and complete heretic and deserved everything that could be thrown at them. A short while later Saul had written permission from the High Priest to 'bury' these 'believers in Jesus' under as much rubble as he could find. So he set off for Jerusalem with a few mates, intent on sorting out the troublemakers.

Approaching Damascus, Saul got the interrogation treatment by God as a bright light blinded him and left his mates speechless. The same eyes that had watched Stephen being stoned now couldn't see to throw a plum stone. Someone took pity on Saul and led him to Damascus where he sat for three days without food or drink.

In the meantime, God had spoken to a bloke called Ananias who also lived in Damascus. Ananias was willing to go wherever God sent him – that was until God told him where he wanted him to go and whom he was to see!

Ananias couldn't believe his ears. God asked him to go and speak to someone who made alligators appear charming. Ananias complained and tried to remind God just who Saul was. God was having none of it and told Ananias to get on with the job.

As soon as Ananias did as God had asked something like fish scales fell from Saul's eyes and he was able to see again. Not only was Saul able to see the physical things around him, he was also able to 'see' (understand) that Jesus was who he claimed to be: the Son of God.

Even though he wasn't confident about what God had asked him to do, Ananias acted in friendship towards Saul by placing his hands on Saul. The placing of hands, usually on the shoulders or head, was a gesture of acceptance and recognition.

Such was the power of this expression of acceptance that a few days later Saul was preaching that Jesus was the Son of God. Saul's preaching was so effective that it wasn't long before the very people who had encouraged Saul to kill the followers of Jesus, were planning to kill Saul. At least now Saul knew who his friends were.   PETE TOWNSEND

Ascension

Ascension Day

Jesus returns to the Father in glory

Luke 24:44-53

(also Acts 1:1-11; Psalm 47 or Psalm 110; Ephesians 1:15-23)

A reading from the Gospel of Luke (24:46-53)

Jesus said to his disciples:

> So it is written that the Christ would suffer and rise again on the third day, and in his name repentance and the forgiveness of sins would be preached to people everywhere. You, my friends, are witnesses to all this. I will send you what has been promised by my Father, but wait in Jerusalem until that time when God's power will come to you.

Jesus then led them to Bethany where he left them and was taken up to heaven. Filled with joy, the disciples returned to Jerusalem and spent their time praising God in the Temple.

This is the Gospel of the Lord
Praise to you, Lord Jesus Christ   KATIE THOMPSON

Introductory material

They had seen death, they had seen resurrection, and for the disciples of Jesus that sight of the risen Christ back among them must have seemed the most wonderful thing they could ever hope to witness. No wonder they asked the question which had been on each one's lips since his return: 'Lord, is this the time when you will restore the kingdom to Israel?' It had to be, surely? What more could be revealed than had been revealed to them already? The answer was just a few moments away, as suddenly Jesus was taken from them, and they were left struggling to come to terms with the unexpected once again. Whatever the precise event behind the language, one thing is clear – their picture of Christ had been far too small, their understanding of his purpose much too narrow. For he came not just to restore Israel but to redeem the world, not to rule on earth but to be enthroned in heaven. They had glimpsed the man but not the face of God beneath. They believed they saw the whole picture, when they saw but one piece of the jigsaw. Suddenly they had to think again, for Jesus was greater than they had begun to imagine. The same, I suspect, may be true for us all.

NICK FAWCETT

Prayers

Praise – The wonder of Ascension

Almighty God,
  we come today reminded of your greatness,
    your glory,
      your sovereign power and eternal purpose
      expressed so wonderfully in Jesus Christ,
      risen and ascended.
  Worthy is the Lamb that was slain
    to receive power and wealth,
    wisdom and might,
    honour and glory and blessing!

We thank you for the wonder of Ascension,
    that marvellous yet mysterious moment
    in the life of the Apostles
    which left them gazing heavenwards in confusion
    yet departing in joy.
  Worthy is the Lamb that was slain
    to receive power and wealth,
    wisdom and might,
    honour and glory and blessing!

We thank you for the way it brought the ministry of Jesus
    to a fitting conclusion,
    testifying decisively to his oneness with you,
    demonstrating your final seal of approval
    on all he had done.
  Worthy is the Lamb that was slain
    to receive power and wealth,
    wisdom and might,
    honour and glory and blessing!

We thank you that through his Ascension
    Jesus was set free to be Lord of all –
    no longer bound to a particular place or time,
but with us always
    and able to reach to the ends of the earth.
  Worthy is the Lamb that was slain
    to receive power and wealth,
    wisdom and might,
    honour and glory and blessing!

We thank you that through his departing
   Jesus prepared the way for his coming again,
   through his Spirit,
   his Church,
   and his coming again in glory.
**Worthy is the Lamb that was slain
   to receive power and wealth,
   wisdom and might,
   honour and glory and blessing!**

Almighty God,
   forgive us for so often failing
      to grasp the wonder of Ascension,
      for living each day as though it had never been.
   Forgive the smallness of our vision,
      the narrowness of our outlook,
      the feebleness of our love,
      the nervousness of our witness,
      our repeated failure to recognise
      the fullness of your revelation in Christ.
**Worthy is the Lamb that was slain
   to receive power and wealth,
   wisdom and might,
   honour and glory and blessing!**

Give us a deeper sense of wonder,
   a stronger faith,
   and a greater understanding of all you have done.
**Worthy is the Lamb that was slain
   to receive power and wealth,
   wisdom and might,
   honour and glory and blessing!**

Almighty God,
   like the Apostles,
      we too will never fully understand
      all Ascension means.
   We accept, but we do not fully understand.
   We believe, yet we have many questions.
   Help us, despite our uncertainty,
      to hold firm to the one great truth
      that the wonder of Christ goes far beyond
      anything we can ever imagine,
      and in that faith may we live each day.

Worthy is the Lamb that was slain
  to receive power and wealth,
  wisdom and might,
  honour and glory and blessing!
Thanks be to God!
Amen.   NICK FAWCETT

Confession – The Lamb of God

Lord Jesus Christ,
  we have failed you in so much,
    our lives, time and again, a denial of our calling.
  We have failed to love our neighbour,
    been slow to forgive,
    swift to pass judgement
    and careless of the needs of others.
  Yet, through the immensity of your grace
    and the awesomeness of your sacrifice,
    you offer us redemption from all our sins
    and renewal of life.
  Lamb of God,
    to you be power and wealth,
    wisdom and might,
    honour and glory and blessing!

We profess to be your followers,
  but our faith has been weak and our commitment poor.
We claim to be your body,
  but we have allowed petty divisions to come between us.
We talk of building your kingdom,
  but our thoughts are all for this world and its pleasures.
Yet, despite our weakness, still you love us,
  accepting us as we are,
  cleansing us from all our faults
  and offering us a new beginning –
  the opportunity to put the past behind us and start afresh.
Lamb of God,
  to you be power and wealth,
  wisdom and might,
  honour and glory and blessing!

We are unworthy to bear your name
  and undeserving of your goodness –
  so much about us that is wrong,
  so little that is right –

yet you went to the cross knowing all that,
taking the punishment that should have been ours,
bringing us healing through your wounds,
and on your shoulders carrying the iniquities of us all.
Lamb of God,
to you be power and wealth,
wisdom and might,
honour and glory and blessing!

Lord Jesus Christ,
through you we have found joy and fulfilment,
love and peace,
grace and mercy.
We have been born again to a living hope,
our sins forgiven,
our lives renewed,
our salvation assured.
Lamb of God,
to you be power and wealth,
wisdom and might,
honour and glory and blessing!
Amen. NICK FAWCETT

Thanksgiving – The Saviour of all

Lord Jesus Christ,
we thank you for the truth at the heart of this day –
that you came to save not just a few,
nor simply your own people,
but all the world.
You are the King of kings and Lord of lords,
your love reaching out to the ends of the earth,
your glory filling the universe!
Mighty Saviour,
in thanks we worship you.

We thank you that, though you were born in Bethlehem
and ministered in Galilee,
though you spent your life in Palestine
and died in Jerusalem,
your love has transformed lives
in every country and continent,
crossing barriers of culture, colour and creed,
unable to be contained by either space or time!
Mighty Saviour,
in thanks we worship you.

We thank you that no one is outside your love,
   whoever they may be,
   whatever they may have done.
You value all,
   have time for all,
   respond to all.
Mighty Saviour,
   in thanks we worship you.

We greet you now as the sovereign Lord –
   the one who reigns in splendour,
   enthroned at the right hand of the Father,
   and the one who, in the fullness of time,
   will reconcile all things to yourself,
   making peace through your blood
   and establishing your eternal kingdom.
Mighty Saviour,
   in thanks we worship you.

Lord Jesus Christ,
   Saviour of all,
      we look forward to that day when every knee shall bow to you,
      and every tongue confess you as Lord and Saviour.
   To you be praise and glory,
      honour and thanksgiving,
      now and always.
   Amen.   NICK FAWCETT

Intercession

*Having paid for our freedom with his life, Jesus our Saviour enters into the full glory
to which he is entitled.*

Loving Father, give encouragement,
vision and deeper faith to all your followers,
so that the church truly expresses your love.
Silence for prayer

You are our God:
with you, nothing is impossible

Dissolve away all fear, suspicion and greed
which lead to corruption in our world.
Silence for prayer

You are our God:
with you, nothing is impossible

Be present in every home,
so that the love increases
and each person is given respect and value.

Silence for prayer

You are our God:
with you, nothing is impossible

Guide those in medical research
and bring wholeness to all who are in any
way distressed.

Silence for prayer

You are our God:
with you, nothing is impossible

Welcome into your heaven all those at the
stage of death,
and give consolation to their loved ones.

Silence for prayer

You are our God:
with you, nothing is impossible

Give us a greater sense of your glory
so that we can worship you
with our whole being.

Silence for prayer

Merciful Father,
accept these prayers
for the sake of your Son,
our Saviour Jesus Christ, Amen.
                                                        SUSAN SAYERS

Short prayer

Lord Jesus Christ,
    we greet you as King of kings and Lord of lords.
We acknowledge your greatness,
    we recognise your authority,
    we celebrate your exaltation,
    we commit ourselves to your kingdom.
Living Lord, open our eyes to the meaning of your Ascension.
Broaden our vision, enlarge our understanding,
    widen our perspectives, deepen our faith.
Equip us for all you would have us do,
    and so may we live to your glory
    and work for your kingdom.
                                                        NICK FAWCETT

All-age-talk material

The complete picture

Reading

Acts 1:6-11

Aim

To show that the Ascension has a vital place in the Christian Year, balancing the humanity of Christ with his divinity, and so offering a complete picture of God's revelation in Christ.

Preparation

First, on a large sheet of card, draw a simple picture, such as the one below, which can be interpreted in two ways – as a vase or as two faces. Display this on a board.

Now, on another large sheet of card, write exactly as written, in large print, the following numbers. (You may be able to print these if your word processor or computer has a similar font.)

73805 1
7 108
7738
805
35007
7735
3807
77 18
57 108
53 17
55378
5537
7 105

Retain this list of numbers for use later in the talk.

Talk

Display the picture you have prepared and ask what people can see. Spend time drawing out a number of responses, and ensure that everybody is finally able to spot both of the ways the picture can be viewed. Bring out the fact that what we see depends on what we are looking for, and that it is very possible for us to see only half the picture.

Now display the list of numbers, and again ask people what they see. Run through the numbers one by one and invite people to confirm the numbers you have written. Ask if anyone can see anything different in what you have written. Turn the display over, and ask again. You should see the following: ISOBEL, BOIL, BELL, SOB, LOOSE, SELL, LOBE, BILL, BOILS, LIES, BLESS, LESS, SOIL.

These are two examples of the way that what we see depends on what we are looking for – examples that remind us how all too easily we can see only half a picture. And Ascension Day reminds us of exactly this truth. It is a day which recalls the departing of Jesus into heaven, lifted up suddenly into the clouds, but what we have here is figurative language used in an attempt to describe an indescribable moment. Precisely what happened we cannot be sure, but what matters is not the manner of Jesus' Ascension, but the truth behind it. And for the Apostles this meant that, for the first time in their lives, they saw the whole picture about Jesus, instead of simply a part. Until then, though they had seen him as the Messiah, revered him as a teacher, and worshipped him as the risen Lord, they had not fully grasped the fact that he was one with God. But at this moment, as he was taken from them, the truth dawned. In this man, who had walked beside them and whom they had followed for three extraordinary years, they had encountered not simply the Son of God, incredible though that was, but God himself, for Jesus and the Father were one.

And in turn the Ascension reminds us that Jesus was not only human like each of us, but also divine – wholly man yet wholly God. Lose sight of either of those truths, stress one at the cost of the other, and we will see only half the picture, missing out on the wonder of God's revelation in Christ.

NICK FAWCETT

Jesus goes to heaven

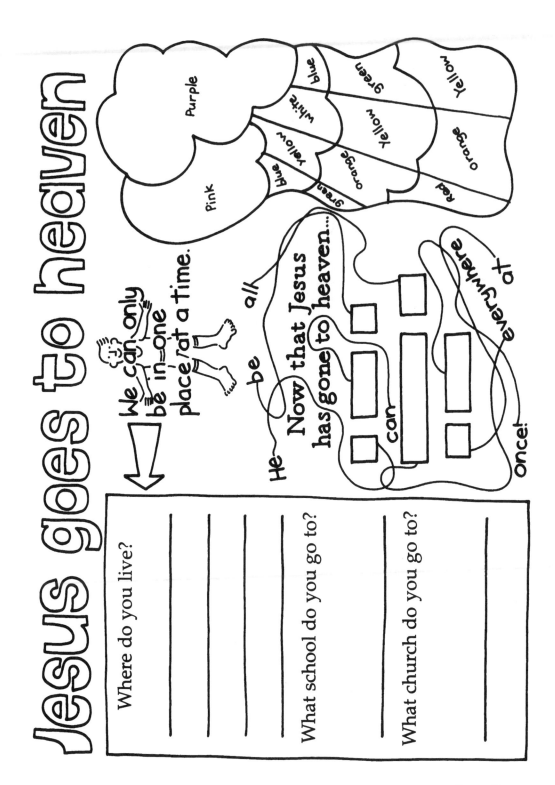

We can only be in one place at a time.

He... be... all... Now that Jesus has gone to heaven... can... everywhere... once!

Where do you live?

_____

_____

What school do you go to?

_____

What church do you go to?

_____

Purple Pink blue white yellow green green orange yellow blue yellow orange Red

SUSAN SAYERS

Jesus is Lord

Beforehand prepare some sheets of paper in large zigzags – computer print-out paper is perfect. On the sets of sheets, write the words LEADING, ORGAN-ISING, RULING and DIRECTING, so that when the sheets are folded up you only see the initial letters of the word, and when they are let down you see the whole word. Fasten the top edges with paper clips.

Begin by reminding everyone of how the people of Israel wanted to have a king, like all the other nations did. They wanted someone important, who would tell them what to do, and ride into battle with them and so on. Samuel wasn't so keen. A king might give them a hard life, and anyway, if they had a king they might forget who was really in charge. Who is that? God himself is really in charge.

Ask four people to come out and arrange the letters you give them into a word. When it says LORD, explain that we are always talking of Jesus as Lord, and today we are going to explore what that means.

Unfasten the letter L so that the word LEADING can be seen. That's one thing about Jesus; when we let him be Lord of our life he will be leading us through all our difficult decisions and hairy, scary moments. Unfasten the O. When we ask Jesus to be our Lord he will be organising our priorities and the things we feel are important, so that our lives fit in with God's plans. Unfasten the R. When Jesus is Lord of our life he will be ruling over us; all the different parts of our territory will be in his kingdom and subject to his law of love. Even those rebellious outlying districts of bad temper, greed or critical gossip can be brought under his rule. Unfasten the D. When Jesus is Lord in our lives he will be directing us, with those tricky decisions, those awkward dilemmas and those nagging temptations.

So when we say 'Jesus is Lord', we mean that Jesus is Leading us, Organising us, Ruling us and Directing us every moment of our lives.   Susan Sayers

You will be my witnesses. (Acts 1:8)

Help Jesus' friends find
their way back to Jerusalem.

Crack the code.

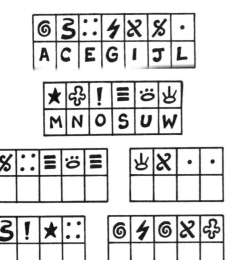

WORDSEARCH
Find the following sentence threaded through
the grid:
YOU WILL RECEIVE POWER WHEN THE
HOLY SPIRIT COMES.
You could also find the following words in the grid:
BAPTISED, HOLY SPIRIT, WAIT, ANGELS,
READY, LIFE, TELL.

MICHAEL FORSTER

Ideas for activities

Play a 'peep-bo' game with some soft toys, and then with people, pointing out the fact that they are still there, even when they can't be seen. Explain how Jesus is close enough to talk to all the time, wherever we are, even though we can't see him.

SUSAN SAYERS

Drama – Wait for it, wait for it . . .

Narrator	Now, you've heard the stories of Jesus – how he was born, and the things he did and taught, and all that stuff. And you've heard about how he suffered, and died – and how God raised him up to new life? Right? Well, now I'm going to tell you what happened next. Of course, the disciples were really glad that Jesus was alive. Well, no, actually, they weren't glad – they were absolutely over-joyed – ecstatic – oh, perhaps you'd better invent your own word, because I don't think there are any in the dictionary that can possibly describe how they felt. Put it this way – if the producers of *Top of the Pops* and *Stars in their Eyes* were fighting over whose show you would star in, you probably wouldn't be one hundredth as happy as the disciples were then. Jesus told them not to get too carried away.
Jesus	You're not ready yet to go telling everybody about me – you just wait until the time's right. Understand, Peter?
Peter	How're we going to know that? I mean, just how much more right can it be?
Jesus	Oh, you don't know the half of it! Look, you remember John the Baptist – how he baptised people by pouring water over them and saying they could have a new beginning in their lives? Well, you're in for a baptism, too – but it won't be water poured all over you. Oh, no – it'll be God's Holy Spirit. And if you think you're feeling good now – well, you just wait, that's all.
James	Yeah, yeah, yeah – but when? Can't you tell us when you're really going to be the top guy?
Jesus	That's not for you to know, James. My Father God's got all that sorted. But when the Holy Spirit comes, you'll get the power you need. You're going to tell everyone about me – in Judea, in Samaria – oh, all over the place, right to the far ends of the earth.
Peter	That's an awfully long way. Will God give me a bigger boat?
Jesus	You worry about that when the time comes. Just wait, that's all.

Narrator	Peter was about to ask another question, but instead he stopped and stared in amazement. Jesus seemed to be floating – then they all realised that he was leaving them. He was taken up into a big cloud, and they couldn't see him any more.
Peter	Where's he gone?
Thomas	Oh, where d'you think? He's gone back to his Father, that's where.
Narrator	Before they could say any more, they found a couple of strangers had joined them: strange-looking people, all white and shining like something out of a washing powder advert on telly – except that automatic washing powder hadn't been invented then. One of them spoke.
Angel 1	Hey there, you Galilean dudes! Like, what gives? I mean, what's the scene, man? Why're you standing looking into the sky?
Narrator	The disciples looked at one another blankly for a moment, and then the light dawned.
All disciples together	Angels!
Angel 2	Gee, man, it takes you guys a long time to catch on! Anyway, just hear this. This Jesus guy, who's just been taken up into heaven, yeah? Well, he's coming back – just like you saw him go, yeah?
Narrator	The disciples turned to look at one another again.
All disciples together	Yeah!
Narrator	A flash made them turn back, and the angels had gone. All that was left was a daisy-chain halo and a hastily scribbled note saying, 'Wait for the power!' So they went back to Jerusalem and joined Jesus' other friends, including his brothers and his mother, Mary.
Peter	Weird experience, that! What are we supposed to do now?
Thomas	What the man said – wait for the power. Isn't that right, Mary?
Mary	That's right. I know all about waiting for God – one way or another I've been doing it all my life. He'll move when he's good and ready – just chill, man. Just chill. MICHAEL FORSTER

Reflective material
(sketches, meditations and poems)

The Prince of Light

The angels crowded round him,
   their faces shining bright.
The air was filled with music
   to greet the Prince of Light.

Heaven was full of laughter,
   its beauty all unmarred –
   when suddenly a voice rang out,
   'Look, his hands are scarred!'

A hush spread through the multitude,
   and heaven held its breath,
   for he who left an empty grave
   still held the marks of death.

'I brought my scars to heaven
   on hands and feet and head
   so it will not be forgotten
   I once was truly dead.'

'These scars are cruel and ugly,
   yet here in heaven they stand.
Where all is light and beauty –
   see now my wounded hand.'

'To you they mar my glory,
   my wounds so raw and red' –
   the hosts looked on in wonder
   and many tears were shed.

'They are my greatest glory,
   not things to make you sad.
These are treasured wounds,
   rejoice and sing – be glad!'

'They are the price of love,
   the reason why I died.
For I chose,' his voice rang out,
   '*chose* to be crucified!'

MARY HATHAWAY

Pentecost

Pentecost Sunday

The gift of God's promised Holy Spirit

John 14:8-17 (25-27)

(also Acts 2:1-21 or Genesis 11:1-9; Psalm 104:24-34, 35b; Romans 8:14-17)

A reading from the Gospel of John (14:15-16, 23-26)

Jesus said:

> If you love me you will do everything I have commanded, and I will ask my Father to send a helper to stay with you for ever. Anyone who keeps my word, which comes from the Father who sent me, will be loved by my Father and me, and we will make our home in their hearts. The Spirit of God will show you the truth and live inside you. This Spirit will teach you and help you to remember everything I have told you.

This is the Gospel of the Lord
Praise to you, Lord Jesus Christ   KATIE THOMPSON

A reading from the Acts of the Apostles (First reading – Acts 2:1-11)

The disciples had gathered together in Jerusalem to celebrate the Feast of Pentecost and to wait for the Holy Spirit that Jesus had promised to send.

One day, as they were praying together, the room was suddenly filled with the sound of a powerful wind which roared through the house. Then, what looked like small tongues of fire appeared and spread out to touch each one of them. So it was that they were filled with the Holy Spirit.

At once, in their excitement, they rushed outside to tell everyone what had happened to them. As they began to speak, they were amazed to find that everyone listening to their words could understand them! People from different regions and countries were astounded to hear these men preaching to them in their own native languages.

This is the Word of the Lord
Thanks be to God   KATIE THOMPSON

Introductory material

'I just can't do it!' How often have we claimed that, or something similar? If so, think again, for today we remember how twelve disciples, who must have said and thought much the same, were transformed in the space of a few moments into those for whom nothing apparently was beyond them. What was their secret? There wasn't one, for the change within them had nothing to do with themselves but everything to do with God. It took simply the breath of his Spirit to bring about one of the most astonishing transformations in history, and to set into motion the extraordinary events of what we call 'the day of Pentecost'. Yet Pentecost is not about *one* day but *every* day, for the gift of the Spirit is a continuous experience intended for all. You and I, like those who have gone before us, are called to be Pentecost people, living and working in ways we might once have thought beyond us to the glory of Christ. Have we risen to the challenge?

NICK FAWCETT

Prayers

Approach – Open to the Spirit

Almighty and loving God,
    we gather together today
        as those joined by your Holy Spirit.

We come remembering your ancient promise
    to send your Spirit upon all people,
        young and old,
        male and female,
        Jew and Gentile.
Move within us we pray.

We come remembering that first Pentecost
    when your Spirit was given to the Apostles,
        renewing their faith and transforming their lives.
Move within us we pray.

We come, on this Pentecost Sunday,
    reminded of the constant work of your Spirit,
    inspiring,
    guiding,
    challenging,
    refining.
Move within us we pray.

Almighty God, Spirit of truth,
    come as you promised
        and reveal to us more of the way of Christ.
    Come and fill us with deeper faith and greater love.
    Give us the gifts we need to work for your kingdom,
        inspire us with new vision and purpose,
        and breathe your power into our lives.
Move within us we pray.

Almighty and loving God,
　　open our hearts and minds and souls to your Spirit,
　　　　whoever we may be,
　　　　and so equip us to live as your people,
　　　　not just this but every day,
　　　　our lives reflecting your glory
　　　　and proclaiming your love.
　　Move within us we pray,
　　　　to the glory of your name.
　　Amen.　　　　　　　　　　　　　　　　　　　　NICK FAWCETT

Confession

Living God,
　　we have rejoiced again today
　　　　at the gift of your Spirit,
　　　　the way you breathed new hope, new faith
　　　　and new life into your people.
　　But we remember also
　　　　that not everyone responded so gladly
　　　　to the Spirit's coming –
　　　　from some there was scorn, ridicule and disbelief,
　　　　suggestions that the apostles were drunk
　　　　or even out of their minds.
　　Lord, have mercy.

Living God,
　　forgive us that we too
　　　　can be guilty of a similar response.
　　Instead of welcoming the Spirit
　　　　we greet him with cautious and suspicious hearts.
　　Instead of opening our lives to the Spirit's movement
　　　　we close our minds to anything
　　　　which challenges our long-held preconceptions.
　　Instead of gladly receiving your Spirit's gifts
　　　　we barricade our souls against change.
　　Lord, have mercy.

Living God,
　　you warn us to test what we think is the Spirit
　　　　and ensure it is of you;
　　　　and there are times when we need to do that,
　　　　when it is right to be aware
　　　　of misplaced enthusiasm and false prophecy.
　　Yet save us from ever quenching,
　　　　obstructing or frustrating the Spirit.

Forgive us all the times we have done that,
   and open our lives now
   to your Holy Spirit's life-giving breath,
   so that we may live more truly as your people.
Lord, have mercy,
   in the name of Christ.
Amen.   NICK FAWCETT

Petition – The renewing Spirit

Spirit of God,
   you swept into the lives of the Apostles,
     and, in a moment, everything was different,
     transformed for ever by your renewing power.
You breathed new vision into them,
   new hope and faith,
   so that the world was suddenly alive again with promise.
Suddenly, you were there,
   deep within,
   cleansing,
   encouraging,
   empowering,
   inspiring,
   turning their lives inside-out
   so that nothing would ever be the same again.
Holy Spirit,
   move in us today.

You came to those looking to serve you
   but uncertain of the way forward,
   to those who believed you could use them
   though they didn't know how,
   to those who recognised the future was full of opportunities
   to serve you,
   but who doubted their ability to respond.
And, suddenly, the future was clear,
   confidence radiating from them
   as you touched their lives with power from on high.
Holy Spirit,
   move in us today.

You came to those who had followed Jesus throughout his ministry
   and who longed to know him better –
   those who had witnessed his preaching and teaching,
   who had watched him suffer and die,
   and, having seen him gloriously raised to life again,

wanted to grasp better what it all meant,
for them and for others.
And, suddenly, you were there,
calling the words of Jesus to mind,
opening their hearts to the truth,
leading them to an ever-deeper understanding
of everything Christ had achieved.
Holy Spirit,
move in us today.

You came to those conscious of their failure and weakness,
all too aware of their limited abilities,
their flawed faith
and their rebellious natures.
And, suddenly, they discovered new life growing within them,
gifts which they scarcely imagined possible,
and fruits which they had never even contemplated.
Holy Spirit,
move in us today.

Spirit of God,
you swept into the lives of the Apostles,
and, in a moment, everything was different.
Move now in us,
so that our service may be enriched,
our faith deepened
and our lives transformed.
Holy Spirit,
move in us today.

Through Jesus Christ our Lord.
Amen.   NICK FAWCETT

Intercession

When God's Spirit is poured out on his people, it shows.

As we still our bodies and open ourselves to God
we think of the church leaders, preachers
and all who minister to God's people.
With them and for them we pray . . .
Silence for prayer
Spirit of the living God:
fall afresh on us

We think of all the world's nations,
the problems, quarrels, misunderstandings
and mistakes.
With them and for them we pray . . .

Silence for prayer

Spirit of the living God:
fall afresh on us

We think of those in our family,
those we like and those we seem to annoy.
With them and for them we pray . . .

Silence for prayer

Spirit of the living God:
fall afresh on us

We think of those in hospitals and hospices,
outpatients at the local accident centre
and those ill at home.
With them and for them we pray . . .

Silence for prayer

Spirit of the living God:
fall afresh on us

We think of those who are close to death,
those who have recently died
and those who miss them.
With them and for them we pray . . .

Silence for prayer

Spirit of the living God:
fall afresh on us

We think of all your amazing creation,
from the microscopic to the cosmic,
and remember with thankfulness that we are part
of this glory you have made.

Silence for prayer

Merciful Father,
**accept these prayers
for the sake of your Son,
our Saviour Jesus Christ, Amen.**

SUSAN SAYERS

Short prayers

Petition

Loving God,
we meet here like your friends so long ago,
praying that you will pour out your Spirit on us
and give us the gifts of faith we need
to be your people in the world.
Please forgive us
for the lack of commitment we sometimes feel,
and give us confidence to go from here full of joy
to tell your Good News to the world. Amen.   MICHAEL FORSTER

Lord,
   I really can't get my head around
   all this 'thee, thou and therefore' stuff.
It drives me round the bend and over the hill.
What does it all mean?
Is it some sort of code for the initiated?
A kind of secret language
   that only those in the know understand?
Do we need a translator or interpreter
   to explain what's going on
   and what we need to do?
Should there be a sort of 'idiots' guide'
   to help us say the 'right' things at the 'right' time? –
   so that we don't stand up when we should be sitting down.
Perhaps you could suggest
   that someone puts a few dictionaries
   next to the hymn books,
   although I really think
   that we'd never sing a word or a note.
We'd be too busy looking in the dictionary
   trying to find out
   what we were singing about,
   or what we were trying to say
   if only we knew what we'd said!
I think we need
   the Holy Spirit
   to descend on a few of the congregation
   and get them to speak
   in a language
   that we can all understand.

Until that time,
    you'll have to guess what I mean
    'cos the only word I've got sorted
    comes at the end of a line. Amen.

PETE TOWNSEND

Loving God, we thank you for sending your Holy Spirit to the Church, to give us the gifts we need to do your work. You've given each of us special gifts to express your love – which is the greatest gift of all – in the world. Thank you for loving us so much you want to make us part of your mission.

We're sorry for the times we hide ourselves away and don't use the gifts you've given us, for those occasions when we could have been open to people and weren't, or when we could have spoken out about something and didn't. Please forgive us, and help us to be better signs of your love in the world. Amen.

MICHAEL FORSTER
SIMON SMITH

Lord Jesus Christ,
    you told the disciples
    to expect the gift of the Holy Spirit,
    yet when it came it took them by surprise,
    bursting into their lives
    in a way beyond all their expectations.
Suddenly life for them was transformed,
    full of untold possibilities.
Lord Jesus Christ,
    you tell us to expect the gift of the Spirit,
    yet we too are taken by surprise.
You want to transform our lives
    to open the door to new horizons,
    but we close our hearts
    or tie you down to our own expectations.
Lord Jesus,
    as we remember today
    that day of Pentecost long ago,
    help us to open our lives
    to the movement of your Spirit now.

NICK FAWCETT

All-age-talk material

Aim

To understand and celebrate what happened at Pentecost.

First help the children to make these streamers (see below) and then read or tell the Pentecost story, with the children using their streamers at the appropriate places. Then have a lively time of singing and dancing, using their streamers and some of these songs:

Jesus is greater than the greatest heroes
The Holy Spirit sets my feet a-dancing
I am a new creation
We are one in the Spirit
(and there are lots of others).

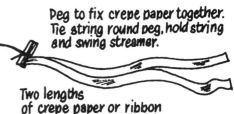

Move from the lively praise into a time of worship, settling down and singing something like:

Jesus, Jesus, let me tell you what I know
Father, we love you
All of my heart

SUSAN SAYERS

Activity

Party games

Pass out sheets of plain A4 paper and ask people to draw a picture of their house – it doesn't matter how rough it is, no one's going to be marking them out of ten. Families can work together on one picture between them, and if there are a number of families you could ask for one person from each to form another 'family', representing the Church, and draw the building. (Alternatively, you could do that one in advance but keep it hidden until the end, when you say, 'What have we missed?') While they're drawing, take a straw poll of the streets represented in the congregation and write each one down in large letters on a piece of paper. Stick the street names around the walls, using Blu-Tack, and then get each family to post up their house drawing under their street name. If some families come from out of the area that's fine – it extends the Church's potential mission field. In those cases you might add the name of their town, village, estate or suburb under the street name.

Now look around. This is the Church's presence in the community: each home full of the special gifts God has given to that family, and a potential mission outpost. It could be simply a place of prayer, or a haven of kindness for visitors. It could be a place where special talents are developed for God, or where coffee mornings are held to draw people together, or – oh, why don't you let them think of their own? After all, they know best!

MICHAEL FORSTER
SIMON SMITH

Tell the children what happened at Pentecost, emphasising that Jesus' friends were keeping in touch with him through prayer, so they were prepared when his life, or Spirit, came to them so powerfully. Explain that we need to keep in touch with him, too, if we want him to live in us (Palm Tree's version of the story is called *Wind and Fire*).

Talk about qualities the Holy Spirit gives us – love, joy, peace, etc. Then help the children to make long streamers out of orange, red and yellow, with these qualities drawn or printed on them. As the children come into church they dance round the aisles waving the streamers and twirling them so that they look like fire.   SUSAN SAYERS

Jesus promised
to send the Holy Spirit
to everyone who keeps
his word

How did
the Spirit appear to
the disciples at
Pentecost?

Write the next letter of the alphabet above the letters given. For example, G will be written above F

‾‾ ‾‾
Z R

‾‾ ‾‾ ‾‾ ‾‾ ‾‾ ‾‾ ‾‾ ‾‾   ‾‾ ‾‾ ‾‾ ‾‾
O N V D Q E T K   V H M C

‾‾ ‾‾ ‾‾
Z M C

‾‾ ‾‾ ‾‾ ‾‾ ‾‾ ‾‾ ‾‾
S N M F T D R

‾‾ ‾‾   ‾‾ ‾‾ ‾‾ ‾‾
N E   E H Q D

Acts
2:2-3

KATIE THOMPSON

Write the first letter of each object

AT

AND

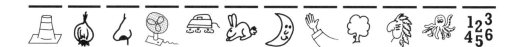

Solve the problem to find out!

$$(4 \times 3) + 24 - 3 + (2 \times 8) \div 7 = \boxed{}$$

KATIE THOMPSON

Abound in hope by the power of the Holy Spirit. (Romans 15:13)

These two pictures may look the same
but can you find 10 differences?

WORDSEARCH

Find the following words in the grid:

PENTECOST, HOLY SPIRIT,
POWER, FIRE, WIND,
LANGUAGES, AMAZING,
JESUS, ALIVE, TELL.

```
P E N T E C O S L L E T
J A M A Z I N P O W E E
P E N T E C O S T E N L
P O S E R A M A Z T R S
E G C U Y F I R E W Y E
N W N G S A G F E S C G
T I R I P S Y L O H O A
E N G U Z O W E R I S U
C D Z A M A W E L L D G
S O W E R I M E W O P N
P E N T E C O A R N G A
A L I V E A M A Z I N L
```

MICHAEL FORSTER

The Spirit gave the disciples the courage and power to preach to the people, just as Jesus had told them to do

These pictures are in the wrong order. Put the letter for each picture in the right order on the lines below

A

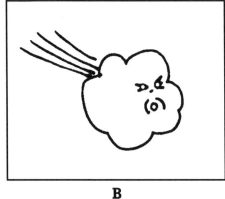

B

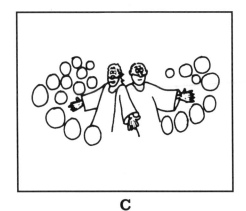

C

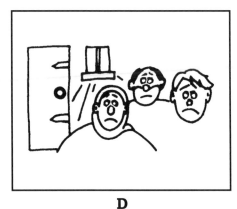

D

KATIE THOMPSON

The Holy Spirit comes!

Jesus asks us to do something for him if we love him. What is it?

Hold this message up to a mirror to read what it says

'Keep my Commandments,'

John 14:15

KATIE THOMPSON

Read Acts 2:1-21

The Feast of Pentecost was a time to celebrate a successful harvest. It was a time when all male Israelites would make a peace offering to God, asking for forgiveness, and would remember God's help in getting them out of captivity in Egypt. Jerusalem would have been bursting at the seams as people gathered to make their peace offering and celebrate God's goodness. Many people would have travelled a long way to celebrate at the temple in Jerusalem. As a result, it would have been possible to hear many different languages in the streets (see verses 7-11).

At this same time God fulfilled a promise that Jesus had made and sent the Holy Spirit on the disciples as God's representative. To their amazement everyone within earshot of the disciples heard these men from Galilee talking in many different languages. The Holy Spirit had given each of the disciples the ability to express their feelings in a foreign language. This demonstration of the Holy Spirit had two purposes. First, it was a fulfilment of a promise and one which gave the followers of Jesus the ability to act with God as their authority. Second, it was a celebration. It was an expression of the disciples' heartfelt thanks for all that God had done and would do.

The use of so many different languages appeared to be God's way of saying that everything that Jesus had accomplished was now to be shared throughout the world; language was no barrier.

Peter, whose education was minimal, stood up in front of a huge crowd and explained what God was doing. The time had come for the disciples (now called Apostles) to spread the good news of Jesus.

Give each member of the group a piece of paper and a pen. In Acts 2:12, the demonstration of the Holy Spirit had left everyone both excited and confused. There may be many things about God, Jesus and the Holy Spirit that are not altogether clear or need some explanation. Invite the group to write a question on the piece of paper about something which has been rattling around their head for a while. Ask the group to be honest and write down, no matter how basic the question might appear, whatever it is that they have trouble getting to grips with.

You may like to respond to some of the questions immediately or set aside a period of time each week to try and answer one question from the group. Make this time an honest, no-holds-barred session where anyone can feel totally comfortable to ask whatever is on their mind. You might like to have a special place on a noticeboard where group members can pin a question.

PETE TOWNSEND

Reflective material
(sketches, meditations and poems)

God breaks the language barrier

Based on Acts 2:1-12

Narrator   The friends of Jesus had a wonderful story to tell. For a time, they'd thought it was all over – the people who hated Jesus had had him killed, but God raised him from the dead and gave him new life – and he'd been seen by all his close friends before he went back to heaven. But they had a promise that he'd always be with them, and he'd told them to tell the whole world the Good News that he was alive – and Peter was getting impatient.

Peter   So what are we waiting for? We must do as he said – tell the world. And instead we're all sitting here together just praying!

Narrator   Peter always was the one who went at everything like a bull at a gate – head down, mouth in gear, brain in neutral!

Andrew   Jesus also told us to wait until we get the power we need. I don't know what he meant, but I'm sure we'll know when we get it.

Peter   But, Andrew, this is the great festival – there are people from all over the world here, and we've got to tell them so they can go home and tell their friends. That's right, isn't it, Thomas?

Thomas   Fine – and just how are you going to talk to foreign visitors when none of us can speak any of their languages?

Narrator   Peter had to admit, Thomas had a point – but before he could answer, something really strange started happening. It sounded like a gale blowing through the room – but the air was completely still. It got louder and louder, but still they didn't feel anything. Philip, another of the friends, knew something important was going on.

Philip   Didn't Jesus say that God's Spirit was like the wind? Didn't he say something about it blowing and you never knew where it came from or where it went?

Peter   Oh, heaven save us, he's getting all intellectual!

Narrator   Peter knew all about nets and fish, but he would never have called himself a deep thinker.

Nathanael   He's right, though – that's exactly what Jesus said, and it's *exactly* what's happening now.

Peter	Never mind the theories, Nathanael. We've got to get out and *do* something. On second thoughts, just get out – the room's on fire!
Philip	(*Calmly*) You know, I do believe he's right – the room *is* on fire. This is very interesting.
Peter	Never mind interesting – let's get out!
Philip	But it's not burning, is it? Lots of fire, but nothing's burning.
Narrator	He was right. Gradually the panic subsided, but Peter was still agitated.
Peter	What's going on? I can't remember anything like this before.
Philip	Yes, you can. Moses – the burning bush – it was on fire but it never got burnt. Don't you see?
Narrator	Peter didn't see. But Nathanael did.
Nathanael	This is the Holy Spirit Jesus promised us! Just like Moses – God's giving us the power we need to go and do his work. Oh, I say – where's everybody gone?
Narrator	When Nathanael got outside he was amazed. Peter was rattling on nineteen to the dozen – nothing strange in that, but he was telling someone from Libya about Jesus – in Arabic. Then he heard Andrew speaking Latin – he'd buttonholed a Roman merchant who just couldn't wait to hear more about Jesus. Just then, a woman came up to Nathanael.
Woman	What's this all about?
Nathanael	I'm really very sorry, but I don't speak Turkish. You'll have to ask someone else.
Woman	I don't understand.
Nathanael	Well, it's really simple enough: I don't speak your language – go and ask someone who does.
Woman	Well, if you don't speak my language, how come I'm understanding every word you're saying?
Narrator	She was right! Everyone was amazed. The Good News about Jesus was being spread to all the foreign visitors *in their own languages*.
Nathanael	So this is God's Holy Spirit at work. Impressive. *Very* impressive!

MICHAEL FORSTER

Meditation of John the Apostle

'You will be my witnesses
    in Jerusalem,
    in all Judea and Samaria,
    and to the ends of the earth.'
Quite a picture, isn't it,
    a prospect to stir the heart and fire the imagination.
But I tell you what,
    huddled there together in that upper room,
    those words seemed a long way off,
    a beautiful but rapidly fading memory.
We were terrified of going out, if the truth be told,
    despite our prayers,
    despite his promise,
    scared stiff our enemies would come for us
    as they'd come for him,
    and send us off to some equally ghastly death.
We wished it were different, of course we did –
    we longed for courage to get out there
    and proclaim the good news,
    to tell the world what Christ had done,
    but, even if we had found that courage,
    it wouldn't have counted for much,
    for we had no idea what to say or how to say it.
We were twelve men with a mission –
    and none of us had the first idea where to start,
    let alone where it all might finish!
So we just sat there,
    and waited,
    and hoped,
    longing to believe it might be true
    but in our heart of hearts wondering if it ever could be –
    for who were we,
    ordinary folk like us,
    to set the world on fire?
It was an unlikely prospect, to say the least.
Only, suddenly, out of the blue, it happened,
    a sound like a mighty rushing wind filling the room,
    tongues of fire leaping and dancing upon us,
    and, all at once, an ecstasy beyond words,
    a peace, a joy and a confidence that defied description.
No more fear or doubt,
    no more hesitation –
    our mouths were opened and we spoke boldly,
    moving out among the multitude that had gathered,

the words flowing freely as we needed them,
and each heard us,
amazed,
bewildered to hear us speaking in their own tongue.
A one-minute wonder?
Don't you believe it!
It was the beginning of an astonishing adventure,
a lifetime of witness,
an incredible journey of discipleship,
out into Jerusalem,
on to Judea and Samaria,
and beyond to the ends of the earth.
As I say, quite a picture, isn't it?
One to stir even the coldest heart
and fire the poorest of imaginations.
At least I hope it does,
for the job's not over, not by a long way,
nor, praise God, is the promise.
The call is there, and the offer is there,
for you and anyone who believes –
the promise of power to be witnesses to the risen Christ.
Wait patiently,
trust in the promise of the Father,
and you, like us, will receive.

NICK FAWCETT

Lead us in a plain path

Leader   Holy Spirit of God,
       we need you so much
       our minds are troubled
       about many things.

       Light up our minds
       as the moon lights up the sky.
All   And lead us in a plain path.

Leader   We don't know what to do
       and there is no one we can
       ask for help but you.

       Light up our minds
       as the moon lights up the sky
All   And lead us in a plain path.

Leader   Without you
              all that is real within us
              will shrivel up
              and die away.

              Light up our minds
              as the moon lights up the sky.
All   And lead us in a plain path.

Leader   Come to us in the gentle
              caress of the wind
              and speak to us
              in the tender shining
              of the summer stars.

              Light up our minds
              as the moon lights up the sky.
All   And lead us in a plain path.

Leader   So Holy Spirit of God,
              come to us and satisfy
              our inward beings
              with your beauty.

              Light up our minds
              as the moon lights up the sky.
All   And lead us in a plain path.   MARY HATHAWAY

Lord, you are like a weaver in our lives –
you have spun each one of us into a unique
and colourful strand . . .
then you wove us together.

Lord, Great Weaver,
open our eyes to the mystery and
power of your Spirit.

Reattach us to your loom
through the power of Christ.
Together in Prayer:
Women's World Day of Prayer, 1993

from *You're Never Alone*
ELIZABETH RUNDLE

Order of Service – Holy Communion
Filled with the Spirit

Order of Service	Directions
1 *Welcome and Notices*	Warm and inviting. Visitors and newcomers should be made particularly welcome.
2 *Introduction to the Theme*	SHORT PAUSE
3 *Acclamation*	Read Acclamation without announcing it. As Acclamation starts, extended introduction to hymn or song begins softly in background.

3 *Acclamation*

Stand

The love of God has been poured into our hearts through the Holy Spirit who has been given to us: **we dwell in him and he in us.**

Give thanks to the Lord and call upon his name: **make known his deeds among the peoples.**

Sing to him, sing praises to him: **and speak of all his marvellous works.**

Holy, holy, holy, is the Lord God almighty: **who was and is and is to come!**

4 *Extended Time of Sung Worship (taking in Confession)*

Move directly into sung worship.

Hymn

Holy, Holy, Holy! (*The Source*) or

Song

Praise God from whom all blessings flow (*The Source*)

Song

As we seek your face (*The Source*)

5 *Open Worship*

(Open to God, open prayer or praise, reflecting, sharing gifts)

Play soft instrumental music in background. Open to the Holy Spirit. The congregation may be encouraged to reflect, pray quietly or out loud and share gifts of the Spirit. It is important for the leader of the worship to direct sensitively at this point.

6 *Silence*

The music ends.

7 *Preparation and Confession*

Let us sit or kneel to pray together:

Almighty God,
to whom all hearts are open,
all desires known,
and from whom no secrets are hidden:
cleanse the thoughts of our hearts
by the inspiration of your Holy Spirit,
that we may perfectly love you,
and worthily magnify your holy name;
through Christ our Lord. Amen.

Remain seated.

Hymn

Breathe on me, Breath of God (verses 1 and 2)
(*The Source*)

Introduction to the hymn begins unannounced.

Holy, holy, holy is the Lord almighty;
the whole earth is full of his glory.
As we too look upon the Lord we cry with Isaiah,
'Woe to me! I am ruined,
for I am a person of unclean lips
and I live among a people of unclean lips
and my eyes have seen the King, the Lord almighty.'
Spirit of God we need you to cleanse us,
to make clean our lips and sweep away our sin,
to breathe new life in us.
We lift our eyes to you, Lord,
and confess the burden of our hearts.

Instrumental music of the hymn continues softly in the background.

O King enthroned on high,
filling the earth with your glory:
holy is your name,
Lord God almighty.
In our sinfulness we cry to you
to take our guilt away,
and to cleanse our lips to speak your word,
through Jesus Christ our Lord. Amen.

May the Father forgive *us*
by the death of his Son
and strengthen *us*
to live in the power of the Spirit
all *our* days. **Amen.**

Towards the conclusion of the Absolution the instrumental music leads into an extended intro to the hymn.

Hymn

Breathe on me, Breath of God (verses 3 and 4)

Verses 3 and 4 should build musically to encourage affirmation of forgiveness and new start.

Collect

God, who at this time
taught the hearts of your faithful people
by sending to them the light of your Holy Spirit:
grant us by the same Spirit
to have a right judgement in all things
and evermore to rejoice in his holy comfort;
through the merits of Christ Jesus our Saviour,
who is alive and reigns with you,
in the unity of the Holy Spirit,
one God, now and for ever.

SHORT PAUSE

8 *The Liturgy of the Word*

Reading 1

Short time of silence

Photograph slide or image of 'a ship's sail' or 'flames' could be projected onto screen during the readings.

Reading 2

Short time of silence

(Visual images off)

Sermon

Sermon linked to theme. Challenging and affirming, giving practical help for life of discipleship filled with the Holy Spirit.

9 *Silence*

Silence for personal reflection on Sermon. How does God want me to respond?

10 *Prayers*

Fill us, Lord – with your Holy Spirit.
May our hearts overflow with thanks,
may our lips sing your praise
and may our lives be renewed with your
    breath of life.

On this occasion the prayers follow the sermon so that 'prayer' is a direct response to conclude the Liturgy of the Word. Prayers are unannounced and follow time of silence.

Silence

We pray:
Holy Spirit, come.

Grant us, Lord – the gifts of your Spirit
that you so desire to pour in us.
Give us the courage and the faith
to receive them gladly and to be released
into new depths of life – life with you.

Silence

Work through our lives and our church in power
so that others may be touched with your love,
and hearts may be won for your kingdom;
all to the glory of your name.

We pray:
Holy Spirit, come.

Awaken us, Lord – to see your purposes
    and your ways.
Holy Spirit, you are the life-giver
and we love to see you at work within creation
and the world in which we live.
As a nation we are in such need
of your power and love.
Breathe new life into the dry bones of faith,
pour living water to quench our thirst for you
and flood this land with hope and healing love.

Silence

We pray:
Holy Spirit, come.

Move, Lord Jesus – within our own community.
Through your saving love reach out to the lost,
the broken and the fallen.
Help us to be your voice calling to those in need
and your hands ministering support and care.
We lift to you now those in need of your healing
Spirit because of sickness and suffering.

Silence

We pray:
Holy Spirit, come.

Thank you, heavenly Father – that through your
Son you have given us the gift of eternal life.
Set this hope in our hearts so that each day
we will live to bring you praise and glory.
Unite your church to be one in heart and mind
so that together we will pray . . .

> Instrumental introduction to song begins softly in the background.

Holy Spirit, come.

Song
Holy Spirit come (*The Source*)

> Song begins unannounced. Sing gently. Music could continue afterwards whilst people pray or sit quietly. Music ends before the Creed.

The Creed

Let us stand to say the Creed:

We believe in one God,
the Father, the almighty,
maker of heaven and earth,
of all that is,
seen and unseen.

We believe in one Lord, Jesus Christ,
the only Son of God,
eternally begotten of the Father,
God from God, Light from Light
true God from true God,
begotten, not made,
of one Being with the Father.
Through him all things were made.
For us and for our salvation
he came down from heaven;
by the power of the Holy Spirit
he became incarnate of the Virgin Mary,
and was made man.
For our sake he was crucified under Pontius Pilate;
he suffered death and was buried.
On the third day he rose again
in accordance with the scriptures;
he ascended into heaven
and is seated at the right hand of the Father.
He will come again in glory
to judge the living and the dead,
and his kingdom will have no end.

We believe in the Holy Spirit,
the Lord, the giver of life,
who proceeds from the Father and the Son.
With the Father and the Son
he is worshipped and glorified.
He has spoken through the Prophets.

We believe in one holy, catholic and apostolic
Church.
We acknowledge one baptism for the forgiveness
of sins.
We look for the resurrection of the dead,
and the life of the world to come. Amen.

11 *The Peace*

God has made us one in Christ.
He has set his seal upon us and,
as a pledge of what is to come,
has given the Spirit to dwell in our hearts. Alleluia.

The peace of the Lord be always with you
and also with you.
Let us offer one another a sign of peace.

All may exchange a sign of peace.

12 *The Eucharistic Prayer (B)*

The Lord is here.
His Spirit is with us.

Lift up your hearts.
We lift them to the Lord.

Let us give thanks to the Lord our God.
It is right to give thanks and praise.

It is indeed right, it is our duty and our joy,
always and everywhere to give you thanks,
holy Father, almighty and everlasting God,
through Jesus Christ, your only Son our Lord.
This day we give you thanks
because in fulfilment of your promise
you pour out your Spirit upon us,
filling us with your gifts, leading us into all truth,
and uniting peoples of many tongues
in the confession of one faith.
Your Spirit gives us grace to call you Father,
to proclaim your gospel to all nations
and to serve you as a royal priesthood.
Therefore we join our voices
with angels and archangels,
and with all those in whom the Spirit dwells,
to proclaim the glory of your name,
for ever praising you and saying:

Holy, holy, holy Lord,
God of power and might,
heaven and earth are full of your glory.
Hosanna in the highest.

Before the Eucharistic prayer begins explain to the congregation that during Communion an anointing with oil will be available. Explain that oil is a symbol of the Holy Spirit and by being anointed you are expressing your desire to be filled with the Spirit of God, his life-giving power. People may wish to renew their life with the Lord, may wish to ask for healing or to ask for a specific gift of the Spirit. Whatever the reason, encourage them to go forward to receive Communion and then go to the appropriate area in the church given over for this particular time of ministry.

A trained prayer or ministry team will be needed to administer the oil (a simple sign of the cross on the forehead in the name of the Father, Son and Holy Spirit) and to pray with each person with the laying on of hands.

Lord, you are holy indeed, the source of all holiness;
grant that by the power of your Holy Spirit,
and according to your holy will,
these gifts of bread and wine
may be to us the body and blood
of our Lord Jesus Christ;

who, in the same night that he was betrayed,
took bread and gave you thanks;
he broke it and gave it to his disciples, saying:
Take, eat; this is my body which is given for you;
do this in remembrance of me.
In the same way, after supper
he took the cup and gave you thanks;
he gave it to them, saying:
Drink this, all of you;
this is my blood of the new covenant,
which is shed for you and for many
for the forgiveness of sins.
Do this, as often as you drink it,
in remembrance of me.

Great is the mystery of faith:
Christ has died:
Christ is risen:
Christ will come again.

And so, Father, calling to mind his death on the cross,
his perfect sacrifice made once
for the sins of the whole world;
rejoicing in his mighty resurrection
and glorious ascension,
and looking for his coming in glory,
we celebrate this memorial of our redemption.
As we offer you this our sacrifice
of praise and thanksgiving,
we bring before you this bread and this cup
and we thank you for counting us worthy
to stand in your presence and serve you.

Send the Holy Spirit on your people
and gather into one in your kingdom
all who share this one bread and one cup,
so that we, in the company of (*N and*) all the saints,

may praise and glorify you for ever,
through Jesus Christ our Lord;
by whom, and with whom, and in whom,
in the unity of the Holy Spirit,
all honour and glory be yours, almighty Father,
for ever and ever. **Amen.**

13   *The Lord's Prayer*

Let us sit or kneel to pray for the coming of God's
kingdom in the words our Saviour taught us:

Our Father in heaven,
hallowed be your name,
your kingdom come,
your will be done,
on earth as in heaven.
Give us today our daily bread.
Forgive us our sins
as we forgive those who sin against us.
Lead us not into temptation
but deliver us from evil.
For the kingdom, the power,
and the glory are yours
now and for ever. Amen.

14   *Breaking of the Bread*

The president breaks the consecrated bread.
We break this bread to share in the body of Christ.
Though we are many, we are one body,
because we all share in one bread.

15   *Giving of Communion*

Alleluia. Christ our Passover is sacrificed for us.
Therefore let us keep the feast. Alleluia.

Songs

By his grace (*The Source*)
The Spirit of the Lord (*The Source* 2)
Holy Spirit, come (*The Source*)

Anointing with oil and prayer
ministry. Singing and music
must be soft and sensitive during
combined Communion and
prayer ministry. The songs could
be linked to form an extended
time of sung worship.

16   *Silence*

Music ends.

17 *Prayer after Communion*

Faithful God,
who fulfilled the promises of Easter
by sending us your Holy Spirit
and opening to every race and nation
the way of life eternal:
open our lips by your Spirit,
that every tongue may tell of your glory;
through Jesus Christ our Lord. **Amen.**

**Almighty God,
we thank you for feeding us
with the body and blood of your Son Jesus Christ.
Through him we offer you our souls and bodies
to be a living sacrifice.
Send us out in the power of your Spirit
to live and work to your praise and glory. Amen.**

Song There is a Redeemer (*The Source*)

18 *The Blessing and Dismissal*

May Christ's holy, healing, enabling Spirit be
      with you
and guide you on your way at every change
      and turn.

And the blessing of God almighty,
the Father, the Son and the Holy Spirit,
be among you and remain with you always.

Go in peace to love and serve the Lord.
In the name of Christ. Amen.

19 *The Grace* (sung) (*The Source 2*)

**The grace of our Lord Jesus Christ
and the love of God
and the fellowship of the Holy Spirit
be with us for evermore.**

20 *Prayer Ministry*

(Continues as needed)

After Communion the service continues whilst people continue to receive prayer ministry.

Before the singing of the Grace offer the opportunity for prayer or anointing with oil after the service. Maybe people felt unable to respond earlier but would like to now.

Soft worship music could be played as people leave or as prayer continues.

TIM LOMAX

Trinity

Trinity Sunday

The inexpressibly awesome nature of God – Father, Son and Holy Spirit

John 16:12-15

(also Proverbs 8:1-4, 22-31; Psalm 8; Romans 5:1-5)

A reading from the Gospel of John 16:12-15

Jesus said to his disciples:

> My friends, there is so much more to tell you, but I will not burden you now. Do not worry; when the Spirit of truth comes he will guide you to the complete truth and reveal the things to come. He will glorify me, because everything he says will come from me, and everything that is mine comes from the Father.

This is the Gospel of the Lord
Praise to you, Lord Jesus Christ   KATIE THOMPSON

Introductory material

'God the Father incomprehensible, God the Son incomprehensible, God the Holy Spirit incomprehensible' – so states the Athanasian Creed. And for most of us that just about sums up the doctrine of the Trinity. We accept it, we believe it – or at least we do our best – but to be honest we find the whole business rather baffling. Yet beneath the religious terminology, Trinity conveys a vital truth – the fact that we today can know Jesus through his Holy Spirit and through knowing Jesus we know God himself. That alone surely makes Trinity Sunday one of the great days of the Christian year!   NICK FAWCETT

Prayers

Praise – Bringing our worship

God of love,
  we rejoice today that you care for each one of us,
    that we matter so much to you
    that you want to share with us your gift of life
    and lead us into a living, loving relationship with you.
  Father, Son and Holy Spirit,
    receive our praise.

God of grace,
    we bless you for expressing your love so wonderfully in Christ,
        through his birth,
        his ministry,
        his death,
        his resurrection
        and his glorious exaltation.
    Father, Son and Holy Spirit,
        receive our praise.

God of power,
    we thank you for continuing to bless us each day
        through your Holy Spirit,
        nurturing our faith,
        renewing our vision,
        guiding our footsteps
        and equipping us for service.
    Father, Son and Holy Spirit,
        receive our praise.

God of all,
    Three in One and One in Three,
        we praise you that you have called us your children,
        your friends, your people,
        and that you are always with us,
        your love surrounding us wherever we may be,
        whatever we may face.
    Receive now our worship,
        offered to you in awe and wonder,
        in joy and thanksgiving.
    Father, Son and Holy Spirit,
        receive our praise.
        Amen.   NICK FAWCETT

Praise –Trinity worship

Mighty God,
    beyond all space and time,
        greater than our minds can fully grasp,
        ruler over all that is and has been and shall be,
        we worship you.

Loving Father,
  kind and merciful,
    full of goodness and compassion,
    constantly watching over us and directing our steps,
    we worship you.

Saviour Christ,
  flesh of our flesh yet the living image of God,
    sharing our humanity yet one with the Father,
    loving to the point of death yet bringer of life,
    we worship you.

Holy Spirit,
  free and mysterious,
    source of guidance and inspiration,
    filling our hearts and minds and lives,
    we worship you.

Father, Son and Holy Spirit,
  God of gods and Lord of lords,
    with awe and wonder,
    joy and gladness,
    love and praise,
    we bring this day,
    we bring our lives,
    we worship you,
    in the name of Christ.
    Amen.

NICK FAWCETT

Intercession – Bringing our world

Father God,
  your purpose is for all,
    for you are the Lord of heaven and earth,
    the Creator of humankind,
    Ruler over history.
  You are always at work,
    always involved in our lives,
    calling,
    guiding,
    speaking
    and responding,
    everyone important to you, no matter who they are,
    each having a place in your purpose.

So, then, we pray for all in our world who feel they are drifting,
   all who search for meaning to their lives,
   a sense of direction,
   a goal to strive for.
May they find in Jesus Christ
   the Way, the Truth and the Life.
In faith we lift them before you:
   hear our prayer.

Son of God,
   your love is for all,
      for you lived and died for others,
      reaching out to both rich and poor,
      Jew and Gentile,
      righteous and unrighteous,
      nobody outside your care,
      no one beyond your grace.
   You gave your all,
      enduring death on a cross,
      so that everyone willing to receive you
      may share in the joy of your kingdom.

So we pray for all in our world today who long for love –
   those who yearn for a meaningful relationship,
   and those whose once-precious relationships have ended in tears;
   those who have been abandoned or orphaned as children,
   and those who cannot have children of their own;
   those cut off from family and friends,
   and those who face the trauma of bereavement.
May they discover in you
   a love that will never let them go.
In faith we lift them before you:
   hear our prayer.

Spirit of God,
   your peace is for all,
      for you are at work in every heart,
      seen or unseen,
      recognised or unrecognised,
      striving to break down the barriers
      which keep us from one another,
      from ourselves
      and from you.

We pray, then, for all in our world who hunger for peace –
   all who are tormented by fear,
   torn by doubt,
   troubled by anxieties,
   or tortured by guilt;
   families separated by feuds,
   communities racked by division,
   and nations ravaged by war.
May they find through you
   peace in body, mind and spirit.
In faith we lift them before you:
   hear our prayer.

Almighty God,
   Father, Son and Holy Spirit,
     we bring you our world,
     thankful that it is also *your* world,
     precious to you
     and shaped ultimately by your will.
   Remake,
     redeem,
     renew it through your sovereign power.
   May all people everywhere
     come to know your purpose,
     experience your love
     and receive your peace,
     and may each rejoice in the new life
     you so yearn to give them.
In faith we lift them before you:
   hear our prayer.
   Amen.   NICK FAWCETT

Short prayers

Almighty God,
   there are no words able to sum up your nature,
   to say everything about you that needs to be said.
We do our best to express our faith,
   but inevitably we fall short,
   for you are greater than our minds can fathom,
   ultimately defying human understanding.
Yet we experience your love day after day
   in a multitude of ways:
   we glimpse your glory in the wonder of the heavens
   and the beauty of the earth;

we see everything we believe to be true about you
   revealed in Jesus Christ,
   his life, death and resurrection;
   and we feel your power at work deep within us
   through what we call your Spirit.
Each reveals different aspects of your character,
   yet it is only when we take them together,
   recognising them as facets of one being,
   one truth,
   that we begin to understand something of your wonder.
Our intellects reel at the mystery of it all,
   yet in our heart and soul we know that you are with us,
   and we rejoice.
Almighty God, Father, Son and Holy Spirit,
   receive our praise.
Amen!   NICK FAWCETT

Eternal God,
   you are greater than our highest thoughts,
   defying full expression
   and ultimately beyond our limited understanding.
Yet through Jesus you have given us
   a glimpse of your glory.
He spoke of you as a Father,
   not just his but ours,
   watching over us from on high.
He personified you as a friend,
   one with us,
   by our sides through thick and thin.
He opened the way to knowing you,
   vitally real within us,
   deepening our faith and enriching our lives.
Eternal God,
   slowly the truth dawned on his disciples,
   that to see Jesus is to see you,
   that to receive the Spirit
   is to receive his power and yours,
   that three is one and one is three.
Help us to recognise that truth
   and to glimpse your glory now,
   in the name of the Father, the Son,
   and the Holy Spirit.   NICK FAWCETT

All-age-talk material

Three in one and one in three

Aim

To demonstrate that the doctrine of the Trinity safeguards an important truth which we cannot afford to ignore.

Preparation

You will need an electrical plug and a length of three-core flex.

Talk

Start by asking how many pins there are in an electrical plug, and how many wires in a flex designed to carry 13 amps. (Three – display the plug and wires.) Ask what happens if one wire becomes disconnected. (The power fails to get through.) Ask what happens if two bare wires touch. (They fuse.)

   Each wire, and each pin, is separate, yet they are all important, each an integral part of the one plug. Take away one and the plug will either fail to work or be dangerously inadequate. And much the same is true when it comes to talking about God, and the doctrine of the Trinity. Three in one and one in three, we are told – words which on the surface don't seem to make much sense. But just as a plug is composed of three wires, so God comprises three persons. To talk about God the Father without God the Son, or God the Son without God the Holy Spirit, is to settle for a dangerously inadequate picture, which ultimately diminishes God and robs him of his full power. It is only when we recognise that God's love flows to us through the Father, within us through the Son, and from us through the Spirit, that we begin to glimpse the wonder of who God is and all he can do.

NICK FAWCETT

One God, three persons

John 16:12-15

How and when does Jesus speak to us?

Copy the letters in order on to the lines above the symbols as shown

Truhhsii / hogteprt

Alhtm / lteie

Can you decode the message?

KATIE THOMPSON

Find these words in the puzzle and circle them

SAVIOUR   HOLY SPIRIT   ADVOCATE
REDEEMER   LORD   FATHER   SON OF GOD
PARACLETE   EMMANUEL   MESSIAH

S	A	O	E	R	U	O	I	V	A	S	B
L	E	T	R	T	M	E	S	S	I	A	H
E	M	I	A	P	A	V	I	A	U	R	O
I	M	R	H	M	C	C	L	D	M	S	E
L	A	I	R	A	A	E	O	T	K	O	T
A	N	P	S	S	I	G	H	V	H	D	E
S	U	S	A	I	F	L	E	R	D	E	L
E	E	Y	S	O	L	O	A	F	O	A	C
O	L	L	N	P	N	R	T	R	S	N	A
N	P	O	S	R	E	D	E	E	M	E	R
M	S	H	E	H	R	I	T	R	S	P	A
L	T	G	R	E	H	T	A	F	T	O	P

KATIE THOMPSON

The Spirit
comes to show us
God's way

Jesus said . . .

'
‾‾‾‾ ‾‾‾‾   ‾‾‾‾ ‾‾‾‾ ‾‾‾‾ ‾‾‾‾
1,6 1,8   1,7 3,8 2,5 2,5

‾‾‾‾ ‾‾‾‾ ‾‾‾‾ ‾‾‾‾   ‾‾‾‾ ‾‾‾‾ ‾‾‾‾
2,5 1,8 3,5 3,7   2,8 2,7 1,5

‾‾‾‾ ‾‾‾‾   ‾‾‾‾ ‾‾‾‾ ‾‾‾‾
2,4 2,7   2,4 1,6 1,8

‾‾‾‾ ‾‾‾‾ ‾‾‾‾ ‾‾‾‾ ‾‾‾‾ ‾‾‾‾ ‾‾‾‾ ‾‾‾‾
1,4 2,7 3,4 2,6 2,5 1,8 2,4 1,8
,
‾‾‾‾ ‾‾‾‾ ‾‾‾‾ ‾‾‾‾ ‾‾‾‾
2,4 3,6 1,5 2,4 1,6

1	C	U	H	W	E
2	T	L	P	O	Y
3	M	A	R	D	I
	4	5	6	7	8

John 16:13

KATIE THOMPSON

Aim

To help the children understand about God's nature.

Have a large sheet of paper entitled: 'What we know about God'. A long strip of lining or wallpaper is ideal, and the larger the paper, the larger their writing can be. Sit all along both sides of the paper, with a variety of felt-tip pens available. Talk together about what God is like, and have every right idea written down colourfully on the paper. If they need some help, see what they can work out from the way the universe is created, the way we are created, the way Jesus behaved and the way God's friends behave.

Have some quiet music playing as all the characteristics of God are read out in turn. Compare these with what Peter says in his post-Pentecost sermon and with what Moses knew of God. Phrases from the psalms can be used instead.

Using felt tips, stickers, or paints and photos, fill in the areas between the words, so that the whole sheet of paper is a blaze of colour expressing the character of God.   SUSAN SAYERS

Ideas for activities

Have lots of lovely pictures and books available, and if possible take the children around outside to look at the sky, plants and flowers. As you enjoy all these things, talk about how lovely they are and how lovely God must be who thought of them and made them happen.   SUSAN SAYERS

Reflecting

As you have time during the week reflect on John 16:12-15.

In this short passage John deftly outlines the mysterious interrelatedness of the life of the Trinity. Jesus Christ, who has everything of the Father, is the centre of the Gospel. The Spirit is the One who 'declares' what is 'of' Jesus Christ. This declaring is not the shouting of a strident voice trying to persuade, but the silent inner pressing home of the knowledge of belonging to God, which shows itself in the self-authenticating truth of lives that are whole. That is the gift of Jesus Christ to receptive hearts – and to a lost world.

When you have found some stillness ask yourself what the phrases of this passage mean to you.   PATRICK WOODHOUSE

Our God, a Trinity of love

Our God is not a lonely God, but a God of happy endings. From always, God the First Person has been the light that nobody lit, the rock based on no other rock, the love that nobody 'loved into existence'.

The Second Person is love-in-return-for-love. Some of the ancient philosophers before Christ arrived at the notion that there must be One who was the origin of truth, of beauty, of justice and of all good. But they did not go on to look at realities like praise, admiration, gratitude, wonder, reliance, trust, in order to find the ultimate origin of those. One person cannot really be the origin of both love and of gratitude for love, of both beauty and of admiration of beauty, without being insufferably vain. Which is easy to see and to say once we know God is a Trinity, and that the one who is wonderful and the one who wonders are two different persons.

The Holy Spirit is the two-way love between the other two divine Persons. The clues are there in the story of the prodigal son. The father loves the son so much that he lets him go and make mistakes, just hoping against hope that he will return some day. From the father's side, a love with no strings. From the son's side comes a love that eventually takes the risk of coming home and trusts that the father's love is still there. Risks on both sides . . . but a happy ending.

When we transfer that to the Trinity, the Father loves the Son with no demands; the Son loves in return, freely. Jesus on the cross was undoubtedly taking a risk, that his Father still loved him. But the risk was well worth taking. Christians believe that when anyone gives unselfish love, it will at last return.

GERALD O'MAHONY

Reflective material
(sketches, meditations and poems)

Lord, you are all around us

(For up to six readers)

Lord, you are all around us.
Open our eyes to see –
   in star and mountain, sun and snow;
   in ocean, flower and tree.

Lord, you are all around us.
Help us to understand –
   in speech and music, book and poem;
   in artist's brush and hand.

Lord, you are all around us.
Give us the faith to know –
    in prayer and worship, bread and wine;
    in cross and candle glow.

Lord, you are all around us.
Fill us with love to care –
    for friend and family, stranger and foe;
    our neighbours everywhere.

Lord, you are deep within us.
Move us to live for you –
    give strength and courage, hope and peace,
    in all we are and do.

Lord, you are close beside us.
Lead us in paths of right –
    through joy and sorrow, laughter and tears,
    journeying to the light.

                                                PETER DAINTY

Meditation of John the Apostle

I didn't know what he was on about at the time,
    not the faintest idea,
    despite the way I nodded
    and attempted to smile in the right places.
The Advocate?
The Son who comes from the Father?
What did it all mean?
We believed he was sent by God, yes –
    called to reveal his will,
    build his kingdom –
    but was he saying more,
    pointing to a closer relationship?
It seemed so,
    yet, try as we might, we just couldn't get our heads round it.
'The Lord our God is one' –
    isn't that what we'd always been told?
Indeed, he said it himself,
    made no bones about it,
    so how could he also tell us, 'He who has seen me
    has seen the Father'?
We were baffled, there's no other word for it,
    and when he went on to talk about the Spirit of truth,
    the one his Father would send in his name,

quite simply, by then, we were reeling,
    unable to make head or tail of what he was getting at.
'Do we understand now, though?' you ask.
Well, no, we don't actually –
    funnily enough if we try to explain it
    we still struggle as much as ever;
    the more we try, the worse the knots we tie ourselves in.
Yet, strange though it may sound, it makes sense despite that –
    for day after day, year after year, we've tasted the truth,
    the reality of Father, Son and Holy Spirit.
We look up,
    to the stars and the sky,
    the wonder of the heavens,
    and God is there, enthroned in splendour,
    sovereign over all.
We look around,
    at the world he's given –
    its awesome beauty,
    its endless interest,
    its bountiful provision –
    and he is there,
    stretching out his hand in love,
    inviting us to share in its wonder.
We look nearby,
    at family and friends,
    beyond, to the nameless faces of the multitude,
    and he is there,
    giving and receiving,
    waiting to feed and to be fed.
We look within,
    at our aching souls,
    our pleading hearts,
    and he is there,
    breathing new life,
    new purpose within us.
One God, yes,
    but a God we meet in different guises,
    different ways,
    three in one and one in three.
It sounds odd, I know,
    and take it from me, you'll never explain it,
    no matter how you try,
    yet don't worry, for what finally matters is this:
    though words may fail you, the experience never will!   NICK FAWCETT

All Saints

All Saints' Day

The great company and blessings of heaven

Luke 6:20-31

(also Daniel 7:1-3, 15-18; Psalm 149; Ephesians 1:11-23)

A reading from the Gospel of Luke (6:17, 20-26)

Jesus and his twelve disciples stopped at a level plain where crowds of people had gathered. The crowds had come from all over Judea and as far as the coastal regions of Tyre and Sidon.

Jesus looked at his disciples and said:

> Happy are you who are poor: the kingdom of God belongs to you.
> Happy are you who go hungry: you shall be satisfied.
> Happy are you who weep with sadness: you shall laugh.
> Happy are you who suffer hatred and abuse because of the Son of Man: give thanks and dance for joy, because a great reward awaits you in heaven.
> The prophets were treated in just the same way by their forebears before them.
> But how terrible for you who are rich: you have had your time of comfort.
> How terrible for you who are well fed now: you shall be hungry.
> How terrible for you who are laughing now: you shall know sadness and tears.
> How terrible if people speak kindly of you! Their ancestors said the same about the false prophets.

This is the Gospel of the Lord
Praise to you, Lord Jesus Christ   Katie Thompson

Prayers

Approach – The steadfast love of God

Almighty God,
> we come together as those you have called into fellowship,
> > to be your people
> > and to share in the rich inheritance of your saints.
> I will sing of your steadfast love, O Lord, for ever;
> > **I will proclaim your faithfulness to all generations.**

We come to worship you,
   not alone,
   but as part of the worldwide family of the Church,
   united with our brothers and sisters in Christ
   across countries and continents,
   centuries and generations,
   bound together by the same Lord and the same faith.
I will sing of your steadfast love, O Lord, for ever;
   I will proclaim your faithfulness to all generations.

We come as part of the great company of your people
   in heaven and on earth,
   following in the footsteps of past generations,
   picking up the torch
   from those who have run the race before us and kept the faith,
   heirs of your age-old promises.
I will sing of your steadfast love, O Lord, for ever;
   I will proclaim your faithfulness to all generations.

We come as those called to build for the future,
   conscious of successive generations that will follow us,
   and mindful of our responsibility to pass on to them
   the message we have received,
   to offer them inspiration and encouragement
   through the example of our commitment.
I will sing of your steadfast love, O Lord, for ever;
   I will proclaim your faithfulness to all generations.

We come then united with all your people of past, present, and future,
   of here, there, and everywhere,
   all those who call upon your name and offer you their service.
I will sing of your steadfast love, O Lord, for ever;
   I will proclaim your faithfulness to all generations.

Remind us of that wider fellowship of which we are a part,
   and may we recognise more fully
   the rich heritage you have given us,
   the great cloud of witnesses to which we belong.
Open our eyes to all we may learn of you,
   through these and one another.
I will sing of your steadfast love, O Lord, for ever;
   I will proclaim your faithfulness to all generations.

Save us from closed and narrow minds,
   forgive us for small and restricted outlooks,
   and restore us with your people
   to the wholeness and fellowship that you desire.

So may we and your Church everywhere
offer our worship and service,
in word and deed,
to the glory of your name.
I will sing of your steadfast love, O Lord, for ever;
I will proclaim your faithfulness to all generations.
In the name of Christ, we pray.
Amen. NICK FAWCETT

Petition

(based on 1 Peter 2:9-10)

Eternal God,
we thank you today that you have called us
to share in the inheritance of your saints,
one with you and all your people across the ages.
By your grace,
help us to fulfil that calling.

Once we were not a people,
but now we are the people of God.
Once we had not received mercy,
but now we have received mercy in all its fullness.
Through you we have become a chosen race,
a royal priesthood,
a holy nation,
called out of darkness into your marvellous light
in order to proclaim your mighty acts.
By your grace,
help us to fulfil that calling.

Teach us to put aside everything that denies our faith
and betrays your love –
anger,
greed,
envy,
bitterness.
Teach us to act honourably and with humility,
loving and gentle in all our actions,
living in unity with you and one another.
By your grace,
help us to fulfil that calling.

Help us to look towards your kingdom,
 to live as those ready for the coming of Christ
 and to offer an example to those around us,
 not superior in our attitudes
 nor thinking of ourselves more highly than we should,
 but offering ourselves in the service of others,
 proclaiming the Gospel through faithful discipleship.
 By your grace,
 help us to fulfil that calling.

Eternal God,
 we come to you as ordinary, everyday people,
 nothing special about us and no particular merits to boast of,
 yet you have welcomed us into your family,
 you have called us to be your Church,
 and you have given us a place
 among the great company of saints in heaven and on earth.
 By your grace,
 help us to fulfil that calling,
 through Jesus Christ our Lord.
 Amen.

NICK FAWCETT

All-age-talk material

Treat each other well!

One day, Jesus began teaching the people on a hillside

Underline the word in each group which doesn't belong. Write those words on the numbered lines

'Happy are the 1_____,

for the 2_____ of God belongs to you.

BACON WEEP SAUSAGE **5**

Happy are the 3_____,

for you shall be 4_____.

POOR BEE FLY **1**

TENNIS SATISFIED FOOTBALL **4**

FLOUR KINGDOM SUGAR **2**

Happy are you who 5_____,

for you shall 6_____.'

APPLE ORANGE LAUGH **6**

STARS MOON HUNGRY **3**

Luke 6:20-21

KATIE THOMPSON

Jesus explained that it is not easy to be his follower!

CODE CRACKER

Use the code breaker to read his words

T	A	E	O	P	Y	H	F	R	S	N	U	M	W	D	B	K
1	2	3	4	5	6	7	8	9	10	11	12	13	14	15	16	17

'
7 2 5 5 6   2 9 3   6 4 12   14 7 4

10 12 8 8 3 9   7 2 1 9 3 15   2 11 15

2 16 12 10 3   8 4 9   1 7 3

10 2 17 3   4 8   1 7 3

,

10 4 11   4 8   13 2 11

Luke 6:22

KATIE THOMPSON

Jesus said . . .

'Treat others as you would like to be treated yourself'

Find and circle these words in the wordsearch

CARE

LOVE

UNDERSTANDING

PATIENCE

FORGIVENESS

KINDNESS

B	J	M	K	O	C	L	Q	T	R	G	S	N
S	K	D	Y	B	O	A	F	S	M	Z	S	R
L	I	E	F	V	E	P	A	P	H	T	E	O
U	N	D	E	R	S	T	A	N	D	I	N	G
G	D	I	V	L	D	T	K	W	X	I	E	S
H	N	U	W	R	I	J	N	S	W	O	V	J
B	E	C	Q	E	M	R	N	V	P	U	I	P
L	S	X	N	O	M	C	A	R	E	B	G	U
Y	S	C	U	Q	X	T	E	A	K	F	R	Q
A	E	J	I	C	Y	V	G	Z	V	B	O	U
Z	Z	K	P	H	S	W	L	A	D	E	F	T

KATIE THOMPSON

Reflective material
(sketches, meditations and poems)

Read Psalm 149

The psalmist doesn't begin with a simple 'Hello and welcome, here are the notices.' Straightaway everyone is encouraged to 'shout praises to the Lord!' Why?

First, the Psalm suggests that we should feel secure in the knowledge that we have God's love. We are acknowledged as being 'his people' (verses 1-2). Second, there is delight in knowing that we are accepted by the Creator. God has gone out of his way to get to know us. He hasn't laid down a library-load of rules and regulations that we need to follow to gain his acceptance, it's already ours (verse 3). Third, if we include God in our life then he is the one who wants to deal with our hassles and problems. We are not expected to sort things out in isolation. We have God with us and the support and encouragement of other Christians (verses 4-5).

There is nothing that God can't handle. Our relationship with him isn't a bunch of 'maybes' and 'sometimes'. He has promised to do the right thing and be with us even though we may be slithering around in a swamp of hopelessness. God has given his word that he'll walk with us every step of the way. There isn't a place or situation where we'll be alone.

It's also good to remind ourselves of what God has done in the past, whether with us or through the example of people in the Bible (verses 6-7).

Finally, no one gets the better of God. Although we may never understand completely how he operates, we should feel confident that he is in control and will deal with things in his own way (verses 8-9).

With the knowledge that God loves us, will be with us always and will not allow situations to ruin our relationship with him, we have a pretty good reason to start and finish each day with a few words of thanks.

PETE TOWNSEND

Endings and beginnings

In you, Lord, there are no endings, only beginnings. Many times in my life I have felt I have come to the end but I did not understand then that you surround all things. Sometimes it feels as if I am dropping into an abyss but the abyss itself is in your hands and even death, the most final ending of all, will become a new beginning.

I can never move outside you, I can never go beyond you. You are the heartbeat of the universe and you are alive for ever. While you live nothing can truly be the end. You are the Alpha and the Omega, the beginning and the end. In you, Lord, there are no endings, only beginnings.   MARY HATHAWAY

Sources of material

Bower, Tony:
Buried Treasure
The Word that Changed the World

Butler, Barbara: *Sharing Ways and Wisdoms*

Castle, Tony: *So Much To Celebrate*

Dainty, Peter: *The Electric Gospel*

Dale, Alan: *The Alan Dale Bible*

Fawcett, Nick:
Getting it Across
No Ordinary Man
No Ordinary Man, Book 2
Prayers for All Seasons
Prayers for All Seasons, Book 2
To Put It Another Way

Forster, Michael:
Act One
The Word in Action
Three + One – A Book of Beginnings
Three + One – Festivals One
Three + One – From Trouble to Triumph
Three + One – Great Kings

Forster, Michael and Simon Smith: *A New Start in All-age Worship*

Fuller, Jill: *Looking Beyond*

Hardwick, John: *Children's Talks with Puppet Sketches*

Hathaway, Mary: *A Word for All Seasons*

Lomax, Tim: *Freedom Within a Framework*

O'Mahony, Gerald: *100 Ways To Hear the Good News*

Richards, H. J.: *Plain English Bible*

Rundle, Elizabeth: *You're Never Alone*

Sayers, Susan:
100 Talks for All-age Worship
Bread and Wine People
Children Too
First Fruits
Including Children
Including Young People

Intercessions for the Church Year
New Intercessions for the Church Year

Thomas, Stuart: *One Lord, One Faith*

Thompson, Katie:
Celebrations for Young People
Footprints in Faith
Hear the Good News

Townsend, Pete:
Café Logos, Year C
Touch Wood

Woodhouse, Patrick: *Beyond Words*

Scriptural index

Bible texts in **bold** refer to main readings and those in *italic*
to references in photocopiable artwork and quizzes;
texts in roman refer to Bible-based reflections